BLACK WRITERS FROM SOUTH AFRICA

Black Writers from South Africa

Towards a Discourse of Liberation

Jane Watts

St. Martin's Press   New York

820.9
W351

© Jane Watts, 1989

First published in the United States of America in 1989

Printed in Great Britain

ISBN 0-312-02732-X

Library of Congress Cataloging-in-Publication Data

Watts, Jane, 1945-
    Black Writers from South Africa / Jane Watts.
        p.   cm.
    Bibliography: p.
    ISBN 0-312-02732-X : $39.95 (est.)
    1. South African literature (English) - Black authors - History and
criticism. 2. South African literature (English) - 20th century—
History and criticism. 3. Blacks - South Africa - Intellectual life.
    I. Title.
PR9358.2.B57W38   1989
820'.9— dc19   88-31415
                                                                    CIP

For Kitty,
my mother,
and the children –
Afrika's and my own

Contents

Acknowledgements

I am deeply grateful to the members of the Medu Arts Ensemble writers' workshop to whom I owe any understanding I may have acquired of what recent black writing is trying to achieve and to all the many people who have helped in so many ways in the preparation of this book. I would like to thank Professor Kenneth Kirkwood and Elizabeth Mackenzie both for advice and for timely and invaluable moral support; Mbulelo Mzamane, whose thesis was my major source for background on Serote and the influence of oral poetry, for his helpful correspondence about his work on *Children of Soweto*; Ezekiel Mphahlele, Wally Serote, Chabani Manganyi and Bessie Head (too late, alas) for the time they so generously gave me to talk about their work; and Terry Eagleton, Frederick Jameson, Christine Howells and Homi Bhabha for their advice and encouragement; the staff of the Bodleian Library and the Commonwealth Library at Queen Elizabeth House for frequent help in locating inaccessible texts; Kitty Watts for checking the manuscript and the children; Eileen McRobbie for typing; Donald Sergeant, John Davie, Paulette Flahavin and Paco Gonzalez for help with word processing; Debby Sander for data searches; Judy Mabro for sensitive and immensely patient editing and, finally, my children, Eileen and Daniel, for enduring it all.

Preface

History, as well as an ever increased output of literature and criticism, has repeatedly overtaken the text of this book. The research upon which it is based was initiated by a Writers' Workshop at the University of Botswana in January 1978, conducted by Mbulelo Mzamane, Mongane Serote and Bob Leshoai. As the work could only be done at intervals, every time I returned to it the focus had to be shifted, another draft begun, as each of the perspectives I employed – first exile, then autobiography, and finally the growth of the Liberation Movement – was sloughed by the collective growth of the body of writers as they lived through the events of the past decade. And since the text was completed in 1986 there has been a further, even more astonishing surge in creativity and now also in criticism that has, in my view, relocated the essential perspective in the field of discourse – a field which demands of the critic an even more rigorous attention to language.

What I have been attempting to do in the course of this pursuit is to explore some of the developments in African writing from South Africa by looking at certain pieces by a few of the writers whose work seems to me to throw some light on the process by which this new literature is being forged and in which fundamental questions are being raised for all literatures in English, about the role of ideology, language and discourse between writer and reader or audience. Obviously, in dealing with such a vast field I have left many gaps and no mention has been made of a number of South Africa's most important African writers or of the best work of some writers who are referred to (for example the poetry of Sepamla). However it would be impossible for a single person working part-time to cover the whole field satisfactorily and omissions are the consequence of lack of time and space, not of judgements about value or importance.

The contents page, listing chapters by genre, would seem an ironical denial of one of the book's major theses about the disruption of western literary constraints, but it has been used, not to make a statement about the kinds of literature discussed in the chapters, but as a convenient structural framework under which to examine what has been happening in the areas formerly covered by the genre divisions. The development of the theoretical underpinning of African literature from South Africa may yield us a more valid foundation upon which to draw for such frameworks.

I do not think it is necessary any longer to embark on the question of the white critic and African literature (I have employed the term 'Black' throughout the text since that was the terminology endorsed by African writers at the time at which I was writing – were I writing today I would no doubt be using African), since the issue with which South Africa's literature is most crucially concerned, the liberation struggle, has by the efforts of the Africans themselves been made into a world issue – the township youth see themselves as fighting for the world, for the global restoration of political integrity, not just for South Africa. Moreover, while I am constantly aware of my limitations in dealing with literature that is nourished by the African rather than the European tradition, I have tried to assimilate to the perspective of African writers, to grow my understanding out of the workshop run by Medu Arts Ensemble, and attendance at social and community occasions on which poetry, drama, song and dance are performed, to learn about African writing from African writers and African people rather than superimpose upon it the literary superstructure or the literary theory of the West. I may not have succeeded, but I can claim an honest effort to have washed my hands, as Ezekiel Mphahlele bids us do, before eating out of the African dish.

The past two years have seen important developments in the proletarianisation of African literature in South Africa. There has been a revival and adaptation of *imbongi* (praise-singer) poetry in the trades unions of Natal and beyond – worker poets such as Alfred Temba Qabula and Mi S'dumo Hlatshwayo have harnessed traditional literary forms for the popular expression of the workers' struggle. Despite all the setbacks of sometimes poor township audiences, lack of venues and resources, township drama has continued to flourish, and plays are workshopped by township and trade union groups and toured not only in the urban but also now in the rural areas. Women's writing is gaining belated recognition with such collections as *Sometimes When It Rains* joining the previously rather isolated voices of Bessie Head, Noni Jabavu, Miriam Tlali and Ellen Kuzwayo. (A deficiency of this book is its failure to take sufficient account of the role of women writers.) A great deal of critical material has been published providing much deeper insights into the significance of the African tradition in the work of earlier writers such as Dhlomo, Plaatje and Mofolo. Were I to begin writing now, all this body of new literature, together with the new evidence and interpretations brought to bear in the recent work of Mphahlele, Couzens, Ndebele, Cronin, Nkosi, Kirkwood and Vassar, would cause me to revise many of my assessments of the language of poetry or the structure of certain novels. It provides interesting proof of intertextuality and the destabilisation of the text for, as more literature is written, so one changes one's readings of earlier texts – always a characteristic of the study of literature, but in this case operating within the space of months rather than within decades or centuries.

The number of post-Soweto novels continues to increase with works such as Sepamla's *Third Generation* and Mandla Langa's *Tenderness of Blood*, while collections of short stories, records of prison life and collections of poems spill from the presses almost as fast as lives are spilled on the streets of the townships or as fast as pressures mount on both sides of the visible and invisible barricades. A literature and a post-revolutionary society is in the making as part of the same process – a process that moves at so swift a speed that the critic can only run gasping behind, catching at tongues of flame streaming and fluttering in the slipstream.

JANE WATTS
Gaborone, Oxford, Beijing, Oxford
1978–1988

Introduction

Black South African literature is no seamless garment with a sustained and continuing literary tradition. It derives from a multiplicity of cultures: the related tribal cultures of the Xhosa, the Zulu, the Tswana, the Tsonga and the Venda have been overlaid by the heavy and alien cultural impact of English and Afrikaans, and touched at various points by Indian, Malay, Portuguese, Italian and East European influences. And from its earliest days it has been subjected to interference ranging from direct missionary intervention and the subtle ideological infiltration of English liberal humanism to the violent overt coercion evident in the Afrikaner Nationalist imposition of Bantu Education, the policy of separate development, the control of the media, the banning of works of literature and the subjection of writers to banning, exile, police harassment, imprisonment and, at times, death. Each generation of writers has had to start afresh with scarcely any access to literary models and in material, political and social circumstances that have changed, generation by generation, for the worse.

Yet in spite of all these obstacles writers have clung to the idea of their literary past. Names such as Sol Plaatje and Thomas Mofolo, Benedict Vilakazi, R. R. and H. I. E. Dhlomo, and those of succeeding writers have been held in deep regard by later black writers, and the mythology of black African writing has been sought out and sustained by those denied its substance. Thus it is possible to trace some tenuous threads of continuity throughout the writing of this century, and to distinguish the survival of African cultural values through all efforts to eradicate or pervert them.[1] The early writers such as Sol Plaatje and Thomas Mofolo or playwrights such as H. I. E. Dhlomo emerged from the mission schools converted not only to Christianity but also, to a large extent, to the cultural values of the West.[2] Yet their choice of African historical subject matter bears witness to their hold upon their own past.

1

Their plays and novels were published in the 1930s by the missionary presses and were followed, in the 1940s, by the publication of Peter Abrahams' first two novels, *Song of the City* and *Mine Boy* and Ezekiel Mphahlele's first collection of short stories, *Man Must Live*, all of which had contemporary themes. (Abrahams' two novels set the fashion for a series of Jim-comes-to-Joburg novels dealing with the gulf between moral life and existence in the urban ghettoes.) These writers were heavily influenced by the outlook of the white liberals to whom they owed their academic education, and their early work focused on the development of individuals and individual moral issues though Mphahlele was later to undergo radical changes in his views. Abrahams on the other hand, despite a brief involvement in the Communist Party, was to pursue the western liberal literary tradition in his later novels written in exile, and in his two autobiographical works, *Tell Freedom* (1953) and *Return to Goli* (1954).

Both of these writers emerged at a time when there was considerable contact, not between blacks and whites, but between the black educated élite and white liberals – a very limited area of racial mixing. It was the stimulating kind of contact that nourished illusions of improvement in the political situation, concentrated attention on the question of racism rather than economic exploitation, and generated optimism about the breaking down of racial barriers. So strong was this illusion that it survived even the election of the Nationalist government in 1948. Indeed the fifties have come to be viewed with nostalgia as a golden age of literary renaissance. And it is true that *Drum Magazine* and its sister publication *The Golden City Post* brought together an extraordinarily talented group of writers: Can Themba, Nat Nakasa, Lewis Nkosi, Bloke Modisane, Todd Matshikiza (creator of the slick jazzy language Matshikese), Arthur Maimane, Casey Motsisi, Bessie Head and Ezekiel Mphahlele. Their typical products were sharp, sparkling essays in a humorous tone celebrating the shebeen[3] culture and the racially mixed vibrant environment that was Sophiatown – South Africa's last and unintentional gesture towards integration. But these writers were not representative of the masses, and the freedoms and culture they enjoyed, for all *Drum*'s populist appeal, had never been and were never to be generally accessible to the black man in the street or on the (white) farm. Nor did these writers have any strong affiliations to the political movements in a way that would impinge upon their writing (though for a time Mphahlele and Modisane were members of the ANC). The musical production *King Kong* was the culmination of literary and theatrical co-operation between the races, and illustrates the general trend of the decade for it depended on capitalist backing and appealed to a cosmopolitan white audience.

While black and white liberals flirted over their cultural collaborations, however, the Nationalist government had been building up its strength to enforce its plans – many of which had been designed in the 1930s and 1940s. The Bantu Education Act of 1953 tried to ensure that future generations of writers would be untainted by English liberalism; the group areas policy sought to impose territorial and physical segregation, and the violent police reaction to the peaceful demonstrations at Sharpeville and Langa in 1960, together with the implementation of the State of Emergency, demonstrated the naked force that would be used to control and dominate the black races. In response, many writers fled into exile rather than face imprisonment, and the Publications and Entertainment Act of 1963 ensured the exile of their writings as effectively as the threat of violence had ensured the exile of their bodies.

Thus a whole generation of writers was effectively obliterated. What we have left is the record of this process: a spate of autobiographies was produced that either covered the writer's life in South Africa up to the point of exile, or the actual journey of exile itself, or the shock of the contrast between South Africa and the non-apartheid West. With the exception of Ezekiel Mphahlele (and one book of critical essays from Lewis Nkosi) all were to fall silent after this autobiographical effort was made: Bloke Modisane, Alfred Hutchinson, Todd Matshikiza, Lewis Nkosi and Dugmore Boetie – an internal exile who died shortly afterwards in South Africa.

It was not the end, however, of western influence on South African writing. The poems of Dennis Brutus and Arthur Nortje, and the novels produced at this time by Bessie Head (*Where Rainclouds Gather*, *Maru* and *A Question of Power*) and Mphahlele (*The Wanderers*) are firmly ensconced in the mainstream of English literature. Exile is a very prominent theme, and the writers are often absorbed with the difficulty of coming to grips with the dislocation of their lives. Where writers do look beyond the question of exile to the political situation of their country, as do Richard Rive in *Emergency* and Alex La Guma in *The Stone Country* and *A Walk in the Night*, they do so within the framework of the traditional novel genre, and their work is looking back at situations rather than indicating a way forward, reflecting the temporary bewilderment of their people after the banning of their political movements – the ANC and the PAC – and the extremely repressive measures enforced both in daily life and in the statutes (notably the Suppression of Communism Act which enabled the government to label all opponents communists and then imprison them).

Meanwhile inside South Africa during the sixties a new generation of writers was maturing. Cut off from the mainstream of western culture by the impoverishment of their Bantu Education they were growing up in symbiosis with their community. It has been claimed that, though inferior, Bantu Education was extended to the majority, instead of a selected élite, and that this was another factor in closing the gap between educated and uneducated: the children of ordinary working people were now at school.[4] They were a generation politicised by Sharpeville, by the blatant manifestations of power that controlled their existence, and by the disillusionment of their elders with the white liberalism that had failed them in their hour of need. It is understandable how the Black Consciousness Movement took root in such soil and how the ideas and ideals of the banned political movements, the ANC and the PAC, were a much more potent influence upon the minds of young writers than they had been in their days as legal organisations.

The Black Consciousness Movement served a threefold purpose. It worked to destroy the negative self-definitions imposed by the white minority; it fostered national unity within the black masses, and it sought to establish traditional African cultural values which had been deliberately perverted by the Nationalist government in order to separate the tribes and divert them, with a toothless and ersatz version of tribal culture, from any kind of political understanding or power struggle. The movement had its base in community efforts to improve basic living conditions, education and health care and aimed to politicise through community action. Writers within the movement turned from white-directed protest to black-directed conscientisation. Populist in orientation, the movement encouraged writers to seek alternative media and distribution systems. The oral tradition was re-established within a new framework as poets sought their audiences by performing at gatherings, meetings and funerals, and thereby reached people print would never have touched. Oswald Mtshali was the first of this group of poets to publish, soon to be followed by Sipho Sepamla, Mongane Serote, Mafika Gwala and Don Mattera. Even James Matthews, a short story writer of an older generation, turned to poetry to escape the censor. *Staffrider Magazine* provided a vehicle for large numbers of less well-known poets, grouping their writing according to areas or workshops, deliberately establishing collective rather than individual identities. Yet the poets' most significant audiences remain those present at their gatherings rather than the purchasers of their published collections and magazines, while the amount of time they devote to work with young poets in regular small workshops, with local children and groups of students reveals their community orientation.

Two factors contributed to a change in direction towards the end of the seventies. One was that the task of the Black Consciousness Movement had been accomplished. Identity had been established and anger channelled into political involvement. The second was the Soweto uprising of 1976 in which ideology became praxis. After 1976 the poets and writers were possessed by the need to record, to seize history as it passed and render it back to those who had made it serve as ammunition in the struggle, and to point the way forward. In the Soweto novels of Miriam Tlali, Sipho Sepamla, Mbulelo Mzamane and Mongane Serote the aggressive assertiveness of the Black Consciousness period has disappeared and the anger has been dissolved into action.

The history of black writing over the last five or six decades in South Africa has been a history of a search for identity: not the *angst*-ridden search of the *Sturm-und-Drang* writer, nor the introspective nihilism of the existentialist, but the purposeful quest of a people who have had to emerge from conscious and subconscious subjugation, rescue their psyche from alienation and near obliteration and forge a collective will to carry out the task allotted to them by history. All these tasks have located themselves within the primary need to appropriate language – a context in which a culture can be created that will articulate their people's demand to take charge of their own lives and their political destiny.

1 The Case for a New Approach

What's poetic
about long-term sentences and
deaths in detention
for those who 'threaten state security'?
Tell me
What's poetic
about shooting defenceless kids
in a Soweto street?
Can there be poetry
in fostering Plural Relations?

    Mafika Gwala: from 'In Defence of Poetry'[1]

INTRODUCTION

It would be futile to embark on any consideration of recent black writing in South Africa without recognising at the outset the need to abandon traditional literary critical assumptions and to forge a new kind of critical framework which will take account of the radically different forces at work within the literary production of that country. Over the past thirty years, writers in South Africa have gradually evolved an approach which has very little in common with western literary tradition. The latter has seen the progressive withdrawal of the writer from communal and political involvement, the evolution of literary forms and linguistic modes increasingly introspective and arcane until art has been 'raised to the status of a solitary fetish'.[2] South African writers have long discerned the inappropriateness of such a convention for their circumstances and for their function within society.

Indeed they have come to question whether literature actually has any real role in the political situation and social milieu which confront them, or whether, as Sartre suggested, they should put down the pen and take up the gun. When Winston expostulates with John in the discussion of their prison performance of *Antigone* on Robben Island over the point of giving the performance at all, he encapsulates the entire South African literary predicament:

> Bloody thing never even happened. Not even history! Look, brother, I got no time for bullshit. Fuck legends. Me? . . . I live my life here! I know why I'm here, and its history, not legends. I had my chat with a magistrate in Cradock and now I'm here. Your Antigone is a child's play, man.[3]

Of what use is literature to a community in prison, at war, totally engrossed in a struggle for survival on literal rather than literary terms? As Mpumalanga so aptly puts it in the opening quotation, 'What's poetic?' about the situation in which his people find themselves? Winston's indictment is one that has to be answered if South African literature is to have any significance.

THE PROBLEMS OF THE WRITER

Material conditions

> Literary production and consumption presuppose certain levels of literacy, physical and mental well-being, leisure and material affluence: the material conditions for writing and reading include economic resources, shelter, lighting and privacy.[4]

In addition to this fundamental query about the basic relevance of their activity, black South African writers have inherited a clutch of other problems, some unique to their country, and others shared with writers all over Africa – the absence of a unified national literary tradition; the pressure from publishers to produce sensational material; the difficulty of reconciling traditional cultural values with modern industrialised society; the need to spend too much of their time and energy dodging censorship, banning or imprisonment, and, at the most basic level of all, the well-nigh impossible obstacle of establishing the basic physical conditions which make writing possible.

It is difficult to conceive of the enormity of this latter impediment without actual experience of the living conditions of the majority of black people in South Africa. Crowded together into locations and housed in shelters varying from tin shacks and cardboard erections to the minute institutional boxes provided by the authorities (with a few fairly luxurious homes for the tiny minority of capitalists and professionals which only serve to draw the attention of the majority to their deprivation), shelters which inevitably have to serve large extended families and numerous homeless friends and dependants, no provision is made for writers to recollect in tranquillity, or even in privacy. Few houses have running water, and those which do often have no electric light: braziers, paraffin, gas and candles serve for lighting, cooking and heating. Through the thin walls come the gumba gumba music, the fights, the shouted conversations, the all-night funeral hymn-singing and the wedding frenzies of song and hooting horns.

One of the material conditions Eagleton fails to note in his basic prerequisites for literary production is freedom from physical harassment – a freedom beyond the experience of any township dweller. The most trivial neighbourhood errand may lead to brutal physical assault, perhaps murder, by the township tsotsis, so that fear becomes a reflex associated with opening the house door. As Biko pointed out, whereas most of us can take our physical survival into adulthood for granted, for the black man it is always a miracle to live to an adult age.[5] If he escapes the knives there is always the possibility of arrest for failure to carry his pass, and as families are not routinely informed of such arrests, a man can disappear for years without trace (and indeed at the time of the Bethal farms scandal, reporters were able to show that men had died without trace too).

If a black person is fortunate enough to have a job (unemployment is high among blacks, although virtually non-existent among whites) its duration is always uncertain and it almost always involves exhausting journeys in appallingly crowded buses or trains from township to city centre and back again, necessitating pre-dawn starts and after-dark returns. A man's right to live in the township depends entirely upon holding a job, and the writing of novels or poems is hardly considered productive work by government agencies. Without a job he is obliged to return to his rural Bantustan – a place he may never have seen, though his great grandfather may conceivably have spent some time there.

For the black people who have the good fortune to go to school and absorb some Bantu Education, any attempts to further their education once they have left will meet with little success: access to libraries,

books, films, theatre, to the whole landscape of the life of the mind is
severely curtailed.

It is true that conditions vary according to the part of the country in
which the writer lives. Richard Rive points out that while it is
impossible for writers to survive the Johannesburg environment, things
are easier for the writer who lives in the Cape, where racial tensions are
less formidable.[6] Yet too often writers are so taken up with the
melodrama of daily life, that they are unable to gain that distance from
experience that is the prerequisite for artistic creation.

Apartheid

Segregation imposes its own restraints on the writer. Nor is apartheid
the simple issue that civil rights are in America, for instance, or racial
prejudice in Britain. The experience of a black South African may
touch at many points the experience of a Southern black in the United
States – an experience of prejudice, ill-treatment, injustice, fanaticism.
But the yawning difference lies in the fact that South Africa is the only
country in the world to build up a whole structure of law and morality
upon the *admitted* supposition that one race is superior and therefore
entitled to all the privileges. In other countries, whatever the attitude of
the masses, at least the law and the conventional moral atmosphere
among the educated frown upon racism, while the official policy is now
based upon equality so that whatever peoples' private views may be,
they are ashamed of racial prejudice except under the cover of mass
meetings led by politicians like Mosley or Powell, or of a party such as
the National Front. In South Africa, by contrast, the government holds
up apartheid not only as the basis of its legal system and its social
order, but also as sanctified by the Dutch Reformed God.

Such a rigid compartmentalising of society has a devastating effect
on the quality of all South African literature, whether it be white, black,
coloured or Indian (to use the artificial categories of apartheid. It is
significant that South Africa has had to develop its own specialised
vocabulary to deal with the anomalies of its social system – yet another
feature by which it cuts itself off from the rest of the world.)

Far more than the rigid class structure which confined successful
nineteenth-century novelists to those sections of society with which
they were most familiar, apartheid confines the writer's imagination
and constricts understanding. He or she is totally unable to penetrate
the behaviour of any other group because, by law, it is forbidden for
groups to mix in any natural setting. Even many radical white South
Africans, dedicated to the removal of the apartheid system, are so

ignorant of their compatriots' way of life that they are often unaware of the language mixtures used in African homes:

> Any writer's attempt to present in South Africa a totality of human experience within his own country is subverted before he sets down a word . . . The black writer in South Africa writes from the 'inside' about the experience of the black masses, because the colour-bar keeps him steeped in its circumstances, confined in a black township and carrying a pass that regulates his movements from the day he is born to the status of 'piccanin' to the day he is buried in a segregated cemetery. The white writer aseptically quarantined in his test-tube élite existence, is cut off by enforced privilege from the greater part of the society in which he lives . . .[7]

And yet, since all South African writers of any significance, by the very nature of their existence, are compelled to draw in some way upon racial tension in almost all of their writings, they inevitably at some point have to include characters from other racial groups. The unavoidable consequence, of course, is that these characters are perforce stereotypes. Nadine Gordimer recognises this in a 1973 footnote to an article written originally in 1969:

> I now believe that Georg Lukács is right when he says that a writer, in imaginative creation and the intuition that comes with it, cannot go beyond the *potential* of his own experience . . . There are some aspects of a black man's life that have been put impossibly beyond the white man's potential experience, and the same applies to the black man and some aspects of the white man's experience.[8]

Lewis Nkosi summarises the situation with an apt bitterness: 'What comes out of the apartheid machine when it has ground to a standstill is not human flesh but cardboard pulp'.[9] He instances Stephen Kumalo in Paton's *Cry the Beloved Country* as an example of this total failure of understanding, pointing out that in his portrait of the humble priest, the author completely fails to take account of 'the fantastic ambiguity, the deliberate self-deception, the ever-present irony behind the mock-humility and moderation of speech'.[10]

Where role-playing is an essential mechanism for survival for one of the groups, there can never be any intimate familiarity between the races. Several black critics have been at pains to point out this two-headed image that is forced on the black man by circumstances which require him, for his own safety's sake, to adopt the role of yes-man, to conform to a pattern fixed by an alien, dominant race, or to risk extermination. As Nat Nakasa freely admits: 'Much of the African's life is lived outside the law.'[11] It is impossible to exist without breaking the law since 'the total effect of the apartheid laws . . . is to make it almost illegal to live.'[12] The white writer is quite unable to penetrate this kind of outlaw life. Aelred Stubbs, in his personal memoir of Biko, notices the different approach to banning between blacks and white, the latter being 'more scrupulous in taking precautions even after they had discovered methods of coming to terms with their restriction'.[13]

This failure of understanding between races is not, I think, merely a result of more stringent measures by the Nationalist government, as Nadine Gordimer suggests,[14] but has grown with South African society from its earliest origins, and is an integral part of its whole history of racial tension. Recent occurrences may have closed every loophole, but South Africans have endured hundreds of years of never living together, and even when there have been crossings of the racial barriers, the circumstances have been tense – as is obvious from Nkosi's accounts of encounters in *Home and Exile* – so that relations must always have been strained and unnatural.

Thus one of the most urgent tasks of writers, if one is to accept the almost unanimous South African concept of literature as an educative force, is to reveal their own racial groups in all the intimacy of their cut-off and segregated life. Alex La Guma stresses this point in his interview with Seraguma:

> I believe that there has been a lot said about South Africa but very little said about what the non-white people in particular are really experiencing . . . For instance, I don't think a great deal has been said about the Coloured community, or about the Indian community and I think even within a framework of racial separateness there is a task which writers have to perform. This is at least letting the world know what is happening – even within their compartments.[15]

It is ironic that literature, which is the only source South Africans have for a knowledge of their compatriots, is always being suppressed. However, it is one of the most heartening aspects of South African writing that, despite all this, several writers are now fulfilling this task. Ahmed Essop is doing for the Indian community what La Guma, himself, Rive and Brutus have done for the coloured community, what Serote, Sepamla, Mtshali, Gwala, Mzamane and Mphahlele are doing for the blacks, and what Gordimer, Gray, Sheila Fugard and others are doing for the whites. Thus, partially at least, and despite the prevention by law of 'any real identification of the writer with his society as a whole', he is struggling with that 'exploration of self'[16] which is essential to any writer's creative survival.

The system also interferes with the actual content of the writer's work. For the consequences of apartheid are so obsessive in the South African situation that they dominate all literature, and leave any writer who attempts to think about something else open to the charge of irrelevance, of failing to grapple with the only important issues of the day. But racial conflict is not the god-given source of inspiration that many weak writers and misdirected critics have assumed it to be. Proof of this lies in the mountainous heap of trashy short stories and weak poems dealing with encounters between white and black or white and coloured, love stories across the colour line, technicolour life among the shebeens with technicolour squalor, technicolour poverty and technicolour wifebeating – all finding a ready market among the curious, the eager publishers with an eye on profits, the sycophantic critics seeking a peg on which to hang their fashionable solidarity with the black masses, and all of it providing acute embarrassment to those black writers who are genuinely attempting to wrest a literature out of the exaggerated misery of their communal life.

In fiction this leads to a concern with what is happening to the exclusion of any concentration on inner motivations or the development of character. Richard Rive's *Emergency* is an example of this at its worst – where the characters are mere mouthpieces for political opinions; but even good craftsmen like La Guma leave us with very little insight into the people he depicts so vividly – apart from what we can glean from their actions. Mphahlele even suspects that 'we, both black and white, unconsciously want to maintain the *status quo* so as to delay as long as we can the coming of the day when we as writers shall be faced with the greater responsibility of inventing plots and reconstructing character in broader human perspective.'[17]

There is also the temptation, ever present, to overplay the situation; its components are in any case so much nearer to melodrama than real life that it requires a very special skill to produce an authentic drawing rather than a grotesque cartoon. Few writers have that skill. Jane Austen achieved the subtlety of her effects by drawing on a very small section of society leading a very humdrum and proper life; for all her genius she would have found it extremely hard to achieve such a skilful effect if faced with Hogarth's London – with the prostitutes, the gin-drinkers and the thieves for her raw material. South African writers have no choice; in addition to the fatuity of segregation of races by skin-colour, they have the distorted, over-coloured life which results from it as their raw material.

Such a situation inevitably produces a blinding anger in the mind of the writer who is identified with it:

> Words, words, words spilled on to the pages . . . you
> had to give an account of your bitterness.[18]

And such anger often urges the writer towards a fruitless didacticism. Yet the old simplistic liberal-humanist rejection of didacticism in literature is irrelevant to a criticism of recent black South African writing, while crude, overt didacticism or propaganda within a literary work may have the opposite effect to the one intended, and prevent the work from performing its social function.

Censorship

The struggle, however, is hardly fostered by those custodians of society who make up the censorship board. A compartmentalised and fragmented society is of course only the beginning of the writer's troubles. A government that is determined to inflict such artificial restraints upon its people finds itself obliged to build up a monolithic structure of laws to enforce its policy. Freedom to write, to read, to publish, and even to think becomes an impossibility, for such a policy can easily be undermined if people are stirred into thinking for themselves. Culture, in any society, is potentially a humanising force. Literature can teach people not only to know themselves but also to know other people. In a society dedicated to the dehumanisation of its whole population, literature and culture can have no place; hence it is entirely logical to attempt to eradicate them by taking out all their teeth. Olive Schreiner foresaw this as long ago as 1883:

> Whenever you come into contact with any book, person, or opinion of which you absolutely comprehend nothing, declare that book, person, or opinion to be immoral. Bespatter it, vituperate against it, strongly insist that any man or woman harbouring it is a fool or a knave, or both. Carefully abstain from studying it. Do all that in you lies to annihilate that book, person or opinion.[19]

It would seem that the governments of South Africa have indeed committed her advice to memory and taken it as a model for their attack on literature and culture in general. One of my first introductions to South African literature was the anthology of *South African Writing Today* edited by Nadine Gordimer and Lionel Abrahams.[20] This was intended to provide a broad spectrum of contemporary writing, it had no political axe to grind, it merely intended to give a glimpse of all kinds of writing then being produced. Of the forty-two writers included in the anthology, fourteen were in exile (five of them permanently, on exit permits), one was under house arrest, one had committed suicide *at the time the book was published*. Since then many others have had books banned and two have died in early middle age. Dennis Brutus cites his own case, not an extreme one, as typical of the contorted double-checks imposed upon writers:

> I was banned from writing, and I was banned from publishing anything. These two bans were not served directly upon me. As the result of an act of around 1961, which was designed to punish people who committed sabotage, and as a result of the interpretation of this act, I was banned from writing. In a strictly legal sense, even to write was construed as sabotage . . . But after I was released from prison in 1965, after I had been on Robben Island, the bans which had been served on me were all lifted . . . and I was served with a new set of bans which ran until 1970. These bans included three which will almost certainly strike you as curious. One was that I was banned from writing at all. This meant you did not have to be published – merely to write was a criminal act. But in addition, I could not even draft anything which might be published. In fact, my Banning Order . . . specifically forbids me to compose slogans so that, in fact, even a string of words could have been illegal. Then there is a further one which says that I may not write, publish or prepare anything which might be published.[21]

The convoluted style echoes the convolutions of the situation.

There are in fact two ways in which literature is subjected to censorship. A particular work may be banned, as was Nadine Gordimer's *The Late Bourgeois World* or Jack Cope's *The Dawn Comes Twice*, or a writer may be banned, in which case everything he or she has ever published is also banned, and it is an offence to print or publish it, produce it, distribute it, display it, exhibit it, sell it or offer it or keep it for sale. Since I wrote this chapter it has also become a criminal offence to possess a banned book.

The Publications Act 1963 decreed that any book could be censored when matter is deemed to be indecent, obscene, offensive or harmful to public morals.[22] The Minister of the Interior, Senator Jan de Kok, explained in a debate on this Bill that 'more freedom is given in this Bill than has ever been given in any existing law. This freedom of thought, of expression and distribution exists in few countries of the world, if it does exist.'[23] A claim which does much to substantiate Nkosi's theory that South African life surpasses the theatre of the absurd.

Yet it seems a harmless enough act, provided one agrees that the government has a right to censor what anyone shall read, watch or hear – and most governments do employ some form of censorship on moral grounds. The teeth of this act lay in its Publications Board – the committee which was to investigate all published material. This board was retained as Directorate of Publications in the Act which replaced it in 1974 – in the application of which 'the constant endeavour of the population of the Republic of South Africa to uphold a Christian view of life shall be recognized.'[24] The new act removed the right of appeal to the courts, and simplified the grounds on which publications were to be censored: they merely had to be 'undesirable'. Those who drafted the Bill defined this word for the confused:

For the purposes of this Act any publication or object, film, public entertainment or intended public entertainment shall be deemed undesirable if it or any part of it –

a) is indecent or obscene or is offensive or harmful to public morals

b) is blasphemous or is offensive to the religious convictions or feelings of any section of the inhabitants of the Republic

c) brings any section of the inhabitants of the Republic into ridicule or contempt

d) is harmful to the relations between any sections of the inhabitants of the Republic

e) is prejudicial to the safety of the State, the general welfare or the peace and good order

f) discloses with reference to any judicial proceedings

   i) any matter which is indecent or obscene or is offensive or harmful to public morals

   ii) any indecent or obscene medical, surgical or physiological details the disclosure of which is likely to be offensive or harmful to public morals etc.[25]

The problem of proving the charge of undesirability is simplified too:

A notice published in the *Gazette* stating that a publication or object is in terms of a decision of a committee undesirable, shall for the purposes of the Act be conclusive proof of the undesirability of that publication or object.[26]

This is only one of the Acts that provide for the censorship of books. Individual books or periodicals can be banned under the Suppression of Communism Act 1950 (as amended) or under the Riotous Assemblies Act 1956 on the grounds that they are calculated to engender feelings of hostility between Europeans and any other section of the inhabitants. And of course writers can be banned under these, and other acts, and all their work consequently censored.

This maze which the government has created for its writers to wander through is so tortuous that it occasionally traps someone it was not intended for. Alfred Hutchinson relates the anecdote of how, in the treason trial, Professor Murray, an expert witness for the Crown whose task was to label speeches and documents communistic 'ended up by labelling an article as communistic which he himself had written a few years before.'[27] The collective effect of these laws is very far-reaching and is channelled in two directions – it affects the writers themselves, and the society for which they write.

The provincialism and narrow-mindedness of South African society and its ability to construct arguments based upon false premises arise from a lack of access to vast areas of intellectual speculation and literary endeavour, both from other countries and its own. In 1969 the number of banned books was estimated at 13,000. I have found no figures for the decade since then, but I would be surprised if the rate at which books are banned has diminished. University teachers complain of the lack of access to certain materials, such as books in the Fontana Modern Masters series: 'One gets the impression that certain sorts of knowledge and intellectual awareness are simply not permitted in this country.'[28]

Almost every writer of note remarks on the sterility which is induced by this situation. Nadine Gordimer articulates the horror which is evoked for many South Africans by such intellectual isolation – a horror at a nation dealing with fear by imposing wilful ignorance and refusing to acknowledge that the rest of the world exists:

The success of censorship must be seen in the completeness with which we are cut off not just from the few books dealing with our own ingrown society, but also from the books which formulated the thinking that is going on all around us, in particular on this continent to which we stake our lives on belonging. From Fanon to Mazrui many African writers are merely names to us. As South

Africans we do not know what the rest of Africa is thinking, just as, as whites, we do not know what the black and coloured population is thinking.[29]

But it is not only the processes of thought that are interfered with by this removal of vitamins from the intellectual diet; it cuts across the population's ability to deal adequately with their emotions, since these can only be dealt with in words, which writers have been made to fear using, and readers to fear reading. (This is a real fear that touches even the comparatively immune: crossing the borders into South Africa with the books required for this piece of work was always a nerve-racking experience, even though, at the time, it was not a criminal offence to be in possession of banned books. The fact that they were irreplaceable made the possibility that an illiterate border guard would seize them and lose them before I could get through the legal processes necessary to recover them a harrowing contingency. If this is so for a white foreigner, what can be the state of mind of black nationals, completely within the power of their government?) When a people fear language itself, their chances of attaining self-knowledge are slim indeed:

> South Africans are, as a nation, a speechless people whose fear of the spoken or written word has created a horrible fatuity in their life both private and public . . . Language must be inhabited, it must be enlarged by usage; South Africans abridge it and stop it from referring too closely to those emotions which they spend all their lives trying to obliterate or deny. We cannot be cowards in the lives we live and be brave in the act of creating plays, novels and poems.[30]

On the question of censorship, Nkosi prophesies a state of barbarism for his country. He insists that South Africa's case is far more desperate than that of a country with a long and sturdy literary tradition. Where there is no tradition for new writers to test themselves against, 'bereaving a few writers of an opportunity to write and publish their work is fatally harmful to the cultural life of the country and to the quality of its thought. Under the circumstances it is difficult to see how South Africans can recover their lost potential for speech.'[31] Nkosi links the whole brutalising, dehumanising quality of life in South Africa with this inability to deal with language. It is a very grave charge to lay against a government – perhaps ultimately more serious than the charge of intellectual paralysis which has been brought against it.

The effect of the censorship laws on the writers themselves varies from a serious interference with their creative process to its total obliteration. Several writers have not only been silenced completely but driven to suicide or to a way of life so savagely self-destructive that it amounts to suicide in all but the technical sense. Nat Nakasa killed himself in the United States; Can Themba drank himself to death in Swaziland; Biko was silenced by death in prison.

There is no way for writers to work untrammelled in South Africa. They may well have no fear of the censorship laws, or even be indifferent to the prospect of being banned, but they must always be conscious of the fact that their books have no chance of being read by their countrymen unless they have ensured that they are either toothless before publication, or so difficult to understand that they defeat the censors' intellects – but then they may also be ignored by a large section of the intended readership. Consciousness of all this cannot fail to percolate into writing, so that the defiant are almost hysterical in their exaggerations, and the timid lose their literary integrity along with their personal integrity.

The government, then, really does have a weapon which enables them to wipe out the creative efforts of a generation. Since writers can only have the working conditions they need abroad, and exile, whether voluntary or on exit permits today always entails banning, it neatly removes them and all their creative endeavour from the reach of the South African public; and those writers who choose to struggle on in South Africa have to face the possibility of censorship with any book they publish. Since the essential function of writing is communication, censorship makes a nonsense of this very craft, and in addition it prevents writers from relying on their craft for a livelihood. (Though of course, if the writer is a black man, the pass laws will do that long before the time comes for the censors, since he will not be able to remain in a town, with access to books and fellow writers, unless he has a job.)

These effects on individual writers also spread to the collective emergent literary tradition. A whole corpus of work can be destroyed by the banning procedures. Thus the short story tradition fostered by the *Drum* writers of the fifties was eradicated by the censorship after Sharpeville; the attempts to come to terms with the Sharpeville era itself in fictional form (Mary Benson, Jack Cope, Richard Rive) were also wiped out; those writers who attempted to work out their experiences in autobiographical form (Todd Matshikiza, Alfred Hutchinson, Bloke Modisane) in the early sixties went the same way. And these books really are killed. Though their publishers might be in England or America, their published life is fairly short once their home market is closed. It becomes impossible to obtain these works as their authors fade into obscurity, revived only in the reminiscences of fellow writers who knew them. Of course in all countries this happens to writers who are not at the top of the literary league tables and taken up by the universities – but they at least have the assurance that their books will be found in the libraries of their native lands. For a South African writer, the grave is unmarked and in an alien land.

In this way the nascent prose tradition among black writers of the fifties and early sixties has been the Censorship Act's first victim. At the moment we are watching the battle between the censors and the new generation of writers who have turned to poetry in an attempt to forestall banning by using jargon and the cryptic turn of phrase. And yet as soon as they attempt to simplify their poetic form, in the interests of their artistic development, the censors are there, like the hounds on the fox – witness the banning of James Matthews's *Cry Rage* and Sipho Sepamla's *The Soweto I Love*.

It is significant however, that there has, until recently, been no way of dealing with contemporary events in literature in South Africa unless it is in a form so cryptic that it is beyond the comprehension of the censors:

> Polymorphous fear cramps the hand. Would-be writers are so affected that they have ignored gigantic contemporary issues that have set their own lives awash.[32]

The damage caused by this repeated breaking of nascent traditions is not to be underestimated. It has always been the case that good writers flourish in groups rather than in isolation (though of course there are such exceptions as Proust). Any glance at the history of western literature will reveal periods of fertility (the Elizabethan dramatists, the Victorian novelists, the Romantic poets) and periods of sterility. Great writers emerge when the genre of the day fits perfectly with their inner compulsions towards expression – thus the Elizabethan dramatists prepared the ground for Shakespeare, the Victorian novelists for George Eliot, the Romantic poets for Keats. Though a good writer will often make considerable innovations in form, the starting point is always the current tradition. James Joyce and Virginia Woolf depended upon a healthy novel tradition for their experimental base; T. S. Eliot is a direct inheritor of the poetic tradition; and Beckett could never have pared down the dramatic form so effectively if there had not been a healthy dramatic form in existence: none of the innovators of literature could have worked in a vacuum. But a vacuum is precisely what the South African writer has to start from: a vacuum deliberately created by the Directorate of Publications. With no access to the seminal writers of the time, writers must create for themselves, in isolation, all over again that 'inner language' which Nkosi refers to and against which the writer needs to 'attest his personal vision.'[33]

The question of African tradition

Writers are not only faced with a lack of any recent literary tradition, any framework within which to take up their own work, but are also faced with the problem that besets all writers in Africa: what to do about African cultural traditions, about the old traditional cultural attitudes and forms of expression with which modern African writers, in a continent jerked so suddenly and violently into the technological era, must come to terms if their work is to remain meaningful for the bulk of the people. This is a question which has been dealt with at great length by most critics discussing African literature, so I will not labour the point, but it needs to be raised very briefly in a summary of the problems facing South African writers, since their position is very different from that of African writers writing in English elsewhere on the continent. Though the majority of black writers are town bred, and links with traditional patterns of living have been broken far more decisively in South Africa than in other African countries – both by the growth of urban populations and the distortion of the tribal pattern by the white government for their own political ends – these writers nevertheless carry within them a consciousness of the traditional role of the artist in African society. And there has been sufficient carry-over of certain social patterns into the townships – the strong bonds of the extended family, the inherent preference for the closely-knit social group (as opposed to the isolated nuclear family of the white suburbs), the retention of group judgements and group pressures, even after the tradition of group decisions has begun to break down, the gatherings for weddings and funerals – for the significance of this traditional role to be readily comprehended, even if the modern writer feels the need, because of political developments, to change it. It is no longer enough to be the conformist celebrant of convention that the oral poet was in the tribal village, strengthening conservative values by creating praise poems for heroes and castigating deviations from the accepted code of behaviour. Now the problem is to bridge the gulf between the old, static culture and the new situation in which black South Africans find themselves – as part of an exploited labour force in a segregated township which is moving in a slow, and as yet, disintegrated way towards social revolution.

Wise authors will attempt to preserve such of the old culture as can be integrated into the new culture they are attempting to forge. They will act as synthesisers, building upon those remnants of tradition that have survived into urban society, rather than razing them to the ground and attempting to impose a totally new approach. At the same time, a weak clinging to out-dated conventions and ideas will not give readers that stimulus to creative perception and thought for which they look to literature. Tradition is only valuable inasmuch as it is alive. The incorporation of dead relics will hardly profit a modern African literature. But it is into this trap that some of those educated in a European tradition (which they later reject) nostalgically fall. Nkosi is rightly suspicious of that 'cry of anguish for a "lost Africa"' that comes from certain of the educated class:

> Traditional Africans do not find the need nor the time to write books extolling the African way of life. They are too busy living it. That we have such a compulsion to rediscover ourselves from the vantage point of the cafe in Paris, Rome or London, is the measure of our profound alienation from that primal vigour and authenticity with which we would so eagerly wish to be associated.[34]

It is here that South African writers find themselves in a very anomalous position. As African writers, they identify with all Africans throughout the continent. And the great mass of Africans, as Nkosi says, still live the traditional life, swayed by traditional values and immersed in traditional culture. As South Africans, however, their own environment is probably urban; and yet it is not the middle-class alienated urban environment of the civil servant in the independent African state. It is that of the suppressed proletariat in a society which ensures that for the Africans education is not the ladder to success. Thus South African writers retain a powerful link with the masses which African writers in an independent state have forfeited in exchange for their education. But the masses in South Africa are not the same as the masses in other African countries.

Achebe recognises this special dilemma of the South African writer in his call for African writers to turn to the past to provide them with the foundations for writing about the present:

> Perhaps they are right to feel this way . . . It is for them to discover how best to explore the human condition in their part of the continent.[35]

Yet despite all that is exceptional in their case, South African writers nevertheless carry over into their work, even in exile, certain influences from their common heritage: in the verse forms for example. In the course of this work I shall trace some of those influences, which occasionally exist even in the work of writers exiled from their birthplace, whose links with their past have been completely sundered.

All South African critics emphasise the need for South African writers to retain in the centre of their consciousness the needs of their own society rather than the developments of those countries from which they take their language – whose literature is becoming increasingly preoccupied with questions of alienation, failures in communication, despair, and all the psychological paraphernalia of the withdrawn individual.

According to Nkosi, writers also have the special task of externalising all the ingredients which have gone into the composition of the African way of looking at the world and at people:

> ... Not only are our European friends ignorant of all the psychological phenomena which form the strands of the African consciousness, but Africans themselves have hardly analysed their societies sufficiently to grasp their motivations. We would therefore need to know how we conceive reality in the traditional African society, and how these insights have helped to shape our social institutions in a particular way.[36]

Mphahlele, South African though he may be, and a South African keenly aware of his differences from his West African counterparts, supports Achebe's claim for the importance of tradition when he insists, like Nkosi, that it is only through an exploration of tradition that modern writers can define themselves.

As mentioned earlier, it is precisely when we come to questions of tradition that the ravages caused by the South African situation come most starkly to light. Nadine Gordimer goes so far as to claim that the social situation has a far more profound influence over the kind of writing produced by South Africans than any of their 'individual differences of talent and temperament'.[37] That is, their whole creative energy is stifled by the atmosphere in which they live to such an extent that the free development of their artistry is a ludicrous and impossible ideal: what they write about and how they write is circumscribed by where they write. And even if they leave South Africa, as many do, perforce and by choice, they carry with them all the preconceptions, all of that world view impressed on them from birth. South Africa, because of its peculiar legal and moral structure, has become Satan's 'hell within' from which there is no escape, no matter where the exile may end up. Ezekiel Mphahlele was a sad example of the prisoner roaming the world, but ultimately pulled back on the chain that linked him to the land of his birth.

The lack of literary tradition

But it is not only the artist's own mind that is interfered with; the very medium of work has been insidiously interfered with by the system. You have to go back several hundred years to find any African literary tradition untouched by white South African society – and it is the fragile oral tradition at that. (The oral tradition is fragile in that the social system in which it operates has broken down.) The links have been broken, so that it is merely an anachronism to attempt the writing of a latterday praise poem. (Recent developments belie this judgement. The publication of the oral poetry of worker poets such as Alfred Temba Qabula, Mi S'dumo Hlatshiwayo and Nise Malange who have revived *imbongi* (praise-singer) poetry not only shows the transformation of the traditional form to celebrate community action, but also puts the work of the Zulu praise poet Mazisi Kunene into a new perspective, as an important developer and sustainer of the tradition in a period of comparative drought). This is not so in neighbouring Botswana where the tribal system has survived automatically and without interference, and where the praise poem is a natural part of any celebration or commemoration.

Even writing in the mother tongue has to a great extent been eviscerated by the eager missionary societies, encouraging platitudinous tracts conducive to good behaviour, baaskap and salvation. And of course any later attempts to forge a new tradition of black writing have been systematically eradicated by censorship. Thus writers are left with no foundation to build upon, no framework within which to work out their own artistic destiny, and no 'inner language' to support them in their utterances.

Nkosi is complaining of the same kind of thing when he instances the lack of any literary hero to identify with when his own generation was growing up.[38] West African literature, untrammelled by censorship, has succeeded in retaining the hero: the hero as rebel. Nkosi and Kunene both compare township life – with its violence, its night-stabbings, its Rabelaisian drinking – to Elizabethan society. But the swashbuckling and violence and vigour of Elizabethan society was that of the rulers of the seas, the defeaters of the Armada, the bold pirates of the Americas, the subjects of a monarchy renowned for its splendour and magnificence. The swashbuckling and drinking and violence of the townships is that of an exploited, subordinated people, not glorying in and boastful of their power, but seeking an escape from the sore-pressing reality of their subjugation. Little wonder that township life does not throw up the heroes of Elizabethan times. And yet it gives to those leaders it has – Biko, Sobukwe, Mandela – a poignancy and force far deeper, a hold over the emotions – the yearning and anger and indignation of all people – which matches up to the hold of the old mad Lear in the storm, if only some South African Shakespeare were to come forth and lend words and form to these muted hero figures. (Several years after this chapter was first written, it is obvious that South African writers have found their own, and quite different solution to the need for documentation in their focus on the contributions of ordinary participants in the struggle rather than focusing on cult figures.)

Problems of consciousness

> Consciousness does not determine life: life determines conscious-ness.[39]

The problems touched on hitherto are all circumstantial: they might weigh upon writers heavily, but they are pressures from outside – from society, from the government, from literary tradition. And so, however pressing they become, they can never devitalise them in quite the same way as pressure from within. Such a pressure is the interference with consciousness, both as human beings and as writers, produced by the sum of all the conditions – political, social, ideological – under which they must live. Marx and Engels argue that, for all men, everywhere

> It is not the consciousness of men that determine their being, but on the contrary, their social being that determines their conscious-ness.[40]

In South Africa, the social being of the majority of the population is geared to produce a mutilated consciousness which is both an accidental consequence of apartheid and a necessary contributor to its continuance. This is a matter to be dealt with at length later in the book, but it is necessary at this point to touch briefly on its importance as a problem facing the black South African writer.

With the growth of black consciousness, writers have come to examine the fundamental interference with self-image which has been an inevitable product of racism and exploitation. In South Africa, where racism and domination have been enshrined in the political *ideal*, the destruction of the very humanity of the majority of the population has become an essential adjunct to a political system based on non-recognition. Denial of a person's humanity renders superfluous any guilt about that person's ill-treatment, and also helps to suppress any fears of retribution. Fugard explains the political situation of South Africa by saying that it is one 'which makes people "rubbish"'.[41] Biko explains how, from birth, the black man aids the system by internalising this view of himself: his very physical environment establishes the extent to which he counts:

> The homes are different, the streets are different, the lighting is different, so you tend to begin to feel that there is something *incomplete in your humanity*, and that completeness goes with whiteness.[42]

The infant's earliest impressions are reinforced by Bantu Education, in which second-rate schools, poor equipment and badly-trained teachers provide a suitable education for subservience. As soon as urban blacks learn to walk they are initiated into the daily violence of the streets – a violence so intense that for a black man to survive into middle-age is, as Biko explains, a miracle in itself. But survival is not the only question: coming to terms with one's own fear, looking one's own cowardice in the face, is a procedure unnecessary to most of us. For the black South African it is a daily inevitability, and one which saps self-confidence. When the time comes to move out of the township to take up employment (often the first real contact with the white world for black South African youths), they find that a subservient manner, an easy, humorous acceptance of insult and crude jest is what is automatically expected of them in the white towns and cities in which they have no place. The adoption of the humble yes-baas role is not a matter of choice, or personality or belief: it is not the refuge of the passive, subservient nature. It is a prerequisite for survival: the compulsory disguise both for the placid and the rebellious, if they are going to have any hope of staying out of prison. Biko illustrates this in his story of the black electrician's mate, who covered his anger, bitterness and resentment of his white 'baas's' intolerable attitude with genial clowning and idiotic good humour: when questioned about the indignity of his behaviour he explained that this was the price of his job.

Thus black people are not only alienated from themselves

circumstantially, by virtue of the environment they have to endure, the privations forced upon them, their legal and social standing, or rather lack of standing, but they are forced into a situation of deliberate self-alienation: they become the accomplices of their oppressors. Sartre's idea of consciousness *pursuing* a self, of consciousness being a self-making process, is obviously not an option open to the black South African writer or reader. The state takes upon itself the 'self-creating process' which by rights should be the province of individuals and the community to which they naturally belong. The self-projection of black people is confined within limits not defined by themselves. The whole apartheid system – the pass laws, influx control, Bantu Education – takes from them the opportunity to develop in any way except the one laid down by the state. In Athol Fugard's *Sizwe Bansi's Dead*, all the anguish of this situation is brought to a head: when he is forced to take on the identity of the murdered man and forfeit his own, Sizwe Bansi is giving up that tiny area of himself which the system has not yet been able to erode. So that the photographer's attempts to record his identity on film for his wife illuminate the entire hideous sham, the cosmic con-trick. Whereas Sartre's free man perpetually remakes the meaning of the past in the light of the future he is in the process of choosing, Sizwe Bansi has no choice: as his past was circumscribed by laws which turned people into an identity number, into a mere porter of a piece of paper – a pass – which exceeds them in importance, so their future will be chosen for them – their work, their place of abode, the food they can afford to eat, the mates they can seek, and the patch of earth that will cover their body after death.

Sartre, whose thinking has percolated into the general literary explorations of African writers (even, despite banning, into South African thinking), takes account of just such a contingency when he examines the limits placed by society upon the opportunities available to the individual engaged in making his consciousness:

> The truth of a man is in his wages, his work, for the external world in which he lives is like a map in which certain roads are open and others are marked 'No entrance', or, perhaps worse, 'No exit'. All these patterns are determined by one thing – scarcity.[43]

And society functions in this way because of scarcity, a condition which fosters competition for resources and entails each man in being either the one to die or the one to cause others to die. In this way, Sartre sees every society as being based on violence, and South Africa is an obvious extreme example of this. However, South Africa differs in three important respects from all other societies: not only does it differ in the degree of violence it entails, but it differs in that it bases the choice of who is to die and who is to cause others to die (literally, not figuratively) upon pigmentation, and also in that it enshrines this process in its laws and its religion. In this it is perhaps more honest than the western democracies where a liberal and humanist philosophy is at odds with the economic and social structure. In South Africa the 'No entrance' and 'No exit' signs are concrete and visible: they add to them the words 'for Non-Europeans'. In other societies they are symbolic and invisible.

Even without the legal and religious superstructure in which South Africa enshrines it, racism is a particularly vicious device to alienate human freedom. Its inevitable consequence is to render blacks prisoners of the situation which others have made for them. Under these conditions the only freedom which South African writers in South Africa can exercise is that of recognising society's denial of freedom to themselves and their readers. But if this is done too vociferously they will still be silenced by the censors. Sartre's exposition of the mechanism of exploitation and alienation fits exactly with the South African black's experience. As Hazel Barnes explains in her exposition of Sartre's philosophy:

> It is not economic laws which are pitiless but men. 'It is freedom which limits freedom'. [i.e. The freedom of the white population entails the inhibition of the freedom of the black population. Or as Manganyi puts it, the creation of a mythological caucasian identity is achieved by crushing the black man's identity out of existence. *My note*.] But what makes of freedom a damnation is the fact that man's creative work, his life, is poured out in efforts which do not reflect his being back to him, which make him 'the product of his product', which alienate him from himself.[44]

The black writer in South Africa is the only hope of the alienated black people of the land: they lack all social and political hopes of self-restitution, of finding their own beings reflected back to them authentically. Only writers, working within the very circumscribed limits laid down both for them and their readers by the state, have any power to reverse the process of self-alienation.

ATTEMPTS TO FIND SOLUTIONS: TOWARDS A NEW IDEOLOGY OF LITERATURE

A time of change: from protest to consciousness

While scholars have been at pains to point out the existence, not only of a long oral tradition of African literature in South Africa, but also of a body of written works which precede the twentieth century, the production of literature by black writers has gathered momentum over the last fifty years or so. And over that period there have been swift and far-reaching changes of direction. Writers like Mphahlele have recorded their own movement towards protest writing in their early years, and by the early sixties a considerable body of such writing had come into existence. Protest writing was directed mainly at a white readership: of course it found enthusiastic supporters among the entire literate black population, whose indignation and resentment it voiced; but while it spoke *for* blacks, it spoke *to* whites in an attempt to force them into a recognition of the injustices and humiliations suffered by the majority of the population. Its motivating force, whether recognized or not, was the hope that, once they became aware of the situation, the powerful white minority would do something to improve matters. One instinctively complains to those who hold the power.

The issue was not, of course, as simple as this might suggest. African writers were (and still are) obliged to go to white publishing houses if they wanted any kind of distribution of their work. (There has been one black publishing house in recent years but it has been prevented from operating effectively by increasingly draconian censorship regulations.) White publishing houses, not unnaturally, directed their sales efforts at a white market. (Lack of education and absence of money for luxuries such as books eliminated any chance, at that time – the situation has changed drastically in recent years – of a black market.) So before black writers took up the pen, their consciousness was already imprinted with a knowledge of the audience they had to address if they wanted to publish.

Thus much of the pre-Soweto 1976 writing was white-oriented: many of Peter Abraham's novels; the short stories of writers like Mphahlele, James Matthews, Bloke Modisane; the autobiographies of the sixties writers like Modisane, Matshikiza, Mphahlele; the poems of Brutus and Nortje; even the early poems of the seventies poets who later became for a time pillars of the Black Consciousness Movement: Gwala, Serote, Sepamla, Kgositsile. And yet, even then, not all writing was white directed. With the emergence of a magazine for Africans in the fifties – *Drum* – Can Themba, Casey Motsisi, Nat Nakasa and others were directing their satirical columns at an almost exclusively African readership.

Gradually, however, black writers became aware of the futility of battering at the closed door of apartheid, despite the friendly liberal glances through the spy-hole, and began to be aware of the need to foster black self-confidence and deal with daily humiliations and injustices by self-healing.

> After we were hurt, after our humanism met with an uncompromisingly cruel rebuff, we thought we could withdraw, take cover in our blackness. This time consciously.[45]

African writers in South Africa, like most African writers everywhere else, had always taken commitment for granted. Now however, they recognised the need to direct their work at the black community, and to use it to transform the consciousness of their people, to reverse the process of alienation. By focusing on the negation of freedom and identity black writers attempt to reflect back to their readers an authentic sense of being. In doing this they have to work within very narrow limits, lacking as they do the free consciousness which Sartre regarded as essential to the task, just as their readers lack the ability to make a free response, for they too have had their freedom removed as a consequence of being born.

And yet, despite the overwhelming conditioning to which they have been subjected, despite all the efforts by the censors to emasculate their writing, black writers do exercise that minimal freedom they have left, 'the small movement' (as Sartre puts it) 'which makes of a totally conditioned social being someone who does not render back completely what his conditioning has given him'.[46] This is done by reflecting back their condition to the readers, rather than reflecting the stereotype image imposed on them by the state. In this way it is possible to make readers less susceptible to the conditioning process of government. As soon as the unconscious processes of oppression are brought into consciousness, the oppressor begins to lose his power. In this way, the black writer achieves what Sartre calls 'the liberating creativity of art'.[47] By using autobiographical material in a totally different way from that of the European tradition, South African writers are able to help their readers out of this deadlock upon their consciousness and urge them into grasping that small degree of freedom they have left – the freedom not to be what they have been conditioned to be. By examining what has happened to them, they offer the readers a reflection of their own fate; by seeking out their own identity, they help the readers to find theirs.

But this is not the full extent of their powers. They are able, through their literary work, to help both themselves and the reader to an active mastery of their traumatic situation. Trilling, in his essay *Freud and Literature*[48] suggests that literature can serve the same function for readers as the dream, in Freudian theory, does for dreamers: that is, give them a chance to recoup their failure to deal with a situation in real life. Thus, just as in the real life situation, so, Trilling suggests, literature can serve the same function, and give both writers and readers a much more dependable control over a situation than the more passive, negative operation of catharsis, which Trilling regards as 'perhaps the result of glossing over terror with beautiful language rather than an evacuation of it'.[49]

This is perhaps why, whatever the literary genre in which it is cast, the content of South African literature is so often autobiographical. Such content forces writers to face up once again to the worst that society has done to them, to drag out of the subconscious all the shadows that have darkened their lives as members of a subjugated group – the systematic obliteration of identity, the emasculation consequent upon being treated as a child in an adult world, the humiliation of the gut reaction of cowardice in the face of authority and in the face of the community violence resulting from the social conditions imposed upon them. And in reworking the entire process of subjugation the writers gain some degree of control over it, and over their own emotional reactions – a control which they also pass on to the reader. South African writers dissect the nightmare of their condition in using their own life as content. All that black individuals have suppressed, in order to make life tolerable, all the roles they play to placate the authorities, to assist the caucasians in the maintenance of their superior identity, the role of yes-man, clown, idiot, all of this the South African writers drag up into the light of day and force both themselves and the reader into confrontation with it. Functioning in this way, literature assumes a therapeutic role.

A time for action: from consciousness to participation

If it was to stop at therapy, though, black consciousness literature, however helpful to the individual writer or reader, would hardly fulfil the function demanded by critics and public alike, of a literature of commitment. Black readers must not only overcome their debased self-image, but commit themselves to a positive, dynamic political role.

There is no place in the South African political arena for the passive disapproval of apartheid: there is no longer, even, a place for non-violent opposition. The demise of the Liberal Party (as much the outcome of a superseded political approach as of the government banning: after all, the ANC has flourished underground despite banning) is an example of this. Acceptance of the need for political change unfortunately involves automatic acceptance of the need for some degree of violence. And it is in the literature of the day that the person in the street seeks the rationale for such an acceptance.

In the early protest writing, literature often proved an outlet for the build-up of tension in the individual. Manganyi specifically sees literature as providing an outlet for the writers' violence, providing both them and the readers with a kind of catharsis. This violence, however, which results from frustration and humiliation in daily life, is useless as a political weapon, and until it has been satisfactorily worked out of the system, the writer is in no position to foster political struggle. Mphahlele frequently refers to the anger that chokes the black writer, and points out that it gives rise to a self-defeating didacticism within a literary work.

Nevertheless, one has to be careful here, not to apply the traditional western literary critical rejection of didacticism and propaganda in literary works to a literature which has a totally different aim. Mphahlele is not rejecting the whole idea of teaching through literary works, when he cites examples of anger undermining the effect of a novel or play or story. He is merely rejecting unresolved didacticism, that is not fused with the work, that stands apart from the story or play so that the personality of the writer intrudes between it and the reader.

Black South African writing *has* to teach, to inform, to motivate the reader or spectator directly as a condition of its validity as literature. In his introduction to *South African People's Plays*[50] – plays by Kente, Mutwa, Shezi and Workshop 71 – Robert Mshengu Kavanagh explains how Kente was pushed from commercial theatre into radical theatre by the increasing militancy of his mass audience – an interesting case of audience manipulation of the writer in a rather more extreme form than usual. A situation has come about in South Africa whereby literature really is the literature of the people, and where such is the militancy of the people that they impatiently reject any works that do not deal with the situation that confronts them. Yet recent writing has begun to move away from the strident self-assertiveness of the early black consciousness writing. Having asserted identity and raised consciousness, writers are shifting to a less defensive role, and one which has indeed more political clout: that of documenting the collective efforts of a people towards the removal of minority rule and apartheid.

A time for experiment: new attitudes to form, language, production and distribution

It is not possible, however, to use conventional literary forms as vehicles for black South African literature's new role. Literary forms inevitably embody the ideologies which give rise to them. Eagleton summarises the belief common both to Hegel and Marx that:

> artistic form is no mere quirk on the part of the individual artist. Forms are historically determined by the kind of 'content' they have to embody: they are changed, transformed, broken down, and revolutionized as that content itself changes.[51]

It is impossible to overestimate the significance of form in literature:

> The true bearers of ideology in art are the very forms, rather than abstractable content, of the work itself. We find the impress of history in the literary work precisely *as literary*, not as some superior form of social documentation.[52]

The writer's resource bank for form, and even for the creation of new form is of course literary tradition, which in turn has been forged out of contemporary ideological structures. (For example, the novel arose, as Ian Watt so carefully demonstrates, out of the bourgeois individualism that became dominant with the rise of capitalism in the eighteenth century.) And the form inevitably dictates the relationship between audience/reader and writer: for example, a play is necessarily a collective and potentially a participatory literary experience, whilst the reading of a novel is an individualistic and solitary undertaking. Therefore, 'in selecting a form . . . the writer finds his choice already ideologically circumscribed.'[53] The form which writers choose determines what they are able to say and how they are able to relate to their audience. It even determines who the audience is: the refined literary work could never reach the people the black South African writer is interested in reaching – the mass of the people. Indeed, for literature to reach out to a mass public at all is a relatively new undertaking (though not, of course, unprecedented, witness medieval mystery plays and Elizabethan drama).

Thus South African authors are brought into immediate

confrontation with the issue. In deciding to write in English they
become heirs to an alien European literary tradition, and a collection
of genres none of which were ideally suited to their tasks. Many
critics writing in the sixties and seventies have commented on the
comparative absence of novels from African writing in that country,
and explained it by the social conditions the writer is subjected to –
crowded living conditions, long working hours, constant harassment
by the police, the pace of life. All these issues render the short,
quickly-finished piece of writing, such as the story, more of a feasible
proposition, and perhaps better-suited to what a writer, living this
kind of life, has to say.

Political conditions also dictate the choice of genres to some extent:
when the short story-writers of the sixties began to be banned and
imprisoned, writers took to the more cryptic form of poetry as a genre
less accessible to the censors – for intellectual understanding has to
precede censorship. The short story writer James Matthews changed to
the poetic form without making any claims for himself as a poet:

> To label my utterings poetry
> and myself a poet
> would be as self-deluding
> as the planners of parallel development.
> I record the anguish of the persecuted . . . [54]

Moreover, a rash of exiles, both forced and self-imposed, elicited a
series of autobiographies from writers who wished to take stock of their
lives and work through those experiences that had brought them to the
point of leaving South Africa. In the eighties, as the liberation
movement has consolidated opposition to the regime, a body of novels
is beginning to emerge which chart the progress of this consolidation
and the growth of action.

But beyond these expediencies lies a dawning understanding of the
need for new forms, the need to break away from the constraints of the
old forms, when social as well as literary revolution is at stake. When
Mutloatse, in his introduction to the anthology *Forced Landing*, says:

> We'll write our poems in narrative form; we'll write journalistic
> pieces in poetry form; we'll dramatise our poetic experiences; we'll
> poeticise our historical dramas. [55]

he is revealing his perception of the interdependence of commitment
and experiment with forms. As Eagleton puts it:

'Commitment' is more than just a matter of presenting correct political opinions in one's art; it reveals itself in how far the artist reconstructs the artistic forms at his disposal, turning authors, readers and spectators into collaborators.[56]

It is not just a matter of trying on forms for size, and tailoring models to suit their own particular needs: it is a question of the interconnection between ideology and form. There is a growing determination not to be hampered by literary conventions or critical demands in the specific task they have set themselves – the furtherance of social and political liberation:

We will have to *donder* conventional literature: old-fashioned critic and reader alike. We are going to pee, spit and shit on literary convention before we are through; we are going to kick and pull and push and drag literature into the form we prefer. We are going to experiment and probe and not give a dam what the critics have to say. Because we are in search of our true selves – undergoing self-discovery as a people.[57]

Mutloatse is discovering for himself, here, what Trotsky described in somewhat more academic terms in *Literature and Revolution*, namely that:

The relationship between form and content is determined by the fact that the new form is discovered, proclaimed and evolved under the pressure of an inner need, of a collective psychological demand which, like everything else . . . has its social roots.[58]

Thus, as Eagleton explains:

Significant developments in literary form, then, result from significant changes in ideology. They embody new ways of perceiving social reality and . . . new relations between artist and audience.[59]

What begins as unformulated resentment of critical failure to understand their aims, as a feeling that literary critics were chastising them for not living up to standards that were totally foreign to their undertaking, has now been thought through to its conclusion and has emerged as a vigorous full-scale search for appropriate literary forms to encompass the very specific goals they have set themselves as committed writers, writing in a state of siege.

And just as they have tried on genres for size and found them fitting badly, so they have rejected the alien literary language they have inherited. At first this was an angry response to patronising critics who pointed out the African writers' deficiencies in the finer points of *belles lettres* or the areas of refined literary skills. As time went on, however, the African writers began to realise how irrelevant western literary language was to what they were attempting to do. They now take the language of the township streets – that vigorous mixture of African grammar, local idiom and jazz rhythm, often incorporating words from English and Afrikaans as well as all the vernaculars – and from it forge their poems and novels and autobiographies. What seems like violence to the language to the mother-tongue speaker of English serves two functions: it enables the township reader to identify with it (even the black middle classes who are often shocked by the public obscenities recognise it as authentic), and it alienates the white readership, and by that very alienation is often able to shock readers into a new awareness of what the writer is trying to convey.

The achievement of black South African writers in establishing the language of the people as the language of their literature cannot be underestimated: publishers now accept, and indeed eagerly demand their work; non-black readers valiantly struggle with the obscurities of unknown vocabulary; critics discuss it in the universities; but more important than any of these, people in the townships and on the farms, children in the schools and men in the shebeens, take these poems and stories and dramas as their own, in the full confidence that their literature speaks not only *to* them, but *for* them; that it expresses in full their social and political and individual being; that it embodies their revolution now in progress.

Of course, such a dissemination of literature among the people was not achieved without a radical change in attitude towards the production and distribution of literature. The individualistic production model and the capitalist distribution model prevalent in the western world in any case conflicts with literary tradition in Africa, which is oral: poems, songs, dances and dramas have always been group activities directed at and participated in by the tribe. Nor was education ever sufficiently widespread or advanced in South Africa to create a black reading public with the leisure and money to devote themselves to novel-reading. As a consequence the western literary tradition did not take root and could not have done so. Nor was it likely that a class of ivory-tower writers would have emerged.

Instead, writers have met together and discussed stories and poems at workshops; actors and producers have fashioned plays together, and performed them in halls and rooms all over the townships to mass audiences that would never dream of entering a regular theatre; poetry readings are no longer elegant, élitist literary affairs, but take their place (as indeed poetry always has done in the African context) at funerals, political meetings, community celebrations or any large gatherings of people. Poetry, stories and excerpts from novels, together with drawings, paintings and photographs are reproduced in magazines like *Staffrider* and hawked from door to door, in crowded buses and trains and at gatherings. Books produced by publishers like Ravan Press or Ad Donker are hawked in the same way, as well as being sold at gatherings.

In this way literature has been brought out of academia and into the streets of the shanty towns. South African writers have begun to forge a genuine literature of the people: a literature in which the spectator and the reader have acquired an importance that is perhaps unprecedented in the history of literature: a literature which reflects back to its readers their struggle for emancipation, and at the same time reinvigorates them for that very struggle: a literature which has abandoned the universities and the comfortable living rooms of the intellectuals in favour of the streets. So that when political meetings were held all over South Africa in September 1983 to commemorate the death of Steve Biko, poetry, folk-singing, plays and photographic exhibitions were an integral part of them, reflecting, as the *Observer* report commented 'an attempt to use culture as a major weapon in the black liberation struggle.'[60]

CRITICISM AND BLACK SOUTH AFRICAN WRITING

Black writing and literary theory

> Breaking with the literary institution does not just mean offering different accounts of Beckett; it means breaking with the very ways literature, literary criticism and its supporting social values are defined.[61]

The emergence over recent decades of this body of vigorous black South African writing which conforms to none of the traditional western literary standards and is not evaluable by any of its conventional critical norms, has posed the critics with almost insuperable difficulties. Conditioned as they are to use ritualistically, well-defined analytical tools to reach universally acceptable value judgements, and so insert the subject of their study into a regular place in the literary hierarchy, they can only be nonplussed when faced with an obviously energetic and thriving corpus of writing which is fulfilling a dynamic and significant role among the people for whom it was written and at the same time making an impact on the western world. Yet most of this writing, measured by the yardsticks which they have at their command, can only be demonstrated to be, at best, second-rate literature, and at worst, not literature at all.

The root of the problem can be traced to a very specific concept of what constitutes literature which has evolved during the last two centuries. Starting with the Romantics' focus on the individual, on the writer as God-like creator, western literature has been hived off as a special occupation, a solitary pursuit, and gradually denuded of the community, political and social functions typical of literary activity in previous centuries. The same period has witnessed the growth of criticism as an academic subject, and this has contributed to the narrowing down of literature to the pursuit (whether for pleasure or profit) of an intellectual élite. In the process an *apparent* divorce between literature and ideology has come to be stressed. This is not to argue that literature throughout this period has always been devoid of social purpose – the Romantics' assertion that the poet was the unacknowledged legislator of the world and the novels of social reform of the Victorian period demonstrate a recurrent consciousness of literature's social function. And even those literary movements and critical theories which stress the disjunction between art and life (the art for art's sake war-cry or the autonomy theories of art) have contributed to the maintenance of a particular social order. Indeed, even the realist writers themselves, by making the universe they presented and the concepts sustaining that universe appear natural, rather than imposed structures, have reinforced the liberal humanist tradition which has emerged as the aesthetic of bourgeois capitalism:

> From the infant school to the University faculty, literature is a vital instrument for the insertion of individuals into the perceptual and symbolic forms of the dominant ideological formation, able to accomplish this function with a 'naturalness', spontaneity and experiential immediacy possible to no other ideological practice.[62]

From Matthew Arnold on, in fact, literature has been openly used to inculcate moral values (hence all the horror when German concentration camp superintendents combined sensitivity to the arts with the ultimate insensitivity towards human beings). And criticism has followed in literature's footsteps, from *Scrutiny* to the present-day Marxist critics. Indeed, Eagleton's whole quarrel with liberal humanist criticism is based on its refusal to recognise itself for what it is:

> Liberal humanist criticism is not wrong to use literature, but wrong to deceive itself that it does not. It uses it to further certain moral values, which . . . are in fact indissociable from certain ideological ones, and in the end imply a particular form of politics.[63]

There is in fact no such thing as non-political criticism, just as there is no such thing as non-political art. The criticism that sees literature as innocent and natural, is in fact making a political statement; its refusal to meddle in the political arena or to consider the social and historical implications of a work of art is actually tacitly condoning the *status quo*. This may not be so obvious in a so-called democratic regime where everyone is apparently free to pursue their own ends, but a situation like the one in South Africa, where an absence of political interest amounts to criminal irresponsibility, compels one to re-examine the situation elsewhere in the world and realise that there, too, a lack of political concern is also a political statement:

> The idea that there are 'non-political' forms of criticism is simply a myth which furthers certain political uses of literature all the more effectively . . . It is not a question of debating whether 'literature' should be related to 'history' or not: it is a question of different readings of history itself.[64]

The apparently neutral critical theories that have emerged this century, fostered as they are within the universities which themselves are in existence in order to nurture perpetrators of the system, have implicit within them whole social ideologies: they, too, contribute to the strengthening of existing power systems. Eagleton comments on critical theory's flight over the years from the living situations of men and women with which literature is supposed to deal – a flight which only underlines the bond between ideology and literature:

> The story of modern literary theory, paradoxically, is the narrative of a flight from such realities into a seemingly endless range of alternatives: the poem itself, the organic society, eternal verities, the imagination, the structure of the human mind, myth, language and so on . . . Even in the act of fleeing modern ideologies, however, literary theory reveals its often unconscious complicity with them,

betraying its élitism, sexism or individualism in the very 'aesthetic' or 'unpolitical' language it finds natural to use of the literary text.[65]

Thus the inappropriateness of western critical methods to deal with the emergent literature in South Africa is more of a statement about literary criticism than about black South African writing. That it provides no methods for the examination and analysis of a different kind of literature is hardly an invalidation of the writing but rather an exposure of an inadequacy in critical theory and critical method. By refusing to comply with literary convention or to bend to critical pressure, South African writers have illuminated a weak spot in the entire institution of literature – a weakness noted in Eagleton's comment on Barthes' discussion of literary narcissism in *Writing Degree Zero*:

> There is no doubt that the 'guilt' of which Barthes speaks is the guilt of the institution of Literature itself – an institution which . . . testifies to the division of languages and the division of classes. To write in a 'literary' way, in modern society, is inevitably to collude with such divisiveness.[66]

Black South African writers, over recent years, have consistently consolidated their refusal to write in a literary way, and thus to collude, not merely with the division of languages and the division of classes, but also with the division of races. (Indeed blacks have come to perceive that their struggle is as much a struggle about class and language as about race.)

There are, however, areas in which aesthetic and literary theory can illuminate the critical analysis of the way black South African writers *have* chosen to write. For example, though structuralist criticism was a response to a problem specific to western Europe – the breakdown of language in an industrial society – its questioning of the assumptions of naturalness, of a fixed and dependable reality that was transferable to literature, provides an essential prerequisite for the examination of black literature from South Africa.

Eagleton's account of the belief underlying structuralism provides a subtle parallel with the dominant white ideology within which and against which black South African culture has had to construct itself:

> Structuralism is a modern inheritor of the belief that reality, and our experience of it, are discontinuous with each other; as such, it threatens the ideological security of those who wish the world to be

within their control, to carry its singular meaning on its face and to yield it up to them in the unblemished mirror of their language.[67]

There are ironical parallels here with the real-life situations of blacks and whites in South Africa. Through black consciousness, blacks have come to know that reality and their experience of it are discontinuous with each other; and the white minority's ideological security rests upon their 'naturalising' of a structured situation which in fact has nothing natural about it, and which depends, for its continuance, on a sufficiently large proportion of the population accepting it as natural; as that proportion dwindles, the amount spent on arms and internal defence automatically increases. Black writers have had to carry over these realisations into their writings; and though their work is a far cry from the European modernists, they, like the modernists, have been forced to a rejection of an earlier mode. In the case of black (and indeed recent white) South African writers it has been a rejection of a literature which evaded confrontation with the crucial issues – nature poetry about the South African bush, or fiction that accepted as the norm, even if it was a norm to be deplored, the segregation of the races by pigmentation.

Ultimately, however, structuralism fails to provide us with a critical method, for, like phenomenology, it springs from 'the ironic act of shutting out the material world in order the better to illuminate our consciousness of it.'[68] Black South African writers have too urgent a grasp of consciousness as an active and purposeful force within their social context for such an introspective literary theory to operate. In structuralism, as Eagleton points out, there is no attempt to grapple with the concept of literature as

a social *practice*, a form of *production* which was not necessarily exhausted by the product itself. Structuralism could dissect that product, but it refused to enquire into the material conditions of its making, since this might mean surrendering to the myth of an 'origin'. Nor were many structuralists worried about how the product was actually consumed – about what happened when people actually read works of literature, what role such works played in social relations as a whole.[69]

But where black writing is concerned, the material conditions of its making and consumption are crucial to an understanding of what it is all about. No critical account can be rendered without taking these into consideration.

Black writing and theories of artistic consciousness

This apprehension of consciousness as an active and purposeful force is the reason why Jung's notion of the objectivity and impersonality of the artist is totally foreign to black writers' ideas about writing. For them impersonality is a rejection of the burden of commitment, a refusal to face up to the sickness of their society, an irresponsible repudiation of the knowledge of the cancer at the heart of things. In any case, the autobiographical approach, which most writers have adopted, makes this kind of impersonality impossible of attainment. For the method adopted by most contemporary writers in their self-imposed task is to examine the traumatic effects of the situation in which everyone lives by examining what has been done to themselves. We shall see that this method sets up its own limits and circumscribes the effectiveness of the work of art conceived under its influence, unless the writer develops techniques to over-come the problem.

But Jung's 'collective man', carrying and shaping the unconscious and psychic life of, not mankind, but his own people, is exactly their apprehension of the artist: though they would give this a much more practical, less metaphysical implication than Jung would. There is also an element in their image of the artist that would concur with Eliot's view of the need for artists to work towards the extinction of their own personality. But whereas, for Eliot, the artist undergoes this self-sacrifice for the platonic ideal of Art, South African writers do so for People: they submerge their personality, the better to represent the community, just as they forego their individual needs and aims in order to further the movement to which they are committed. There cannot be the separation of the man who suffers and the mind which creates demanded by Eliot, in a committed literature. There, the life of the writer is significant in a way it can never be in conventional European literature: but it is significant in a communal rather than an auto-biographical way.

This is why Eliot's unqualified dismissal of the realms of psychology and sociology as areas of exploration for the critic is nonsensical where South African writing is concerned. Such writing cannot be examined unless the critic takes into account the mind of the person who writes and the circumstances *in* which and *for* which he or she creates, and recognises that the South African writer gives priority to the *function* of the work as a catalyst within a specific community, rather than to the notions of literary tradition and literary value so important to Eliot. There nevertheless remains a question of how best the literary work achieves such a function and whether or not some degree of objectivity is necessary for this purpose.

Sartre, in *What is Literature* goes some way towards examining this whole question of the mind of the writer and its effect upon the mind of the readers, then, via them, upon society at large – the most pressing concern of black South African literature. Examining the motives for artistic creation, he infers that its chief motive is

> the need of feeling that we are essential in relationship to the world. If I fix on canvas or in writing a certain aspect of the fields or sea or a look on someone's face which I have disclosed, I am conscious of having produced them by condensing relationships, by introducing order where there was none, by imposing the unity of mind on the diversity of things. That is, I feel myself essential in relation to my creation.[70]

In order to do this he requires the co-operation of the reader, and this involves certain restraints upon the writer. He is obliged to appeal to the reader's freedom – a task which necessitates the purging of his own passions as an individual, since these would interfere with the reader's response:

> If I appeal to my reader so that we may carry the enterprise which I have begun to a successful conclusion, it is self-evident that I consider him as a pure freedom, as an unconditioned activity; thus, in no case can I address myself to his passivity, that is, try to *affect* him, to communicate to him, from the very first, emotions of fear, desire, or anger . . . Freedom is alienated in the state of passion; it is abruptly engaged in partial enterprises; it loses sight of its task which is to produce an absolute end. And the book is no longer anything but a means for feeding hate or desire. The writer should not seek to *overwhelm* otherwise he is in contradiction with himself.[71] (Sartre's emphasis)

He also castigates those writers who do concern themselves with rousing emotions as an easy way out of the task of artistic creation, since it is easy to provoke such emotions, and they are 'foreseeable' and 'manageable'. This charge has particular bearing on the question of South African literature, since so many writers concentrate their efforts on precisely this end.

But as Sartre insists, if the work of art is to produce an authentic effect upon the reader, 'the reader must be able to make a certain aesthetic withdrawal'.[72] Here Sartre is taking one stage further the arguments of Eliot and Jung for the impersonality of the artist and the work, and applying them also to the reader, without whose co-operation the work of art has no significant existence of its own. Just as the artist has to surrender himself to the collective unconscious, to sacrifice himself to a consciousness of the past, so the reader has also to lend himself to the work of art, to create for its reception a state of passivity, to make himself credulous that the artefact may do its work on him.

> It is a Passion, in the Christian sense of the word, that is, a freedom which resolutely puts itself into a state of passivity to obtain a certain transcendent effect by this sacrifice . . . Thus reading is an exercise in generosity.[73]

In such a situation the artist is doubly beholden not to betray the generosity of the reader, but to demand of him 'the gift of his whole person, with his passion, his prepossessions, his sympathies, his sexual temperament and his scale of values'.[74] If he writes in passion, then he inevitably forfeits the trust and confidence of his reader:

> Certainly I do not deny when I am reading that the author may be impassioned, nor even that he might have conceived the first plan of his work under the sway of passion. But his decision to write supposes that he withdraws somewhat from his feelings, in short that he has transformed his emotions into free emotions as I do mine while reading him; that is, that he is in an attitude of generosity.[75]

What Eliot and Jung conceive of as the prerequisites of great art – the surrender of the artist's personality to the forces of the collective unconscious or the consciousness of the past – Sartre sees as an obligation on the part of the artist to the reader, in a contract which involves the freedom and the generosity of each, in order that the final goal of art might be achieved; 'to recover this world by giving it to be seen as it is, but as if it had its source in human freedom'.[76]

It is at this point that Sartre sees aesthetic considerations as merging with moral considerations. For he shows how impossible it is, in a situation in which art draws upon the freedom of the artist and the freedom of the reader, and their mutual generosity, to achieve its goal, for an artist to lend his work to support injustice or oppression. If he gives the world to the reader, together with the injustices it comprehends, it is only that the reader might 'animate them with (his) indignation . . . as abuses to be suppressed'.[77] Hence his argument for the withdrawal from feelings on the part of the writer, the transformation of emotions into free emotions, is by no means an argument for the impartiality of the artist, only an argument for the objective control of his approach. His ultimate object is to incite the reader to the suppression of abuses, but he must achieve this not by rousing the reader's emotions directly, as a didactic work attempts to do, where the writer tries to manipulate the reader by telling him how to react and what to think, but by freely allowing his re-creation of the world freely to play upon the reader. Thus we arrive at a point where aesthetic considerations automatically involve moral considerations, where aesthetics and ethics have a common goal: 'At the heart of the aesthetic imperative we discern the moral imperative.'[78] It may be that the destruction of ethics within South African society, whereby the normal rules for civilised behaviour have been turned upside down, has seriously interfered with the establishment of valid aesthetics. For South African writers, in their particular situation, the transformation of emotions into free emotions has not only become impossible, but would be reprehensibly laissez-faire.

Yet Sartre sees artistic freedom as inextricably linked to social and political freedom:

> It would be inconceivable that this unleashing of generosity provoked by the writer could be used to authorize an injustice, and that the reader could enjoy his freedom while reading a work which approves or accepts or simply abstains from condemning the subjection of man by man.[79]

He finds it impossible to imagine a good novel written in praise of anti-Semitism, since the freedom of the writer is so bound up with the freedom of all other men, and this freedom cannot be used to approve of the enslavement of a section of mankind. He claims that no writer can write for slaves, and that the art of prose, by its very nature, is bound to democracy. So that if democracy is threatened, there comes a point where the writer must cease writing and take up arms:

> Writing is a certain way of wanting freedom; once you have begun, you are engaged, willy-nilly.[80]

So much for the state of mind of the artist and the attitude of the critic. All the critics mentioned so far would be inclined to agree with Wimsatt and Beardsley's dictum that:

> The evaluation of the work of art remains public; the work is measured against something outside the author.[81]

Indeed this conviction lies at the heart of South African beliefs about the role of art in society.

But what *is* the function of art, and how are we to distinguish great art from the second-rate, if we are neither to assess how far the authors have fulfilled their intention nor to ask ourselves how the work of art has affected us as readers? Now even the New Critics, for all their rejection of value judgements, reverted to testing the effect of a work of art for establishing the boundaries of great art. Northrop Frye points out how different is the study of masterpieces from the study of mediocre works of art:

> The study of mediocre works of art, however energetic, obstinately remains a random and peripheral form of critical experience, whereas the profound masterpiece seems to draw us to a point at which we can see an enormous number of converging patterns of significance.[82]

Here again we see the need for withdrawal on the part of the artist, since the retention of 'private memories and associations, his desire for self-expression, and all the other navel-strings and feeding-tubes of his ego'[83] can only obstruct the emergence of 'converging patterns of significance'. (South African writers are in a different position in this respect in that they have renounced their private, egotistical emotions in favour of the community in any case.) Artists must purge themselves of their identity as a person in order to provide the more perfect instrument for the work of art. Jung points out that, as a consequence of this theory, it is unreasonable to expect the artist to interpret his work. His job is merely to give it form, the interpretation is the task of the readers:

> A great work of art is like a dream; for all its apparent obviousness it does not explain itself and is never unequivocal.[84]

And if something is necessarily equivocal, it is useless to expect it to provide clear moral imperatives or categorical statements of the truth. It presents its images in the same way that nature allows a plant to grow, suggests Jung, and leaves the reader to draw his own conclusions. Such assumptions are obviously alien to the majority of South African writers.

Sartre, however, puts forward as one of the functions of art an idea with which most South African writers would find themselves in sympathy – that in seeking to enlist the readers' sympathies for the oppressed, literature needs to make us not only '*know* what it is like to be a victim, but also to *feel* it'.[85]

In fact their approach to literature and its function lies closer to Sartre's ideals than to those of any other critic mentioned so far, with the exception perhaps of the Marxist critics touched on in passing. South African writers emphasise the point that, in the circumstances in which they write, any approach which is not wholly pragmatic is totally irrelevant. They dismiss with scorn the recent dedication of western literature to the analysis of metaphysical neuroses. Their literature has to serve a much more down-to-earth function – it has to express the victimisation of an entire community, to speak for its humiliation and shame, to bring home to the readers a consciousness of their state of being, and to help them come to terms with the violence evoked by the situation in which they find themselves:

> Art, like an unconscious process, possesses the quality of shocking us out of our complacency by reflecting those contradictions and dimensions of human existence which prey on us while we sleep.[86]

Manganyi sees literature as fulfilling a distinct social role, by mediating 'the dissonances between violence against the self and violence as a social act'[87] – that is, art acts as a surrogate for violence. While ordinary black people in South Africa can only escape violence against themselves through violence against others, writers are able to resolve anguish into images, to substitute artistic creation for the violent or rebellious act:

> The image forces itself from formlessness into clarity and through the creative act the artist also transforms subjective experience into the realm of the universal.[88]

Thus their writing achieves for themselves and for their readers 'a long-term unmasking of the false consciousness'[89] – that false consciousness which encouraged the victims to smile, to appear to co-operate with the oppressor in the continuance of their submission. In this unmasking of the false consciousness, we can see the operation of Sartre's principle of artistic freedom, by which both writer and reader are released through the work of art from the false consciousness that had held them bound.

South African writers do not, perhaps, lay as much stress as Sartre does on the necessity of transforming their emotions into free emotions – undoubtedly because of a difference in artistic purpose. Sartre's approach to commitment passed through three distinct stages: his earliest phase was one of non-engagement – creative writing would provide the writer with a way to escape the meaningless contingency of the world. Later he was to insist that the writer committed himself, accepted responsibility for changing the world to save others. Finally he reached the point where he questioned the privileged position of the writer and suggested that literature had no role to play in freeing the oppressed; and that the writer should either restrict himself to the political tract or put down his pen and take up arms. South African writers on the other hand, have been devotees of committed literature since they first began to think about the role of the artist. And since the rise of the Black Consciousness Movement there has never been any question of separating writing from actual political activity: both are demanded of the writer simultaneously. Not only must their literary works foster the struggle, but they must take upon themselves the revolutionary tasks of any other section of the community. In black South Africa the alienation of writers from society that besets the western world is annulled: writers feed not only their words, but also their deeds into the struggle. The black writers' explorations of their literary consciousness have a completely pragmatic aim: that of perfecting the functioning of their art within the community.

Black writing and socio-historical criticism

Given the positivist base of black writing in South Africa, the most useful critical methods currently available are to be found in the approaches of the Marxist critics who always, whatever particular slant they give to Marxist critical theory, take into account social and historical factors in their assessment of a work of art, and consider the conditions of production and consumption – that is, they examine its function within the social structure as a social practice, and do not look at it as a thing apart from the everyday world of social reality. Literature is seen as one form of production among many others, and the story or poem as an artefact, similar to other craft products, to be consumed by the reader.

Marxist critics are also the ones to recognise the extent to which literature is a privilege accorded to the few at the expense of the many – a recognition especially relevant to South Africa:

Men and women do not live by culture alone, the vast majority of them throughout history have been deprived of the chance of living by it at all, and those few who are fortunate enough to live by it now are able to do so because of the labour of those who do not.[90]

For this reason, Benjamin demanded careful 'dissociation' on the part of the historical materialist critic:

> According to traditional practice, the spoils are carried along in the procession. They are called cultural treasures, and a historical materialist views them with cautious detachment. For without exception the cultural treasures he surveys have an origin which he cannot contemplate without horror. They owe their existence not only to the efforts of the great minds and talents which have created them, but also to the anonymous toil of their contemporaries. There is no document of civilisation which is not at the same time a document of barbarism.[91]

A large part of the rejection of western culture by black South African writers on the grounds of irrelevance, can be traced to this élitist factor: to the reality that European writers were, and still are, the privileged few, writing for the privileged few: that their leisure was made possible by the physical labour of the majority, who were left with neither time, energy nor money to indulge in culture. South African writers, on the other hand, in refusing to write in a literary way, in aiming their stories and poems at the ordinary man and woman, assert their identification with their people: they are, even now, attempting to answer with their work Slaughter's question in *Marxism, Ideology and Literature*:

> Can the writer change the actual practice in which his 'educational privilege', his means of production, is manifested?[92]

And yet they face many problems in this task. For, as Trotsky was careful to point out in *Literature and Revolution*, there is no such thing as proletarian culture, for, by definition, the proletariat have always been deprived of the means to acquire it: property, education, leisure and so on.[93] And, as I have shown earlier in this chapter, the problem is compounded in South Africa by a number of factors which have prevented any kind of literary tradition emerging.

It is for these reasons that the culture presently manifesting itself is perforce a political culture. They really have now politicised art, as Benjamin once demanded of the European socialists: their fight is not only a fight against apartheid, but also a fight against a history of imperialism and a present of exploitation:

> Imperialism is not only the exploitation of cheap labour-power, raw materials and easy markets but the uprooting of languages and customs – not just the imposition of foreign armies, but of alien ways of experiencing. It manifests itself not only in company balance sheets and in air-bases, but can be tracked to the most intimate roots of speech and signification. In such situations . . . culture is so vitally bound up with one's common identity that there is no need to argue for its relation to political struggle. It is arguing against it which would seem incomprehensible.[94]

The Black Consciousness Movement is itself a history of the attempt to come to terms with an endurance of imperialism, exploitation, with uprooted languages and customs and the imposition of alien ways of experiencing. Eagleton explains how literature can function both on behalf of imperialists to establish hegemony, and on behalf of the oppressed, to preserve their identity:

> Literature is . . . a crucial mechanism by which the language and ideology of an imperialist class establishes its hegemony, or by which a subordinated state, class or region preserves and perpetuates at the ideological level an historical identity shattered or eroded at the political. It is also a zone in which such struggles achieve stabilization.[95]

And the role black consciousness writers have assigned to literature in this attempt is more or less the role Marxist critics accord it within a revolutionary situation. Black writers answer with a vigorous affirmative Slaughter's questions:

> Cannot art have an essential role in preparing man for the practice in which he needs to engage to break the rigid institutional and ideological framework?[96]

and

> Does [the artist's] work help to engage the reader, the onlooker, the listener, as a whole man endowed with passion, will, thought and the capacity for action, to confront, or in some cases simple [sic] to accomplish the feat of not succumbing to, those human creations

which have assumed independence of his control and have taken on the appearance of unalterable obstacles.[97]

One of the human creations which have assumed independence of the artist's control and taken on the appearance of an unalterable obstacle is, of course, the entire institution of literary criticism:

> Critical discourse is power. To be on the inside of the discourse itself is to be blind to this power, for what is more natural and non-dominative than to speak one's own tongue.[98]

But black writers are *outside* this discourse, and when it is applied to their work they are quick to perceive the power – a power which they have to break completely if their writing is to accomplish its object:

> The power of critical discourse moves on several levels. It is the power of 'policing' language – of determining that certain statements must be excluded because they do not conform to what is acceptably sayable. It is the power of policing writing itself, classifying it into the 'literary' and the 'non-literary', the enduringly great and the ephemerally popular. It is the power of authority vis-a-vis others – the power relations between those who define and preserve the discourse, and those who are selectively admitted to it.[99]

Hence the statements by black writers already examined earlier in the chapter dismissing the critical standards and critical assumptions of the west. However, in the last two or three years, as writers and critics have begun to develop a distinctly South African critical discourse, the African writer is now speaking from *within* his own different discourse rather than from *outside* the western critical discourse.

So black writers in South Africa have taken on a double task: to break through the existing ideological framework as part of the liberation struggle, and to undermine the power of western critical discourse: to put a stop, within their own environment, to the policing of language, to the ideological support system provided to the power structure by the literary institution:

> Art and literature educate for the winning and the living of that freedom to which revolution opens the door. For this revolution not only an ideological crisis is required but knowledge. That knowledge is not imposed on the working class from outside by an intellectual

élite which has somehow freed itself from reification. Nor is the great work of art produced by the imprint on inert material reality of some 'possible consciousness' or 'world vision'. Revolution, like the work of art, is achieved not by some wondrously efficacious subjective conception . . . but by a practice which brings cognition of reality.[100]

The writer's role, then, in the revolutionary situation, is to bring to their readers the requisite knowledge to allow them to act; in South Africa this has been defined as a consciousness of oppression combined with a sense of their own worth and value as human beings – two elements which, united, lead logically to resistance and assertion. Benjamin, writing in the context of the rise of fascism, shows a similar perception of the necessity for the artist (and consequently for the reader, listener or spectator) to apprehend the changed reality of the capitalist (and for Benjamin, the fascist) social structure:

> The artist must use and develop the means of artistic production to penetrate, to understand, to prise out of the changed reality the truth, which he cannot do without developing the means of penetration and presentation themselves.[101]

Both Eagleton and Slaughter (following Benjamin) and the black consciousness writers in South Africa are in agreement on the essential place that literary form has in such a process:

> The writer's political tendency must be judged not by the progressiveness of his explicit subject matter, but by whether he is technically progressive. And the latter depends on how deeply he has found himself compelled to pose the question of how artists can do their work in the present situation of insoluble conflict between productive forces and property relations.[102]

This, of course, is the underlying reason for South African writers' impatience with literary forms developed to perpetuate a western, bourgeois ideology. They are not youthful rebels impatient with old forms, but political agents intent on establishing a new ideology as part of the establishment of a new political structure: they would agree with Eagleton's analysis of the operation of literary forms within an ideology:

> The text establishes a relationship with ideology by means of its

forms, but does so on the basis of the *character* of the ideology it works. It is the character of that ideology, *in conjunction with* the transmutative operations of the literary forms it produces or enables, which determines the degree to which the text achieves significant or nugatory perceptions . . . The process of the text is the process whereby ideology produces the forms which produce it, thus determining in general both the instruments and devices which work it, and the nature of the work-process itself.[103]

His argument explains the reason for much of the confusion surrounding current experiment with literary forms in black South African writing: where both ideology and form are in flux together – and necessarily so where the character of the new ideology is in the process of being worked out simultaneously with the working out of literary forms – it is hardly surprising that a literature which is at once vibrant and yet rough-hewn, varying in effectiveness and power, should be the result. But unevenness of impact does not undermine the basic integrity of the attempt to change the function of the novel, drama and poetry in order to make them more accessible to the people and consequently more applicable to the liberation struggle.

The black consciousness writers share with these three Marxist critics a recognition of the importance of readers as consumers of and participators in the literary work: 'For literature to happen, the reader is quite as vital as the author.'[104] And Eagleton pursues this maxim to its logical conclusion: if readers must, of necessity, participate in the production of literature, they must also, of necessity, shoulder a share of the responsibility. Not only is no reading innocent, or without presuppositions but

> there is no such thing as a purely 'literary' response: all such responses, not least those to literary *form*, to the aspects of a work which are sometimes jealously reserved to the 'aesthetic', are deeply imbricated with the kind of social and historic individuals we are.[105]

This is perhaps more of a European temptation than a black South African one. In a society where literature is an élitist pursuit, it might be possible for readers to attempt to evade responsibility by confining themselves to questions of aesthetics: in the black townships, no one is interested in aesthetics: everyone reads to learn, to find a reflection of their oppression or a confirmation of their commitment to liberation. People vote with their feet, and walk away from 'literary' writing.

In South Africa, not only have black writers come round to the Marxist view of literature as an artefact which emerges *from* the community, to be consumed as a product *by* that community, but they ensure that consumption does not become the vapid end in itself typical of other forms of superfluous consumption within capitalist society. It has to activate something within the readers; it must set in train a social transformation that will lead, eventually, to social revolution:

> Literary texts are 'code-productive' and 'code-transgressive' as well as 'code-confirming': they may teach us new ways of reading, not just reinforce the ones with which we come equipped.[106]

Brecht took this dynamic role one stage further, and demanded of the work of art, not just that it should *change* the reader, but that it should dismantle his given identity and produce a new kind of human subject.[107]

And the fundamental reason for such dismantling is the replacement of bourgeois individualism with human solidarity: Marx's ideas upon consciousness stress this relinquishing of preoccupation with self in favour of a larger social ideal:

> Marx's target is not the self-consciousness of the spirit, or of actual men for that matter, but the self-creation of the individual in his social relations, in all its dimensions, with the individual able to educate and develop his humanity, refine his needs and his manner of fulfilling them, not in the narrow 'individual' sense taught by capitalist society, but with the historically developed needs and satisfactions of the 'universal' individual. For Marx the 'aesthetic education' of men is at the core of this real and continuous transformation, and of the revolution men must make to initiate 'the realm of freedom'.[108]

It is not that individuals are no longer valued, but that their development is seen as essentially linked to their social context. Within the South African context, the personal has become increasingly submerged in the group struggle, but writers have not lost sight of the greater potential for human development once that group struggle has been won. They have merely shifted the emphasis to the self-creation of individuals within their social relations. In their preoccupation with the consciousness of the group, their emphasis upon group identity and community action, black writers in South Africa affirm the validity of Eagleton's definition:

> The ideological function of art is to affirm human solidarity against disintegrative individualism.[109]

2 The Construction of a Framework: Ezekiel Mphahlele

INTRODUCTION

There is one writer in whose work it is possible to trace, over a period of forty years, both the problems of literary production experienced by South African writers and the stages in the development of an appropriate critical approach: for Ezekiel Mphahlele functioned as artist and critic throughout that period, encountering in his creative and confronting in his critical work the alienation of consciousness and the appropriation of discourse, while his later criticism records the efforts of black writers towards reappropriation.

While it would distort the corpus of his writing to divide it, whether critical or creative, into stages, there are nevertheless certain identifiable features appearing progressively within it, which sometimes correspond to, and sometimes seem to be partially responsible for precipitating changes in the attitudes of black writers. In his earliest years, his writing is white-oriented: he addresses a predominantly white readership, in the forms and language of white culture, to record his protests on behalf of his black brothers. The events and pressures leading to his exile together with the distancing effect of that experience produce a raised consciousness that eventually resolves itself into an identification with the general ideas and aims of the Black Consciousness Movement, despite his removal from the scene of its inception and growth. Lastly, with his return to South Africa, he was compelled to confront the whole issue of the liberation struggle, which had finally and reluctantly moved beyond the long years of patient non-violence.

We shall see in later chapters how the pattern of his critical and theoretical development is echoed both in the literature itself and in the individual development of other writers. In the course of the study we shall be looking at examples of autobiographical writing, poetry and novels, and in each genre, if that is the appropriate term, there are interesting correspondences. The autobiographical writers work mainly in a white-oriented framework, though their move into exile produces in them the first signs of raised consciousness; Mongane Serote, perhaps the most representative poet of the seventies, starts with white-directed protest poems but quickly moves, during his period in America, into the mainstream of black consciousness and then finally, as a novelist, together with the other eighties novelists examined in this study, focuses exclusively on the liberation struggle itself.

Ezekiel Mphahlele wrote his critical works during periods when he felt too barren and infertile to attempt creative writing: they became, I would argue, far more than his fiction or poetry, seminal forces in the development of South African literature. He used both versions of *The African Image* and *Voices in the Whirlwind* as a search for personal intellectual and cultural identity, and they helped the establishment of a communal cultural identity in his country. The resonances of his work can be traced throughout the Black Consciousness Movement in South Africa and beyond it into the eighties, providing young writers with aspirations and goals, and helping them to develop the means – the literary skills, styles and genres – with which to attain them. He is the grand old man of South African letters, to which he has contributed, inside and outside South Africa, for forty years. His criticism helped to launch a self-propagating cultural theory – feeding into the work of younger writers, then, years later, taking up what they produced and analysing their contributions in such a way as to prepare the ground for further cultivation.

The fact that he has written more, and at greater length than any other critic is one of the reasons for the extent of his influence. He has been able, despite the banning of his work in South Africa, to reach a wider audience, over a longer period, through a wider variety of genres, than any other South African writer in English. (I am not making a claim here in terms of values or standards; I have explained earlier my reservations about such criteria with regard to South African literature.)

His struggle to help articulate a black aesthetic for South Africa is immeasurably augmented by his attempts to come to grips with three other areas of literary endeavour: the presentation of black characters in western fiction, the West African negritude movement and the writing of black Americans. Indeed these three areas may well appear to take up the major part of his critical attention, but the reason for his interest in them is betrayed by his recurrent application of any conclusions he draws from his examinations to the South African literary situation. His search for images, for a black aesthetic in these other three regions, however, indisputably gives his reflections on the South African literary scene a much firmer base as he brings to it a much wider perspective. His interest in them was initially academic: his early reading had touched on them all, and his first critical endeavour, his M.A. thesis, bears witness to their fascination for him. This scholarly interest was transformed by actual experience of the different cultures during his sojourns in West Africa (though he lived in Nigeria, not French-speaking West Africa, he was in closer contact there than he had been in South Africa with the intellectual climate of negritude), Paris and America. His absorption of black American culture – a culture of protest against oppression – proved especially fertile.

This interweaving of life experience and intellectual pursuit is an indication of the impossibility of separating out, in Mphahlele's case, critical development from emotional and personal growth. Indeed he makes a clear statement of their indivisibility in his prefaces to the two editions of *The African Image*. There is no pretence, in his critical writing, of an objective critical stance, of an academic panorama of literary movements. Indeed his first edition concludes with a series of very long personal memoirs concerning his experiences after leaving South Africa. In the preface to the first edition he states very clearly the personal nature of his search:

> My purpose in raising it all [i.e. the political and social content of his book] in this book is as much to try and clear my own mind about things as to try and evaluate the sense and nonsense that is often said and thought by whites and blacks . . . [1]

He emphasises this once again, and expands on his reasons for such a course, in the preface to the second and very different edition published twelve years later:

> This is largely a personal book. I chose to explore images, a phenomenon which through the imagination and intuition can cut across the barrier that lies between literary activity and social studies. Observation, through every possible means available, imagination and intuition – these have been my tools. [2]

It would be extremely difficult for a black South African, whose intellectual development, educational progress and academic career is so severely hampered by the oppressive conditions of the racial society to which he is subjected, to make the clear division between the intellectual and emotional spheres so characteristic of western capitalism. For every intellectual step is hedged about by so many overwhelming emotional barriers that academic progress can only be won by parallel gains in emotional strength and self-confidence. While for all of us there is a personal element in academic direction and our choice of intellectual pursuits, for the black South African the personal is often the motive and elective force behind each move. Manganyi confesses in his introduction to his biography of Mphahlele how the attraction of biography for him was that it was a part of his own search for identity:

> This interest was not an entirely intellectual offshoot of my immediate academic surroundings; it was, no doubt, part of my personal soul-searching at the time. I was, on the one hand, dealing with the prospect of life in exile, and searching for a creative solution to the problem of a satisfactory research direction for a black South African psychologist, on the other.[3]

There is, however, an additional, more comprehensive reason for not attempting to chart Mphahlele's intellectual development in isolation, and that is the fundamental differences in world view, in metaphysical schemata, between Africa and the West. For as Mphahlele himself explains, Africa has no tradition of dualism, separating spirit from body, intellect from emotions, and indeed lacks the entire western analytical tradition into which he and his fellow Africans have been educated by Europeans. In fact he bluntly describes African intellectual activity as derivative, 'because traditionally we did not analyze and formulate intellectual systems'.[4] Africa, like the Orient, has a more holistic approach that focuses more directly upon human beings.

It is understandable, then, that knowledge both of the course of Mphahlele's education and of its significance to himself, his family and his community should be a prerequisite for an analysis of his critical evolution. He makes it quite clear in the interview upon which the relevant section of Manganyi's biography is based, that his struggle to search out an educational direction, unaided by parental guidance and with financial support severely limited by the economic constraints on his and all other black families, had a profound effect on him. Moreover, any achievement at school, at teacher training college, or later on university courses, had for him and his family and their neighbourhood a symbolic significance that it is difficult for even the poorest of Europeans to grasp. Hence the intensity of his vocation as a teacher and the depth of his opposition to the fraudulent and oppressive intentions of Bantu Education. His intellectual direction was set, first by his own education, then by his experiences as a teacher; as he moved into the wider sphere of education's significance for the community through his union work, it prepared him for his battle with the authorities over the introduction of Bantu Education – a battle which helped him to develop a conception of the kind of education necessary for black development in South Africa. His involvement in education and culture in West Africa and East Africa then brought about a wider understanding of the educational and cultural needs of the entire continent, bedevilled as it has been by the aftermath of colonialism and by racism; and finally, his experiences in America deepened his awareness of the needs of the whole African diaspora.

And just as his educational activities as a teacher and organiser led him to perceive the inter-relationship between literature and education and the need for mass education to promote meaningful mass culture, so his conflict with the authorities over the introduction of Bantu Education initiated him into the interconnection between literature and politics, and between his own critical development and his political development. The very circumstances of his upbringing had obviously given him an unequivocal apprehension of the mechanisms of oppression, and his first (and indeed lifelong) obsession as a critic was with the literary response to this. Although in his early criticism he was not consciously political, the examination of white images of black people inevitably set his course in a political direction. As negritude brought him face to face with black assertion, he also came to measure the inadequacies of the literary movement and locate what was missing in the sphere of politics. His immersion in black American writing provided him with the missing link at a time when he had realised that poetry was not only a means of coping with conflict for the individual but could provide a tool for the community as well. Mphahlele's later critical work is markedly functional in its outlook: he systematically examines different bodies of literature for what they can achieve in the communities from which they emerge. For this reason he is one of the earliest critics to question the whole applicability of value judgements in relation to African literature, and to call for their suspension, not in order to dispense with literary standards (for which he has ever had a very high, sometimes one feels too high, respect) but in favour of a different set of critical tools more finely attuned to the literatures upon which he focuses.

Subject at different periods in his life to different influences, Mphahlele's ideas changed at intervals, often fairly radically. It is a tribute to his rigorous intellectual honesty that he has never made any attempt to veil these changes, or even to synthesise them into a coherent pattern as so many of us do. There is no tendency towards totalisation in his criticism. In his conversations with Manganyi after his return to South Africa, he does, with Manganyi's help, make some attempt to *trace* a pattern in his life and writing, but it is Manganyi, in his biography, not Mphahlele, who *superimposes* it. And at the time of writing he not only holds back from such pattern-seeking but he actually draws the reader's attention to the discrepancies in his ideas. In the preface to the second edition of *The African Image* he warns the reader not only of these changes, but also of his tendency to repeat himself as he works over material again and again in his mind. This open-ended approach to the presentation of ideas in books leads to a certain amount of confusion – sophistry is always neater, clearer and more finished than straightforward accounts of thinking in progress. And indeed his arguments are not always wholly explicit, coherent and completed; though this is not to say that his statements, even if they are retracted later in his critical career, lack force of utterance or that his judgements, when he makes them, are tentative.

It is perhaps this openness towards change, this willingness to review and reconsider which gives him the sensitivity necessary to his near-prophetic insights into the future needs of South African literary culture. It is astounding that many of his statements of South Africa's needs in the field of literature – the need for novels by blacks instead of the short stories and poems that have been so prolific; the need for white South Africans to assimilate African culture and cut their ties with the European tradition; the need for politically conscious writing – are stated many years before they become part of the general currency of black writing and white writing in the country. It is as though Mphahlele, throughout his career, has ever been so receptive to social and cultural undercurrents that he has always had his critical finger on South Africa's literary pulse, even though he was out of the country for twenty years. He has articulated, not so much for the people, the masses (though he has done that too in his short stories), but for those writers who were to articulate for the masses, their innermost conflicts, contradictions and afflictions.

It is also this tendency to present explorations rather than discoveries in his criticism which leads me to classify the work as intellectual autobiography. Each stage is charted as it occurs, his theories are presented as they evolve, without any effort to conceal lacunae or flux. Systematisation is not merely rejected, it is never even in question. It is, as Mphahlele himself points out (though not in reference to this particular question of his own work of course) a western approach, not an African one, to systematise.

Consequently I shall not attempt a conventional structure in this chapter, analysing the development of his critical theories as though they followed a logical and coherent progression. Rather I shall attempt to follow his interests, ideas, revisions and rejections as they occur chronologically in his growth as a writer and teacher, and were impinged upon by influences and circumstances in his life. Since these evolved as a series of progressions, contradictions, syntheses and conflicts, the imposition of a rigorous and systematic pattern would inevitably distort the history.

THE WEST VERSUS AFRICA

Throughout his writing, creative as well as critical, the impact of Europe on himself and his community provides a leitmotif – a leitmotif which is given different emphases at different periods, at times being overshadowed almost completely by contemporary preoccupations, but repeatedly surfacing and always, after such a period of dormancy, having suffered a sea-change. His attitude to the effects of European culture and education were equivocal from the outset. He was always aware of the conflicts set up by its introduction into an African context even when he was most receptive to the potential benefits it brought with it. However, throughout his life the balance shifts consistently, to the point where he is acutely aware of the damage it has inflicted, though even then he recognises that there is much to be salvaged from the wreckage.

Through the course of his three major critical works, we can chart a growing awareness of his own emergence from a western-style education. At the beginning when he embarked on English literature courses he was too involved, too subordinated to the structure, too much an agent of the power that had produced him, to be conscious of the implications of its operations upon himself as an individual and upon the African community as a societal network. With his incursions into negritude and black American literature he gained the necessary distance from his own educational background to achieve his consciousness.

From the very beginning, however, he was aware that the content and structure of school and university education had set up a conflict within himself and between himself and his people. One aspect of that conflict is the contending expectations of the family and surrounding community of any African that enters into the western educational process. The family's complete ignorance of the process inhibits them from fulfilling the traditional role of counsellors and guides, and sets up reactions in them against the traditionally submissive and inferior young. At the same time the young person is also fulfilling their deepest aspirations both for the family and for the community in taking this road to personal, familial and communal advancement. Thus the child grows up at once made to conform to traditional modes in the role allocated to the child by traditional society, and yet at the same time alienated from family and community by that education they themselves had striven to help him attain: and so

> communication becomes difficult, sometimes impossible between your people who are still not tuned in to western intellectual systems and yourself.[5]

There are simple physical difficulties too: not only the financial hardship for those deliberately exploited and kept below the breadline to find money for fees and books for their children, but the students themselves lack the conditions for study in the overcrowded townships with their vibrant streetlife. Moreover the whole orientation of European education and the values it inculcates jars against African values:

> Formal education throws up individual talent which in turn, side by side with a money economy, builds up an individualism that creates problems unknown in traditional societies, where the welfare of the group took precedence over that of the individual.[6]

He is beginning here in his essay on 'The Fabric of African Cultures' to probe the symbiosis between education and culture and the economic and political structures – an enterprise that forms the basis of all his later critical activity. For he is aware that the differences between Western and African cultures and values are the radical essentials of modes of being, rather than the accidental by-products of different social systems. Intellectual systems are inextricably bound up with the perceptual sets that gave rise to them and there is a fundamental difference between those of the West and those of Africa. Mphahlele points out the aggressive nature of western culture as opposed to the passive cultures of Africa and the East. This inevitably sets up constraints especially when an intellectual is compelled, as the African intellectual is, to operate through the alien culture, using its language and concepts to communicate essentially incompatible ideas:

> You try to express their (the African people's) philosophy in a European language whose allegory, metaphor and so on are alien to the spirit of that philosophy: something that can best be understood in terms of allegory and metaphor that are centred heavily on human relationships and external nature ... Your mind operates in a foreign language, even while you are actually talking your mother tongue, at the moment you are engaged in your profession.[7]

Both languages and culture operate in totally different ways in the two areas. In Africa language has become a ritual, heavily dependent on metaphor and symbol; in western society language is primarily a tool for the conduct of business and government – its use for aesthetic purposes totally divided into a separate category. Mphahlele illustrates the African lack of division, with the poetic content of the language spilling over into the analytical, by comparing the sensuous poetic language involved in the trial of a case by the traditional court with the disconcerting effect such language has if it is used in a western court case (as it often is by African people):

> Even the rhetoric that a lawyer may indulge in is primarily a thing of the brain rather than of the heart. In African languages, activities overlap a great deal and there are no sharp dividing lines between various functions.[8]

It is another face of the same coin that just as African languages incorporate the aesthetic in the functional, so African culture is primarily functional rather than a mechanism for aesthetic enjoyment. He censures the post-colonial inheritance of the attitude towards culture that sees it as entertainment for the wealthy and leisured:

> Such an idea is opposed to the traditional African idea of culture as a way of growing up, as fundamental to education.[9]

Functional culture is part of the community-oriented (as opposed to individualistic) social structure referred to above. It is no mere difference of emphasis between the two cultures but a question of basic set. Whereas western culture is rooted in surplus production, traditional

African culture is not yet hived off from the process of production, but an essential part of it:

> In traditional society where culture is a process of growing up and not a thing separate from human activity in general, comfort and abundance would not be necessary for the growth of culture.[10]

A writer like Mphahlele is therefore caught between the polarities of Africa and the West in all aspects of his growth and development, and from his earliest critical work he has been acutely conscious of the need to find some way of resolving the conflicts this entails. And interestingly enough he sees the very education that sets up the conflicts as providing some of the mechanisms for resolution:

> Education sets up conflicts but also reconciles them in degrees that depend upon the subject's innate personality equipment. It seems to me a writer in an African setting must possess this equipment and must strive toward some workable reconciliation inside himself.[11]

He does not, however, offer this course as a benign, easy and natural process of totalisation: he is aware of the cost of it, the losses and the suffering it entails:

> It is an agonizing journey. It can also be humiliating to feel that one has continually to be reassessing oneself with reference to the long line of tradition he has entered – the tradition of the West.[12]

Yet the writer's background (and Mphahlele speaks here from the heart of his own experience) provides an instinctive compulsion to integrate the two philosophies:

> Of course you cannot help using your African setting as your field of reference; you cannot help going out of the queue of Western orientation now and again to consult those of your people who are not physically in it.[13]

And it is his assimilation of western patterns of thought and argument 'from an alien culture in an alien language'[14] that equips him to do this.

Yet the introduction of alien languages and culture into Africa, and the necessity for Africa's people to work towards this reconciliation was not an accident of history. It was a part of the colonial process; and Mphahlele's efforts at assimilation were always permeated with the psychological responses to oppressive subjugation. At the beginning of his academic career he had concentrated on absorbing as much European culture as possible. He plunged into English literature in his university course with the voracious appetite of the semi-starved, and his friend Norah Taylor was a powerful influence upon him, contributing to his vision of the synthesis of western and African culture as the most fruitful way forward for African writers. Yet even at this stage, it was the reflections of black people in western literature which took possession of him and formed the basis of his M.A. thesis.

It was inevitable that such an examination of the literary ramifications of cross-cultural intertextuality should bring him up against the political nuances of all social interaction or literary portrayal between black and white, and that as he came to political consciousness he should undergo radical changes in his attitude towards white culture. From high hopes of amelioration and faith in the potential of those whites working towards reform, from a nagging frustration at his inability to penetrate the racial barriers sufficiently to create anything other than a white stereotype in his writing, he arrived, by the time he was writing the preface to the second edition of *The African Image* at an indifference that led him to dismiss equally his hopes of political improvement and his concern about the proper understanding of white characters in fiction: 'Over the last ten years I have ceased to care. It is not worth the trouble. The white man's inhumanity in South Africa has proved that much to me. To feel his muscle in real life is to understand him.'[15] But more important than his hopes of whites, or his relations with them, either literary or social, is the gradual refinement of his understanding of the political manipulation of which the cultural influences were the tool: 'Being brought up on the white man's textbooks, you assimilate his thought. You make his goals yours.'[16] Mphahlele elucidates the entire process when he talks about the colonisation of the mind. The excitement of new horizons opened up by English education was qualified, not at the time, but in the reflections of later life, by the realisation that this gain was perforce countered by a similar loss: 'These things came to you in English. Which meant that you were simultaneously absorbing English ways of thinking, which were to modify or condition some of your own indigenous ways of thinking.'[17] In the chapter 'Blackness on My Mind' in the second edition of *The African Image* Mphahlele examines the deliberate cultural, religious, political and economic infiltrations by Christianity and Islam in Africa, the price they extorted for the benefits they offered and the toll paid by the more passive African humanism the alien religions encountered on arrival:

We know . . . that this proselytizing mania is a western and Islamic thing. To see it continue at economic and political levels today is even more frightening. The Grand Blackmail: if you want the hospital, the clinic, the school, you've got to take the bible, Christ. We'll trade with you, teach you to master the alphabet and the art of disputation, but you must take the Koran too.[18]

Along with Mphahlele's growing awareness of the fact that the individual's absorption into the dominant culture is but an element in the social, political, economic and ideological engulfment of Africa by the West, comes a change in his perception of the functions of culture that parallels his change of attitude to the West:

The white man's language, the technology he initiated, conveniences that accrue from this technology, the middle-class syndrome, the areas of individual ownership that you were born into – all these and others that are associated with white living – become part of your personality equipment. Your values unconsciously have reference to white values. Because the things to which you have to attach *some* value, positive or negative, come to you on a white caravan.[19]

The colonisation process, for the intellectuals at least, has usurped their native consciousness and made them white inside. Though this was only a partially conscious domination on the part of the missionaries and settlers (conscious to the extent that they genuinely believed European customs and traditions superior and considered themselves benefactors in sharing them, and unconscious to the extent that they were the oblivious tools of western hegemony), it was a manifestation of the general need of whites to control Africans – a need which Mphahlele and others force into the open in the process of their self-analyses.

As a consequence it becomes a most pressing business for Mphahlele and his people to reverse this transmutation, to begin the process of decolonisation: a process which is not only political and economic, but cultural and educational: 'One thing is certain, if nothing else is: it is that the African wants to determine his cultural organization himself. And in many areas he wants to decolonize his mind.'[20] His people, both in South Africa and in the recently independent states, need to rethink the impact of western culture and colonialism in black terms, from outside the expropriation of the mind which they have endured. The irony of this position had been with Mphahlele from the beginning of his critical career. As early as the first edition of *The African Image* he had seen the implications, and understood that they were of more than local significance, and had to do with the African tendency to absorb foreign influences rather than resist them:

> For the African Negro the problem lies in the struggle to express the larger irony which is the meeting point between acceptance and rejection, once he has felt the impact of Western civilization. This problem is superimposed on the one of local political commitment. And for a long time to come yet, such ironies are going to provide him with literary material.[21]

By the time he came to rewrite the book, the emphasis has shifted, the tone hardened, the demand sharpened, but the message is still the same: the ambiguity forced upon the African by his historical context:

> Ambivalence, ambivalence. Always having to maintain equilibrium. You walk with this double personality as a colonized man. You had to cope with the presence of foreign rule and its white minions. Now you cope with what they left on your mind. So you will always be a colonized man. Only, political independence ought to help you turn that state of mind into something dynamic. The dialogue between the two selves never ends.[22]

Yet he avoids the trap of over-simplification: there is no trace in his critical work of a belief that cultural colonisation can be disposed of by mere denial and focus on things African. Mphahlele accepts inevitability and calls for an incorporative procedure of which the black man is in charge. Indeed he castigates negritude for its failure to make this necessary historical acknowledgement: 'It is a dialogue between two selves in the African and only indirectly addressed to Western civilization.'[23] Mphahlele goes on to make it clear that this is not a plea for western-directed African writing in his later charge of élitism. (Much of his later criticism in *Voices in the Whirlwind* and the second edition of *The African Image* is focused especially on the need for African writers to address their work specifically to the African masses, and to evolve methods and forms for reaching their audience.) He accepts the inexorable need for the black man to work out his identity through the medium of the sum total of his experience, rather than attempting it by the negation of a large part of it:

> We are pioneers at the frontier, seeking a definition of ourselves and the past from which we have come. The frontier lies between us and

the white man's technology, religion, mores, economics and so on. We try to address him and ourselves at the same time.[24]

His concern for addressing the white man was to become much less emphatic by the time he wrote the second edition of *The African Image*, by which time the Black Consciousness Movement was in full spate, and Mphahlele, together with the majority of other black South African writers had become caught up in the urgency of addressing the black masses of his country to the exclusion of their white oppressors and well-wishers alike. Yet even here he was never to deny the inter-relationship of the two cultures, and while he was writing *Voices in the Whirlwind* he was anxious to impress on his black readership the imperative necessity for recognising this fact:

> What I am trying to warn against is the danger of finding ourselves having, out of sheer crusading zeal, dismissed elements of Western aesthetics which are . . . built into our new modes of expression.[25]

But this plan for intellectual acknowledgement is very different from his initial acolyte's delight in white culture, evident in his early letters written at the time of his university courses. And by the seventies he had worked out very clearly the terms on which black writers needed to analyse the connection – conscious black terms that have no time for the reformism of the white liberal of the fifties.

By 1984 he was viewing the black acquisition of white education and white culture as part of the process of blacks equipping themselves for the struggle to liberate themselves from the domination of that very culture. It is the political tone of the seventies, by virtue of considerable hindsight, which speaks in his justification in the second edition of *The African Image*: 'We had to try to grab the tools by which the white man pillaged and plundered his way to power. The arms, we couldn't have. Education we could have, albeit literally at a price.'[26] There is a kind of glee in his contemplation of the African's power to steal back from the whites the necessary instruments for the recovery of what the whites had stolen from them on their arrival in Africa:

> We felt it a great triumph to have been able to store in our minds things we could never have dreamed ourselves capable of; things stolen as it were from the great store of western technological civilization that he took so much for granted he wasn't aware of what was happening. It is the things you are denied that you go after.[27]

Such intentions and feelings were at most semi-conscious in Mphah-lele's youth. It was an instinctive drive towards a final goal at the school and university stage of his career, and it was only in later life, with the growth of political maturity and contact with black cultural and political movements in other parts of the world, that the direction in which he and others had consistently been moving came into consciousness:

> Even when you realize later that you didn't need to justify yourself, give an account of yourself in those terms, you felt the exercise had given you a purpose, a sense of discipline that could be channelled in the direction of a revolution.[28]

And it is important not to underestimate the violence and the strength of the feelings involved here. Despite Mphahlele's obvious enjoyment of the irony of the situation, he is keenly aware of the desperation occasioned by the no-exit situation of South Africa: 'You just want to use these tools to murder.'[29]

But Mphahlele's most important perception, in the second edition of *The African Image*, a perception made on the empirical level some years before the cultural theorists had provided exhaustive analyses on a theoretical level (though of course the basic idea had been in circulation since Gramsci's work on hegemony) is the manipulation by the South African government of the entire cultural and educational spheres as part of the mechanism of oppression. And the logical issue of this recognition is the construction of a counter-culture and a counter-education that will enable them to construct a revolutionary condition among the people:

> Meantime, we have got to wrench the tools of power from the white man's hand: one of these is literacy and the sophistication that goes with it. Our culture will interact with our political aspirations. At the moment the government appears to have things under control: African political and trade union organization is prohibited; our leaders are in jail or in exile; the curricula for primary and high school and university have been reduced to a level that is a shame and a mockery to human decency; literature that is suspected to possess a liberating power is banned for both black and white.[30]

Originally the construction of black culture in South Africa was a process of self-identification for blacks. It was only as the Black Consciousness Movement got underway that this culture's political function began to come clear. Obviously, its political potential had been there from the very beginning, as it had in the young Mphahlele's struggle for education, but it was white interference that brought that political potential into consciousness, and once it had come into consciousness it posed a threat to the entire fabric, not only of white culture, but also of white society. Mphahlele dates that consciousness from the attempt to impose an artificial 'Bantu culture', which he brands very clearly as a 'technique of oppression':

> We know where we stand culturally, but the whites are out to confuse our people by making them believe that fragmented tribal cultures are the ultimate in our black consciousness. The whites know very well that they are safe as long as our cultural development is fragmented into tribal compartments. They fear the day when we will take things in hand as the majority race and direct our own cultural destiny, mightier than their own miserable dead-end racism will ever attain.[31]

Mphahlele has been aware of the dead-end of racist white culture in South Africa since he first began writing criticism. Already in 1962 when he published his first edition of *The African Image*, he was calling, not only for an integrated society, but for a common stream of culture 'in which two or more streams of consciousness influence one another'.[32] At this stage in his thinking he was still heavily influenced by the advantages offered by white culture, and tended to think in terms of integration on an equal basis. Later he began to apprehend the greater significance of black culture for all of Africa, including white-dominated South Africa, and he began to consider that any integration called for the assimilation of the white minority into the majority culture. Moreover the terms of his demands became much harsher and more implacable:

> In South Africa . . . the dominant culture (dominant only because it is economically prosperous and has the political patronage of the ruling class) happens to be that of a minority Caucasian group. It has refused by constitutional and statutory physical apartheid to share in the wealth of African culture. Come the day when the tables are turned, the white man will have to choose to quit or adopt the majority African culture or be marooned by history . . .[33]

In a later section, 'Black on Black', he characterises the urban African culture that has struggled into existence in spite of all attempts to eradicate it and that is possessed of sufficient strength to lay siege to the economically dominant minority culture:

> This (African culture) is a fugitive culture: borrowing here, incorporating there, retaining this, rejecting that. But it is a virile culture. The clamour of it is going to keep beating on the walls surrounding the already fragmented culture of the whites until they crumble, until the white chooses to be assimilated or spat out.[34]

The astringent and indeed aggressive vocabulary denotes the hardening of attitudes since his early writing, and bears the stamp of the more assertive tone of the Black Consciousness Movement.

And it is interesting to note that in the work of white writers at the end of the seventies and during the eighties, there is a noticeable shift towards not only African culture but also African as opposed to a European consciousness, though the consciousness arrives, ironically, in the recognition and acceptance of difference. In André Brink's *A Dry White Season*, it is when Ben finally recognises that he is white and that his very efforts to identify himself with Gordon Ngubene were obscene in the eyes of the blacks who had just attacked him and stoned his car, though he was on their side, that he finally internalises the African world view.[35] And in Nadine Gordimer's *July's People*, Maureen, born the white pariah dog in a black continent[36] only understands July's being when he speaks to her, at the end of the novel in his own language – a language she cannot understand – and she recognises that her standards, her life, her culture, were irrelevant to him all along: 'His measure as a man was taken elsewhere and by others.'[37] All of this ties in with Mphahlele's declared aim in the rewriting of *The African Image*:

> I attempt in a very personal impressionistic way to evaluate various areas of African life and thought by way of pointing out what order an African consciousness can impose upon our social systems.[38]

Beginning with his education into white culture, Mphahlele has worked through, via his immersion in the writings of negritude and black American writers and a study of the influence of African traditions, to an extensive and ample conception of an African culture which can assimilate outside influences in such a way that they lend vigour without threatening domination. It is to his encounters with negritude and black American writing that I will now turn.

NEGRITUDE

When Mphahlele began to consider studying African writing in his young adulthood South Africa itself had little by way of an African literary tradition. East African writing was to emerge later as Ngugi Wa Thiong'o's work became known; Nigeria and Ghana were producing work which originally, as far as style and genre were concerned, was in step with the mainstream of European tradition though its content was obviously African. The only literary innovation in the continent was the work of the negritude writers of French West Africa. So whatever Mphahlele's critical response to their work, he was obliged to take cognisance of their contribution to African literature. They were among the first writers in Africa to be conscious of a need to foster a pride in being black, to identify the pride to be taken in African traditions, to uncover the worth of all that was African beneath the accretions of white value systems, white standards of beauty, white conceptions of civilisation and progress. It might seem, on the surface, to one familiar with Mphahlele's value system, that all this would be found entirely appropriate by him, and the severity with which he took issue with the negritude philosophy may come as something of a shock. There are, I think, two elements in this response to negritude, one personal and one intellectual, and in order to understand his attitude it is necessary to take both into account. Moreover his personal response is, as he would be the first to admit, ambivalent, and often so closely interwoven with his intellectual objections that it would be difficult to separate out the two. To a large extent this complex response is a consequence of the amorphous nature of the concept of negritude: it covers a wide range of beliefs and ideas, to which there have been many and often contradictory responses.

  Mphahlele seems to have been irritated by the 'back-to-Mother Africa' conceit of African intellectuals – many of them concocting the passion at the café tables of Paris, and all of them out of touch with the common people of the continent with whom they think they have so romantically identified. He is also somewhat impatient with the notion of the African Personality despite being caught up in the enthusiasm at the Accra All-African People's Conference in 1958, for 'something that could express the longings and ambitions, aches and torments, the anger and hunger of our people and shout them out to the outside world'.[39] Despite the fellowship which the concept initiated, as it was put to the test of practical discussions of joint action and political accord it gradually shrank back into the confines of a myth; 'a glorious myth'[40] perhaps, he concedes, but nevertheless one ill-adapted to help to cope with the reality of Africa in the present day.

And it is in similar terms that he views the cultural impact of negritude – an intellectual and emotional romanticism of great comfort to the élite who perpetrate it, but ultimately of no relevance to the mass of the African people on whose behalf it falsely claims to speak. Though he can see that the African Personality debate might be useful as 'a focus, a coming into consciousness',[41] it has little practical value, and like the protestations of some of the negritude poets, it offends him by its sloganising, its emphasis on emotionalism and romanticism.

Perhaps at the root of his objections lies his understanding of the unsuitability of any such cultural movement for his own country, and their unique situation as Africans initially divorced from their tribal culture and then inflicted with a synthetic brand of it imposed by the white oppressors as a form of social and political control. In such a situation any romance about the tribal past is sure to have a hollow ring about it. Linked to this is his genuine identification with the people and his contempt for those over-civilised 'been-tos' who elevate nostalgic hygienic tribalism into literary theory.

Yet for all his initial rejection of negritude as manifested in its early writers, there is an ambivalence in Mphahlele's attitude. He endorses the need of artists to keep searching for the African Personality inasmuch as it is a search for their own personality. He acknowledges that the negritude movement and the cult of the African Personality embodies a very real necessity for individual writers and for African culture as a whole to define themselves in African terms – a process which hitherto had been hindered by the cultural and political dominance of the West.

What he dislikes about the way negritude attempts to carry out this task is that it oversimplifies and omits elements of the character of the African people and African writers, and that it fails to provide a sufficiently far-reaching framework for the essential political reference of any significant cultural theory. He objects to the way that negritude implies that all African writers can be put into a sociological category, and to the fact that it takes no account of the violence in the African character in its idealised presentation of the African humanist – the warm, loving, caring, socially-oriented being negritude opposes to the cold technology-oriented whites. The omission of violence is not a mere accidental off-shoot of romanticism, but an essentially emasculating dismissal of the African's revolutionary potential.

It is on this social and political level that Mphahlele's gravest charges against negritude are brought. Mphahlele, whatever his final political standpoint or his real, as opposed to his desired audience for his writing, has been consistently anti-élitist throughout his writing life. And it is negritude's self-conscious address to the small public of the like-minded, its failure either to acknowledge, or to seek communication with the larger public of the masses, which disqualifies it in Mphahlele's eyes for what he considers the essential function of any African literary movement: the voicing of the struggles and the afflictions, the oppressions and aspirations of the African people. For as early as 1967, when he first published the essays in *Voices in the Whirlwind* he recognized not only negritude's fear of technology and refusal to come to terms with it (an atavistic stance in the modern world) – that is the necessity for culture to come to terms with economics – but its subservience to western political autocracy by its failure to root its cultural message in a political context:

> *Negritude* can tell us nothing about how to plan for the second revolution. How can it when it never addressed itself to power, even when it was most necessary to do so.[42]

He condemns it for its ultimate frivolity, its failure to harness any of its insights or concepts to social function, thus evading literature's principal purpose for Mphahlele and a significant majority of African writers:

> *Negritude* was content to lie and sprawl in the African sun, laugh and jeer at Western civilization as a way of life, without organizing the mind against it as an instrument of white power.[43]

The consequence of this failure was that the ground was prepared by this cultural manifestation for neo-colonialism. Culture's failure to engage in the growth and formulation of a new political consciousness, its adherence to western patterns of non-involvement meant that it lent passive support to a new regime of oppression, differing from the old only in the skin-colour of the apparent dominators (the real dominators remaining tactfully off-stage in the West).

Mphahlele is trying to point out here a truth which many western literary theorists have laboured to elucidate: that if culture cultivates a stance of non-engagement, it is inevitably lending itself to the perpetuation of the *status quo*, and as such operating as a tool of those in power. In his essay on 'African Writers and Commitment' in the same book, he points out the dangers of a cultural propaganda that emphasises black pride without placing that pride in an appropriate social context or political framework and providing the critical armaments necessary to prevent its mis-appropriation:

> Black pride need not blind us to our own weaknesses. Also, I do not care for black pride that drugs us into a condition of stupor or inertia. I do not care for it if leaders use it to dupe the masses so that they forget to clamour for the bread and decent shelter and education they have a right to.[44]

It is negritude's 'stale presidential, ambassadorial, conference, festival élite platforms'[45] that he objects to – its diversification into publicity exercises and prestige projects that prop up the exploitation and oppression of the vast numbers of the starving and malnourished: 'Let it stop telling the masses how beautiful they are while they are starving.'[46] He regards this development of negritude, in which it collaborates with the global structures of oppression, and permits white intervention into Africa's rediscovery of its past, colluding with the various cultural operators who enthusiastically subject themselves to the scourge, as the ultimate stage of self-denigration:

> You glory in your corporate blackness, you keep telling the white world about yourself, your inscrutable 'being', you do nothing to decolonize the mind of your elite, to put more effort into the social and economic welfare of the masses. And you still do your song and dance for the amusement of the white world.[47]

Basically what angers Mphahlele most is negritude's failure to recognise the powerlessness of their constructed Africa that was 'beautiful, innocent, non-violent, bountiful, vibrant':

> They did not, and still do not, realize that the white man can easily concede your black pride, give you the freedom to do your song and dance while he manipulates you from a position of political and economic strength.[48]

There is some confusion in the entire body of Mphahlele's criticism in regard to negritude. This is owing, in part, to a shift in Mphahlele's own attitudes and in part to changes in the dominant ideas of the literary movement itself. The poets differ widely among themselves in their perceptions of the interconnections between literature, the state and politics. Mphahlele considers that Senghor and his disciples never 'really understood the essence and workings of white power – political and economic',[49] whereas he has a healthy respect for Césaire's approach, for he saw negritude as a weapon against that power. And Mphahlele is open to his own shifts and ambivalences: as he came to understand western and neo-colonialist manipulation of negritude, institutionalising it on the international-conference–national-celebration level in order to defuse it on the political level, he also began to visualise a way to evade this defusion and channel it into a social and political function.

Thus Mphahlele's later writing on negritude in the second edition of *The African Image* is as much an exploration of his own desideration as it is of the development of a literary movement. By 1974, when he published this second edition, he had lived in West Africa, close to, though not actually at the source of negritude, and in America where he had been in contact with black Americans, another and much more politically-oriented manifestation of black consciousness. As a result of these experiences he was beginning to feel towards a new interpretation of negritude, that took account of Fanon, Marxist criticism, the growing Black Consciousness Movement in America and Césaire's global concept of the African diaspora:

> He [Césaire] arrived at the idea that there was a 'Negro situation' which expressed itself in various parts of the world. Negritude became for him the meeting point in Africa, the Caribbean and the black Americas.[50]

It is easy to see how Mphahlele might sympathise with such a vision since it chimed in with so much of his own experience, loath as he might be to surrender his original objections to negritude's politically harmful aspects.

He had always acknowledged negritude's usefulness as a transition process for the establishment of black self-definition. In his later thinking, however, he concentrates on negritude as function – social function, that is to say, not the personal function of self-definition. Function had by now become Mphahlele's critical yardstick for any literary artefact or school. And he began in this second edition to speak to negritude, to confront it with functional imperatives:

> Negritude needs to confront modern Africa with a sense of revolution. With a sense of mission that emphasizes the enlightenment of Africa rather than the outside world, the enrichment of Africa rather than that of a universal civilization.[51]

He proposes negritude as a social concept and makes the plea 'that it comes to terms with the revolution that is necessary in social organization'.[52] And he repeats the call that it should cease speaking to the world and look inward. It is to this projected negritude that he can give his assent, this negritude as black consciousness in which he feels he can participate – an affinity which is in accord with the Black Consciousness Movement then coming into force in his own country.

This later apprehension of negritude shares with American and South African black consciousness a more aggressive, assertive grain than the nostalgic romanticism of early negritude. Mphahlele sees it as forced into adopting this new tone if it is to remain relevant to black aspirations of the day:

> In any case, a breed of Africans is emerging that will demand institutions of culture that represent a real African consciousness.[53]

His ultimate demand upon negritude is stringent and rigorous, for he demands not only the integration of cultural and political momenta but also the subordination, in the last resort, of the cultural to the political:

> *Let negritude, then, be defined by the second African revolution rather than try to define it for the people without being involved with the people.*[54] (Mphahlele's emphasis).

Note, as always, the supremacy of the people in Mphahlele's cultural demands.

AMERICAN BLACK WRITING

It was to a large extent his analysis of American black writing that had strengthened his awareness of the political potential of literature. In negritude he had recognised the shortcomings of a literature that had failed to connect with urgent political and social issues; in black American writing he located some of the possible channels of access.

However, his relationship to black American culture was not the adult, intellectual initiation of his association with negritude. Popular black American music had taken hold of the South African townships from an early period, and the young Mphahlele was exposed to this jazz in much the same way as to American gangster films and New York fashions. From here he was able to slip naturally and easily into a familiarity with black American writing which offered him heroes and situations he could identify with in a way that no European writing had done, and which linked into his people's life in the townships through the popular culture of which it was a part, in the way élitist western literature could never hope to do. Black American writing served a cohesive function while western writing served an alienating function within the black community, both in America and South Africa.

Though black American culture formed a part of his environment, it was his experience of living in America, of physical contact with that culture and its artists which provided the catalyst in his thinking about black culture and the African diaspora. It opened up his thinking on the question of the awakening of the black masses because it was much more political in approach than negritude, more overtly addressed to interaction with power. And because black Americans also spoke to an oppressive situation, their creation could be used as a fairly direct comparison with the black deadlock in South Africa: 'My encounter with American Negro poetry set me thinking about . . . the meaning and function of poetry . . . It is a poetry born out of situations of political controversy or conflict.'[55] Obviously, in his examination of black and white images of negritude, Mphahlele had been seeking a form of cultural expression applicable to the South African context, and much of what excited him about black American writing was its applicability to that context. His reading among the critics of that writing, people like Gwendolyn Brooks, Quentin Hill and Larry Neal confirmed for him that he had found what he was seeking, a poetry which had its being in function – the function of awakening the black masses for whom it speaks. Black American poetry had very deliberately set political goals for itself, and its writers had recognised that political action had its roots in aroused consciousness.

Mphahlele began to realise that it was poetry's function in consciousness-raising that was going to form the basis for a significant black aesthetic (as opposed to the impotent and irrelevant aesthetic of early negritude). He took up Caudwell's idea 'that poetry comes to express the collective conscious and unconscious of a community'[56] and argued that:

> When the black aesthetic comes to demonstrate itself in poetry, we are most likely to find that we have merely returned poetry to its original purpose; that we are simply talking about the black experience in a communicable language, and that in the process we are pushing Black Power.[57]

He is raising here the criterion which he is to press so forcefully when he considers black consciousness in South Africa: the importance of poetry speaking *for* the entire community and *to* it in language which it can understand. Audience is the crucial element in the poetic function for Mphahlele, who has no time for a literature which, though it may claim to speak for the masses, addresses itself to the educated élite. It is for this reason that he dismisses the formalist critics without even attempting to answer their objections. And though, in the essay 'Poetry in Conflict' in *Voices in the Whirlwind*, as everywhere else in his critical writing, it is the problems of South Africa that drive him to his analyses, he explains that: 'I have tried to focus on the concept of a black aesthetic only in the context of American political conflict because here it has been most consciously canvassed.'[58] Indeed this analysis of the operation of a black aesthetic as part of a political conflict was one of the factors which enabled South African writers to develop their own aesthetic of struggle. And black writers in South Africa were to experience for themselves the need for new forms, new values, new history, 'new symbols, myths and legends'[59] in exactly the same way, in order to ask questions about the nature of truth, and whose truth was valid, that of the oppressor or oppressed?'[60] He also noted the degree of self-negation demanded of a writer who had decided to participate in such a cultural venture as that initiated by the black American writers:

> The black American poets of this half of the twentieth century have, by and large, tacitly and aloud, made a pact to subordinate the individual temperament or will to the creation of a poetry that will be a black expression, a black revolt, a realization of a black consciousness, available to all black men who respond to the battle cry. Not only should the individual personality be subordinated to this major purpose: it must be made to serve the purpose.[61]

Not only had the indissolubility of politics and literature been reinforced for him in America, after striking him first on his examination of negritude writing, but he had gained a number of essential insights into the nature of the bond and the necessary operative procedures for any writer consciously attempting to accept this imperative in their own work.

Obviously he was aware of the fact that no exact parallel could be made between America and South Africa. The lack of a common identity between the two peoples was apparent to him from the strained relationship that often arose out of the fact that their idealistic conceptions of each other as African brothers were not matched by their cultural reality. Moreover their cultural positions *vis-à-vis* the white populations of the two countries were quite different: in America because the black population is a minority it suffers a longer-term threat from white culture even though it is less brutally oppressed than the black majority in South Africa:

> They [the Afro-Americans] are fighting an almost last-ditch battle to assert an ethnic identity. Apartheid or no apartheid, we could never be swamped by the white man's culture in South Africa because whites have not constructed anything like the formidable social structure the dominant group has done in the United States. South African whites are still a hybrid extension of Europe, teetering between reality and dream.[62]

Mphahlele recognises that while it is possible to make connections between the black American and the black South African struggles – and indeed such was his object in critically examining the cultural constructions of the Americans – it is not possible to integrate them. Each group, while it can learn from and support the other, needs to focus very closely on the specific practical problems it faces if its literature is not to dissolve into the kind of idealistic universalism of which he had accused negritude. Mphahlele's search for an underlying common black cultural aesthetic in American writing was to have no finite result; but this does not undermine the value of the search itself which has an important, one might say a crucial function in contributing to the development of a black aesthetic to serve the South African cause.

THE AFRICAN TRADITION

It may seem a long journey from black American writing to the roots of traditional African culture; but for Mphahlele both areas were to provide strands in his literary search for a South African cultural identity. It was impossible for him to make a straightforward analysis of African tradition in the way that writers like Ngugi and Achebe or even the French West African writers were able to do, examining the disintegration consequent upon white intervention, urbanisation and the introduction of alien social, cultural, educational and political values, because of the interrupted and ambiguous history of this inter-relationship between the two in South Africa, and its manipulation by Europeans for various kinds of social engineering and repression. When it suited European capitalists to break up the tribal societies in order to provide labour for their ventures, the government introduced a poll tax, so that each man living in an economy that was only very marginally based on money was forced to go and find work in the towns or farms in order to pay it. As with all urbanisation movements it precipitated the partial disintegration of rural social networks, moral structures and cultural patterns. As the white government became aware of the numbers of black people flocking to the towns, however, and of its own unwillingness to take on board social services (education, health care, provision for old age, housing and urban infrastructure) for such numbers, it developed the bantustan policy, removing all but the productive labourers to rural areas and re-introducing a spurious tribalism under puppet chiefs as a form of social control. This abuse of African tradition and its misappropriation by the oppressor may well account for some of Mphahlele's ferocity in his reaction to negritude.

And yet he is careful, throughout all his critical works, to explain the powerful influence of tradition in his own and his people's milieu. This is not the straightforward traditional culture in which he was steeped during his childhood in Maupaneng, herding cattle for his harsh unyielding grandmother and sitting around the men's fire listening to the traditional tales. Many urban South Africans have something of this rural culture in their background – relatives they visit periodically or with whom they may have lived for a time during childhood. But for Mphahlele the most significant traditional influences are those which have survived in the urban environment itself, the urban transformations which provide the community support system for the townspeople under their apartheid stresses: the large gatherings for the funerals, the singing in the months approaching a wedding, the training of children by their elders in the traditional discipline and courtesies appropriate to the young.

The very strength of these residues, however, sets up ambiguities and conflicts. Mphahlele recognises the strength of tradition's hold upon himself and his people and the necessity for them to confront this in their communal search for identity – 'It is as if we wanted to account for tradition, because it won't let us be.'[63] The past is not something that can be looked *back* on by Africans, it lives on in present communities to a much greater extent than it does in western communities where social patterns have radically changed and the past is enshrined for the majority in monuments and libraries. Mphahlele is at great pains to attempt to characterise this shifting relationship and to enable his readers to understand its effect upon the development of an African writer:

> All that I have said so far has been an attempt to indicate the relative distances between tradition and the present – some shifting, others freezing, some thawing, others again presenting formidable barriers . . . We need to appreciate these distances if we are to understand what the African writer is about. He is part of the whole pattern.[64]

One of these shifting elements is the symbiosis between Christianity and ancestor-worship. It is not merely a question of the two religions being present in the same community, but of the majority of the population incorporating elements from the two systems within their own make-up. Intellectuals such as Mphahlele find a rationalisation for all this, rejecting Christianity in adulthood, while holding aloof in a practical way from overt ancestor-worship. Yet fundamentally it is a wholly irrational, instinctive element in people's make-up and Mphahlele is sage enough to acknowledge this:

> I later rejected Christianity. And yet I could not return to ancestral worship in any overt way. But this does not invalidate my ancestors for me. Deep down there inside my agnostic self, I feel a reverence for them.[65]

Another area of flux is in language itself, and this is perhaps the root of the entire problem, for interference at the level of discourse is an interference ultimately at the level of being. Mphahlele first examines the question at the beginning of 'Poetry and Conflict', the first essay in *Voices in the Whirlwind* when he points out the kinship between poetry and everyday language which is much more pronounced in African languages than in the more analytical languages of the West. There is, for example, a direct link between forms of address in a legal trial and oral poetry in an African context, which would be inconceivable in a western language that rigidly sets aside aesthetic and ritual language from the conduct of everyday business. Thus the oral poetry that enshrines the traditional African life has a significance much more powerful and far-reaching for the African than, for example, Shakespeare has for the twentieth-century English person. For while we may carry over much of the vocabulary and some of the speech patterns from Shakespeare's English, there is a large gap, in general, between his poetry and our own daily greetings or our conduct of the business of daily life – a gap which has yet to appear in African speech patterns where communication is in the mother tongue. The demands of modern life are conveniently separated out by being dealt with in a foreign tongue. And Mphahlele admits:

> Those of us who write in the metropolitan languages know that *we have abandoned the direct route leading from tradition* which is the mother tongue, for the more intricate and perilous one of interpreting experience in a language and genre that belong to a historical tradition outside our own origins.[66] (My emphasis)

The whole debate about the African Personality is part of the search for reconciliation between the two elements – traditional and western – in the make-up of individuals and communities:

> The real African Personality is a dialogue between two selves. A dialogue between two streams of consciousness: the present and the living past. We realise it is an ever-changing personality.[67]

And for writers, of all people, it is essential to come to terms with these two streams of consciousness, for unless they do, they lack an identity. They use their writing to communicate with tradition and by attempting to define tradition they arrive at a definition of self. And yet this process cannot be one of absorption into the mysteries of the past, an attempt to slough off its adulteration by colonialism, as early negritude attempted to make it. Particularly it cannot be so for South African writers, who are primarily preoccupied with the brutality of everyday reality. Tradition is there for them, deep within themselves, but it is something to be used in the confrontation with the present – they cannot devote their entire attention as writers to working out the niceties of a literary version of African traditional culture.

This project of reconciliation is difficult enough in its own right, but the use of African culture by the minority white government renders it almost impossibly complex for the black South African writer:

> Now because the government is using institutions of a fragmented and almost unrecognizable Bantu culture as an instrument of oppression, we dare not look back.[68]

Exactly how complex it has become is witnessed by the course of Mphahlele's life: his withdrawal first from Bantu Education as an instrument of oppression, and ultimately from South Africa itself:

I suspect when conditions do allow me to sit back and reflect more necessarily upon tradition, we in South Africa will find it is laced with just this suffering. I suspect that because the ruling class is forcing us into traditional ethnic groups in an attempt to frustrate nationalism of a non-racial kind, when one day we decide on a pilgrimage to the source if we shall ever need to do that, we shall find it poisoned.[69]

In exile, after the rejection of the sentimentalisation of the past by the negritude writers, Mphahlele did find himself needing to return to the source – a need that had its parallel in South Africa in the Black Consciousness Movement. And Mphahlele was quick to recognise the white encroachment on the Movement for white political ends: their exploitation of the traditional heritage to foster their own version of 'Bantu Culture', confusing 'our people by making them believe that fragmented tribal cultures are the ultimate in our black consciousness'.[70] And here we have the root of Mphahlele's misgivings about the writer's relation to his past: a distrust of its distortion by the authorities to serve disruptive political ends. So although he recognises the writer's role in fusing the tradition and the present, he is conscious of the fact that this, in itself, is too simplistic a solution for the situation that exists in his country. Mphahlele's (and black consciousness's) ultimate answer was to call for the adoption of the aspects of African tradition that were functional within the liberation struggle, and to leave all the other aspects to one side.

MPHAHLELE AND THE
BLACK CONSCIOUSNESS MOVEMENT

The evolution of black consciousness in South Africa was to bring into prominence a great many of the ideas broadcast long before by Ezekiel Mphahlele. Though he was out of the country, perforce addressing a mainly white western audience (publishing in England and America) and though the movement was intrinsically focused on South Africa's black population and the life within the townships (despite the movement's wish to reach the rural populations, it only impinged on them in a fairly peripheral way in the seventies), Mphahlele's intellectual explorations of the function of culture ran so closely parallel to the practical aspirations of the black consciousness writers that it is difficult not to assume that a number of them had read his critical writings, banned though they were, and had been influenced by him. We know that he met with certain writers at various conferences and there is no doubt but that his ideas must have percolated through in discussions. Unquestionably many of the demands he had made of black South African literature, black writers and black culture in the early sixties formed part of the intellectual foundation of the Movement.

In his earliest critical work, his M.A. thesis, he took cognisance of the vast volume of black literature which agonised about blacks' relationships with whites, and of the relatively small amount of white literature that gave so much attention to relationships with blacks. This lack of balance alerted Mphahlele and others to their failure to concentrate on their relationships and activities within their own communities. Added to the total failure of whites to respond to any of the protest or cries for reform, this led first Mphahlele (who initially had addressed his work almost entirely to white intellectuals and academics) and later black consciousness writers, to withdraw their attention entirely both from whites as subjects and from whites as audience.

When, later, he took on board many of Christopher Caudwell's ideas about poetry and its community function – that it developed the collective conscious and unconscious – he identified also with Caudwell's concern with a community's cultural destiny; indeed this became Mphahlele's principal pursuit in all his later criticism: he was to articulate it before it emerged in South Africa as the main focus of black consciousness thinking. Even when former black consciousness writers were to reject the movement as having been over-concerned with cultural alienation and insufficiently aware of historical and economic components, the analysis of a community's cultural destiny was to survive into the liberation writing of the eighties. Mphahlele had never, however, been unaware of the connections between culture and power, and his African humanism had always engaged with politics in its clear grasp of the avenues of cultural and economic dominance. His ideas naturally clarified as his critical career progressed, and it is in his second edition of *The African Image* (where, incidentally, he notes the emergence of the South African Students' Organisation – the organization that was to form the backbone of the Black Consciousness Movement – as a hopeful sign) that he gives his fullest exposition of this humanism, demanding that:

We must stop placing ourselves on show to the outside world and begin teaching our people, creating bonds where national political life is torn and poisoned by the manipulation of language and ethnic interest.[71]

This concept of humanism had, not surprisingly, originated from his commitment to people. Just as his objections to negritude rested on its élitist character, so in his earliest deliberations on culture he had insisted on the importance of participation:

> Africans . . . want a *social* climate where they can *make* music and fun and not just *listen* to music and *look* at a performance . . . Culture is a part of the very process of living, of a stream of consciousness, in which a whole community takes part.[72]

South African writers, he felt, had always been in a specially privileged position to provide such culture, because they were not an élite either socially or intellectually, but detribalised writers living in the heart of their communities (in contrast to West African inheritors of the colonial suburbs) and producing unavoidably proletarian art. (In fact his whole search through African literature in Africa and the diaspora was perhaps prompted by his indignant query: 'Where do we come in? . . . Has the society of African Culture no room for us?'[73])

In his rejection of élitist poetry and championship of people's poetry, he was quick to dismiss that kind of poetry that only *purports* to appeal to the emotions of the people, written by poets who claim to be able to speak for a community with whom they have no significant contact. And he is systematic in following through the implications of such a call: with a continent where the majority is illiterate no written poetry can ever really claim to speak either for or to the masses: it is spoken poetry which is required, poetry 'that deliberately uses the speech rhythms and diction of the street or market place'[74] and he sees that the recording industry might have a greater part to play here than the publishing industry. Oral poetry had of course traditionally filled this role in Africa, and what Mphahlele is seeking here is not a return to the original, unsullied traditions, but the creation of a new tradition in the old mode, a spoken poetry that speaks to the current situation and the new kind of people. He has witnessed experiments made on these lines by black writers in America, and calls for critical tolerance as such writers endure the birth pangs while they make their almost desperate efforts

> to perform their works orally for large audiences and to write a poetic language that will excite, move, and elevate ever larger segments of the public by speaking to both their plight and their resilience and survival – such efforts should not be belittled or sneered at.[75]

Even though, at this stage, Mphahlele has more faith in the theatre's capacity to fill the popular role than in poetry's, he resolutely refuses to apply the western critical standards which by now come naturally to him as an academic in the western tradition, to a kind of literature conceived out of that tradition.

Though this is not a dominant feature of Mphahlele's criticism – the need to construct a new kind of critical engagement – he sounds warning notes against traditional critical judgements throughout his work. Both as creator and critic he is conscious of the unique predicament of the South African writer recreating the drama of the black ghettoes in language that is inevitably overcharged:

> I have got to stay with it. I bleed inside. My people bleed. But I must stay with it . . . I say I must speak for a public, an oppressed public. My voice is their voice.[76]

His attempt, in his criticism as in his creative work, is to *locate* the aspirations of black South African literature.

But in order to be the voice of the people, black writers have to forge a language that engages with them, and as African writers all over the continent have pointed out, a difficult problem for all writers in all countries becomes almost insurmountable when an alienating language in which the majority do not communicate with each other is introduced. Earlier in this book I have gone into the special circumstances obtaining in South Africa that call in question approaches such as Ngugi's in Kenya, for South Africa not only has a large number of different vernaculars, but these languages have themselves been used as instruments of domination in such a way as to give their speakers and writers an ambivalent attitude. Yet the burden lies on the South African writer to provide discourse for all his people – 'The strong sense of community makes it imperative that you hammer out a way of talking to your people.'[77] And he makes it clear that to opt out of this almost impossible task is to opt out of relevance and join the élite.

It is not only a question of the writer providing the voice, either, but of experienced writers helping the inarticulate to find their own voice. And one of Mphahlele's most interesting calls in this last major critical work is for an end to prestige writers' conferences and a great increase in writers' workshops at the grassroots level: he emphasises the need for practical workshops that travel around – which will facilitate access *to* and *for* the ordinary people seeking to express themselves. And it is interesting that one of the major products of the Black Consciousness Movement is the large number of small writers' workshops that have sprung up all over South Africa and in the countries of exile, and the corresponding number of small magazines and newsletters that publish these writers' first efforts. It seems to be another instance of Mphahlele expressing the dominant needs and wishes of his people, even from his segregated position of exile, of perceiving developments at a time when the outside world was scarcely aware of them, and drawing public attention to them in a symbiotic process that fostered awareness at the same time as it nourished growth: Mphahlele in his critical works, especially in *Voices in the Whirlwind* and the second *African Image*, pricked out the seeds of black consciousness, giving them the space and nourishment necessary for sturdy growth.

One important feature of Mphahlele's attempts to define a black aesthetic has been his understanding of the radical engagement of culture with power. He had never made the mistake of ignoring the social, political and indeed economic context of literature, as had the middle-class black writers, who by focusing only on their cultural alienation had 'dismissed the economic laws and historical processes'[78] and so led to the split in the Black Consciousness Movement and the dissociation from it of so many writers today.

On the other hand, Mphahlele laboured under no illusions about the potency of literature or the literary critic, whatever his insight into its incorporation or otherwise into the power structure of the day. He acknowledged poetry as 'a ready tool for the expression or dramatization of protest and indignation'[79] but he did not deceive himself into believing that poetic will constitutes social force:

> Neither our perception of the 'unified sensibility' in literature nor the critic's revelation of this seems to have influenced for the better the corporate will of a society, even in countries where literature has been produced in written form for centuries. It has not, for instance, been a brake on the march of racism, fascism, the acquisitive drive and its corollary, the rat race, in developed countries.[80]

However, he does not allow literature's failure to exert direct pressure to be accepted as an excuse for cultural disengagement. His realistic assessment of literature's effect is a part of his attempt to construct a valid theory of a literature of commitment unhampered by romantic and idealistic illusions. While, like the American poet Don L. Lee, he doesn't see poetry ever taking the place of the gun or stopping it,[81] he nevertheless considers that poetry, and indeed all literature and the culture of which it is a part, has a role to play in the confrontation with power:

I am interested in the frontal attack on power and its instruments. Long after we have attained culturally integrated personalities, power will still be a problem. And poetry in such a conflict may have something to tell us that will be relevant for all time.'[82]

Naturally the conflict to which he refers, and with which he has been concerned all his writing life, is that between power and the under-privileged, and the poetry he would foster is that which speaks for the latter and arrives at 'the most intensive articulation of a people's yearnings'.[83]

Indeed he considers that poetry is most truly itself when it is caught up in that conflict and at the same time most fully expresses the writer's intention. At one point in the essay 'Poetry and Conflict' he almost seems to contradict his initial dismissal of poetry as an active social force, and seems to suggest that it does have a potential revolutionary role:

When poetry can be a vehicle of revolutionary passion and ideas and at the same time be what the writer wants to say, and that as memorable speech, we have the 'truest poetry'. It can anticipate the historical moment of armed revolution, it can promote it while the conflict is in process, and it can stay on as ritual during and after the event.[84]

Yet I think he clarified this point in an interview with Manganyi after he returned to South Africa when he explained that he did not think a specific piece of literature could specifically mobilise a reader into political action. In this interview, perhaps because he was speaking in South Africa and there is an involuntary tendency towards self-censorship, he does not elucidate in exactly what ways literature can have political potential. It is difficult to be sure here whether he is trying to create a climate for less censorship or expressing his genuine opinion at that time. But he has never, at any stage in his critical career, suggested that the promotion, by literature, of armed revolution should be on a reductionist cause and effect basis. This does not prevent him from endorsing Castro's insistence that the artist should create primarily for his contemporaries or from quoting with approval his dictum:

For the revolutionary . . . those goals and objectives are directed towards *the change of reality* . . . towards the redemption of man.[85]
(My emphasis)

But the quotation is accompanied by his customary warning against idealism, and a personal note on the limits to the capacities of the revolutionary poet:

> Poetry is not going to help us resolve social conflict. But through it we are going to see ourselves as we are and perhaps as we want to be.[86]

Perhaps the value of Mphahlele's cautious examinations of literature's revolutionary potential lies in his intense commitment, despite all tendencies to puncture idealism or romantic fervour, to the realities of the struggle, and his acceptance of all the implications and consequences. He can accept the apparent irrelevance of educational and cultural philosophies to those engaged in the life and death conflict in Southern Africa without faltering in his own conviction of the interrelationship:

> And yet that very bloody struggle helps determine the shape of their (Mozambique's, Angola's, Zimbabwe's, South Africa's) culture . . . The cut and thrust of guerilla warfare must also give an account of itself in the theatre of the mind.[87]

And he voices, in his criticism, the will of the Southern African people to take charge of their own cultural destiny – a will that is manifest in all contemporary publications by black writers.

THE INFLUENCE OF MARXIST CULTURAL THEORY

It is hardly surprising that, along with Mphahlele's convictions concerning the centrality of the people in any cultural theory, and his identification of the conjunctions between culture and power, his thinking should to some extent converge with that of Marxist literary critics and cultural theorists, even though Mphahlele makes no particular identification with Marxism in general. And certain Marxist writers had especial relevance for him while he was in the process of working out his own ideas – writers such as Christopher Caudwell, whose *Illusion and Reality* was a seminal force in the preparation of *Voices in the Whirlwind* and Frantz Fanon whose *The Wretched of the Earth*, *Towards the African Revolution* and *Black Skin White Masks* are evident in the thinking behind the radical revision of *The African Image*. It is not so much that Mphahlele adopts a Marxist position, as that his reading of Marxist thinking helps him to frame some of his questions and establish some of his priorities.

He came to literature and criticism by a route that was anything but Marxist. As he struggled towards higher education through all the difficulties in his path he plunged enthusiastically into the realms of English literature, imbued with the liberal humanist ethic of his 'mentor', Norah Taylor, and saturating himself in 'the study of poetics, practical criticism, the Victorians, Shakespeare and the Elizabethans, and Middle English'.[88] Even his first consideration of black characters in fiction, in his M.A. thesis, is based to a large extent on European writing.

One of the values he absorbed so strongly that it was to dog him for the rest of his life and play havoc with his responses to African writing was a prejudice against didacticism. This is not the exclusive property of western bourgeois ideology – Marx and Engels had also expressed reservations about didactic writing in their day, but Mphahlele had contracted a particularly virulent form of the disease which militated against the politicisation of art, spreading into theories about the autonomy and universality of all great art. Thus in his first version of *The African Image* he is loud in praise of Faulkener, Conrad and Forster for their freedom from didactic standards in the creation of their characters. And even as he began to look much more closely at the imperatives of African literature he was unable to shake off this initial prejudice. Though he modified his rejection of the didactic by the time he came to write *Voices in the Whirlwind*, to the point of admitting that 'all meaningful art has moral implications', he was careful to qualify this concession – 'We should be free enough to say this without necessarily asking the writer to preach to or at us.'[89] He goes on to suggest, in the regular English liberal humanist tradition, that the writer should 'suggest the moral implications through metaphor or symbolism'.[90] Even when he comes to endorse Achebe's interpretation of his role as a teacher, he feels constrained to insist that the actual teaching in his novels must have been unconscious at the time of writing or they would have turned out to be bad novels:

> The power in Achebe's novels is evidence that the motive to teach could hardly have dominated the forefront of his consciousness at the time of writing.[91]

And it is those who can 'distil propaganda through the individual sensibility so that it comes through as a beautiful synthesis between reflection and battle cry'[92] who earn his fullest commendation.

For a writer in a fairly stable, relatively unoppressive society the question of didacticism might perhaps be kept on an academic level. But for South African writers the question of bitterness and anger was the one which had to be faced before anything else – for it constituted their content and dictated their style. In his early critical writing Mphahlele consistently saw this as a disadvantage, hampering writers in their attempt to express themselves, interfering with the effect upon their readership and preventing their work from qualifying for a place in the literary hierarchy.

Another effect of his immersion in the western literary tradition was his preoccupation with standards, and his tendency to weigh black South Africa on the scales of the English literary heritage. In his efforts to formulate a black aesthetic (that is, an aesthetic both for Africa and for its diaspora) he returns compulsively to this question – 'Clearly we have still to arrive at the standards of the aesthetic we are talking about.'[93] The most dangerous residue from the west, however, as far as South African writing is concerned, is its tendency to separate art from politics, which Mphahlele inherited along with the rest of the bourgeois liberal tradition, and which affected his attitude towards African writing for many years and which accounts for many of the contradictions in his theorising. His instinctive response, for example, to the All-African Peoples' Conference in December 1958 in Accra (albeit an acquired instinct rather than a hereditary one) was to condemn the confusion of art with national politics:

> It was already clear that the artist at work and the nationalist who blabbers all this political jargon are not one and the same person: something happens in one's art which does not support, and is not supported by, another man's platform theories.[94]

This is so far from his later position (albeit he retains some traces of the discrepancies that are the inevitable consequence of conflicting traditions) that it is interesting to trace the path of his development.

As I have already pointed out, when he came to the application of the western values implicit in his education to the African writing that ultimately became his primary concern, he found that it was impossible to make them operate within an African context. He could apply them fairly successfully to any African literary works written in the mainstream of European tradition (for example most of the novels of Peter Abrahams or Achebe), but once writers began to move away from that tradition it was impossible to construct a synthesis. It was necessary either to discard African writing as below standard, or at an inferior stage of development, or to discard the values as irrelevant criteria.

Even at the time when the hold of the western literary tradition was strongest, when he was writing his first version of *The African Image*, Mphahlele was aware of the distortions imposed by the social context of South Africa that forced a writer, before all else, to find his identity among the oppressed majority or the oppressing minority, subjecting him to an extraordinary pressure to 'preach, protest, hand out propaganda'.[95] It was this pressure which brought Mphahlele, by no means an instinctive politician, to declare himself in *Voices in the Whirlwind* as a socialist and humanist. And gradually, though he was never to withdraw absolutely his objections to didacticism, he began to give that element more space within the context of African writing, and to dissociate himself from the failure of certain regions of western aesthetics to 'assert the moral purpose of art'.[96] It is here that he begins to admit that anger and bitterness need not necessarily have a detrimental effect on art – a step forward from his position in the first edition of *The African Image*:

> I cannot support the common assertion among some Western critics who claim that bitterness must always produce bad art.[97]

By this time he is also beginning to call for a suspension of the standard practice of automatically applying statutory value judgements, when he begins to analyse some black American poetry:

> It is easy to slip into a value judgement between, on the one hand, a poetry that hits the level of local response and at the same time has a relevance for the larger world audience and, on the other hand, a poetry that is only or largely local in appeal. The former is often considered to be superior, or 'more meaningful'. *We need not make a value judgement here.* Particularly as between two worlds that consider themselves culturally opposed, and when the black world is at least partially in the process of withdrawing from a Western scheme of aesthetic values.[98] (My emphasis)

Mphahlele is one of the first critics to point out the need for caution in this area, and to confront the academic public with the notion that literary values differ in the West and Africa:

> A novel may be badly written by Western standards, in terms of language and still portray life vividly and meaningfully for us.[99]

He is careful to add that this is not a question of good or bad language – for the African story-teller has traditionally been very skilled linguistically – but of attitudes to language. (Mphahlele does not expand this point, but it is easy to grasp his meaning if one looks at the use of language by the poets writing in the seventies.) In this whole issue Mphahlele is not out merely to discard standards or values but to contribute to the discovery of specifically African values which are the only ones to have significance within the African context:

> My discussion of images has been a way of getting closer to the writer's intention, to probe his index of *value* in the context of the social milieu.[100] (Mphahlele's emphasis)

But it was more than a confrontation of literary traditions and values that Mphahlele experienced as he groped towards the construction of a black aesthetic. He began to realise that the whole complex of relations between literature and society which had been worked out in the West were inapposite for his purposes, and that his own social values, on which he drew for his literary judgements, were out of step with the social values of the society from which he had received his formal cultural education and academic initiation. *People* were always central to Mphahlele's scenario, people, not as individuals wrestling in solitude with their private *Sturm und Drang*, but people within their social context, people as social beings related to their communities. This is a priority that he shares both with the Black Consciousness Movement and with Marxism, and it is one which is fundamental to his aesthetic – for it is only in relation to people within their communities that art can have any validity in Mphahlele's eyes. For him the poet's 'only justification lies in the communal consciousness that he represents and is shaped by'.[101] And literature and art attain greatness by the degree to which the artist is able to achieve this:

> Great art thus endures because it integrates private instincts with those common to man in general within a cultural context.[102]

This preoccupation with people and the community leads naturally to an overwhelming concern with the vast majority of the population of Africa – the poor, the exploited, the oppressed and an agonised search for the ways in which literature can become significant for this majority. And this brings him very speedily to the conclusion that élitist literature concerned with the niceties of literature, style, autonomy can never have any significance whatsoever in Africa, and that the only literature which approaches relevance is that which is fairly based on a socialist ethic:

> It seems that one of the very few times literature strives to reach the underprivileged strata of society is when it is concerned with socio–political causes, with the suffering of man as a victim of power. Because the creators of such literature care desperately about man, they must engage his sensibilities, using the simple and basic proposition that man recreates a poem or a story for himself as he reads.[103]

This last concern – with the reader of the work of literature – is something else which Mphahlele has in common with Marxist and related criticism. It was obviously Mphahlele's humanism – a community-oriented humanism – which caused him to focus his attention as much on the consumer as on the producer of literature, and this was to become a major emphasis among black consciousness writers as they strove to undermine western traditions of the writer as a deified creator and replace it with the concept of the writer as a cultural worker working with and for the community in a workshop fashion.

Of course Marxist criticism does not monopolise concern with the reader. Mphahlele recalls E. M. Forster's emphasis on the reader in his preface to the second edition of *The African Image* – an emphasis which he obviously takes for one of his own guidelines. And throughout this book he repeatedly reminds the reader of the need for African literature to take on board this whole problem of audience (with all that entails when there is a great deal of illiteracy), and together with it the related problem of publishing which until very recently was a white monopoly. Without very thorough attention to such matters and very practical solutions, Mphahlele realised there could be no question of a realistic mass African culture emerging.

For Mphahlele himself, as for all other banned and exiled South African writers, the issue has a particular poignancy. He identifies very strongly with Kgositsile's difficulty in writing in America a poetry strongly influenced by black American traditions, and commends him for his success in working out in the much more difficult sphere of poetry the easier intellectual and emotional alignments of African and Afro-American interests and aspirations:

> Most of the time Kgositsile succeeds. His focus will always be in danger of losing its sharpness when he becomes uncertain of his audience on either side of the Atlantic . . . Kgositsile has to find the

solution *himself*: that is how one earns his exile as an artist.[104]

For a writer with Mphahlele's convictions about the overriding importance of the audience and of the writer's community role, the deprivation caused by exile and banning is inestimable, for it empties his role of all its significance. And, as so often, he is speaking here not only for himself, but also for all the writers exiled from and banned in South Africa.

Mphahlele had come increasingly, throughout his writing career, to look upon literature in terms of its function. He, in common with the writers who began to publish during the Black Consciousness Movement, had come to judge a literary work not by a literary scale of values, or according to a traditional hierarchy, but by the way it operated in the social context for which it had been designed. That is, he was not only concerned, as are the Marxist critics, with the content of the novels, plays or poems, but with the way they interacted, as elements of the superstructure, with other elements in the super-structure, and with the base.

Even as early as *The African Image* 1, where he is still thinking in terms of the autonomy of art, he demands that the work of art carry out a social function:

> If the autonomy of art means anything at all, it is that art should order our experiences and responses and help resolve conflicts inside ourselves as individuals in such a way that we each bring to our groups a personality that could never justify race, colour, and religious discrimination, intellectual dishonesty, poverty and inequality of privilege.[105]

There is nothing here, of course, that any traditional English literary critic over the last eighty years would take exception to. The demand owes nothing to any Marxist influence, and could indeed be construed as part of the mainstream of critical tradition already prevalent among the major critics of the nineteenth century. It is interesting only as marking his starting point as a socialist critic. However, by the time he came to write 'Poetry and Conflict', the first of the essays in *Voices in the Whirlwind*, the demand was hardening and he was focusing upon 'poetry that, consciously or unconsciously, seeks to meet socio–political imperatives of a con-temporary order'.[106] And he was very dismissive of new criticism's dismissal of authorial intention and effect upon readers. He pointed out that for African writers such as those of the negritude school these two criteria embodied the purpose of writing, and such poets 'would . . . like their poetry to be judged according to whether it is a successful mouthpiece of the ideology'.[107] Not only did he see poetry as crucially affecting the consciousness both of the writer and the reader, he also considered that the ultimate aim of literature as social practice was to intervene in the communal consciousness in such a way as to bring about a greater depth of understanding of the socio–political as well as the interpersonal forces at work. It is for this reason that he commended Oswald Mtshali's first publication *Sounds of a Cowhide Drum* as an 'image of a man grappling with life in his own ghetto, trying to understand it in the context of social chaos'.[108]

It was perhaps his observation of what happened at Sharpeville and after, when the viciousness of the repression obliterated literature in South Africa and he realised that 'at the moment, the function of literature in the South African context is in a state of suspension',[109] that spurred him to formulate his theory of the function of literature within a revolutionary context referred to earlier. Though even at this stage (during the writing of 'Poetry and Conflict' in 1972) he accords poetry a revolutionary role, and indeed asserts that the truest poetry is that which carries out this role, he still considers the most effective way of mobilising people is through everyday speech in prose or through song.[110]

But more significant than his shifting view of poetry's revolutionary potential is his vision, long before the fairly orthodox Marxist view of the black consciousness writers, of the integration of and interaction between literature and politics, and the crucial question he asks of the entire literary world in the process of examining the link between ethics and aesthetics in the black American cultural tradition: 'Whose vision of the world is finally more meaningful – ours or the white oppressors? What is truth? Whose truth will be valid – that of the oppressor or oppressed?'[111] For it was on these basically challenging questions that the Black Consciousness Movement was able to build the confidence to construct its own black South African universe.

Once such questions had been asked, it was possible to move forward to an analysis of the way black cultural movements had been manipulated by whites – and later by the black bourgeoisie as yet unliberated from western standards, values and aims – in order to retain political control of the masses. Once the process of demystification had been undertaken, it was possible to read off the manoeuverings beneath the surface of economic, political and cultural life, which culture had formerly helped to conceal. Mphahlele warns:

When I talk about white power, it may be political, economic, military, religious authority. Power may even be only implied, understood, while in the foreground Africans act out their own dramas, either in the theater of the mind or that of communal life.[112]

This change in Mphahlele's stance, from a liberal acceptance of white cultural myths masking the realities of power to a revolutionary rejection of compromise and challenge to these underlying forces on a level which does not dissociate culture from power, is brought out most clearly in his chapter on 'The Nationalist' in the second version of *The African Image*. And it was the recognition of the way that 'European systems of economy and politics have brought about a dissociation in African life between a way of life and a way of governing'[113] that made such a change possible.

It was at this stage in his intellectual development, after he had analysed the problem and visualised the solution, that Mphahlele experienced one of his most anguished personal dilemmas. For to accept the necessity for revolution is to accept the necessity for violence. Only reform can provide escape from violent confrontation, and over the years it had become very clear that reform was not a possibility in South Africa. But to accept the necessity for violence was not enough for Mphahlele, himself incapable of violent action and morally scrupulous about accepting it on behalf of others who would have to carry it out. At this time in his life those writers who commanded his admiration were those like Brutus and Kunene who had resolved this conflict satisfactorily and become men of action. Ultimately he had the intellectual honesty not to back down from either issue: the need for a degree of violence and his own inability to participate in this area of the struggle.

So perhaps his concentration on the cultural end of the struggle, and his attempt to drive home its political character is as much the outcome of his need to find a personal role as of his intellectual interest in the cultural and academic field. Whatever the reason, he takes every opportunity to drive home his message. Having identified the inherent weakness of the negritude philosophy as lying in the fact that 'political revolution in Africa preceded cultural revolution'[114] he repeatedly directs attention towards the need to integrate political and cultural struggle in the future: 'My speculation about South Africa would be idle if I did not take into consideration the fact that political struggle interacts with cultural patterns.'[115] His recognition that an élitist culture fails to shift the balance of power, fails to construct a milieu in which the oppressed can take control of their lives is crucial in helping to define the parameters of the struggle in South Africa. He focuses his demand for the unification of political, economic, military and cultural struggle in his country by applying Fanon's ultimatum:

> There is no other fight for culture which can develop apart from the popular struggle . . . No one can truly wish for the spread of African culture if he does not give practical support to the creation of the conditions necessary to the existence of that culture.[116]

His strategies in that struggle are concerned with education (the evolvement of specifically African curricula and educational policies that reinforce the aspirations of the people for whom they are designed and who should participate in their formulation) and with culture (he demands the institutionalisation of culture at a non-élitist, non-exhibitionist level). He stresses the need for cultural theory to be involved with the social and economic welfare of the masses, and announces, with a surge of confidence in the strength of those masses that 'Our culture will interact without political aspirations.'[117] This absorption of culture into the political struggle has consequences for the writer which the Black Consciousness Movement was efficacious in promulgating. While it closed certain options to him that had been open throughout the long hegemony of bourgeois ideology, it also opened others that gave him a place and a function within the most significant arena of his era, the liberation struggle:

> The African writer in this part of Africa has an urgent dual responsibility . . . At one level, he has to act as political man, and that means literally think and *act*. At another he has to practice the art and craft of interpreting his world through images and symbols.[118] (Mphahlele's emphasis)

Mphahlele is really implying that the amalgamation of action and creative writing is not an option for the South African writer, but a condition forced upon him by his social circumstances: that necessity has in fact forged for him, and for culture as a whole, a role that is much more dynamic and significant than the peripheral role of the writer in more stable societies:

> In self-governed communities, there is more time to reflect on the

relative degree of withdrawal into one's private world. In Southern Africa, there is hardly time: as long as one decides to live and work in the center of the whirlwind.[119]

This role is not confined to the writer in Southern Africa. Mphahlele quotes Achebe, later in the book, on the same issue, making similar demands on the writer and on his contribution to a culture that is not confined to books, but made by the people:

> He had better understand that Africa is undergoing a revolution and that this also involves culture. The writer's place, Achebe insists, is 'right in the thick of it – if possible at the head of it'.[120]

No one, however, is more conscious of ambivalence both in himself and in his social context, than Mphahlele. And his attitude towards culture and revolution is no more free of ambiguities than any of his other intellectual or emotional positions. His revolutionary fervour reaches its peak in 'Poetry and Conflict', at the point at which his analysis of the political and economic situation in Africa and elsewhere meshes with his ideas about culture and its functions. But even at this stage he does not attempt to suggest a straightforward relationship between writing and struggle, and only a year later, in 1973, he was to set out his qualifications of the writer's revolutionary potential:

> I am aware that writers don't make political revolutions, they wield no power that immediately counts in the struggle for political and economic power. Creators of serious imaginative literature are engaged in a middle-class occupation, can only be read by the educated . . . It does not matter if we write about the concerns of the common man sometimes or always. We are not read by *him*. The politicians and financiers run our world, not people who play with images or symbols.[121]

This may seem in direct contradiction with what has gone before; and it would be irresponsible to attempt to conceal or synthesise the contradictions in Mphahlele's thinking for he admits them quite freely himself. However, many of the contradictions are inherent in his content – and indeed have always been inherent in any examination of the function of culture, though they were artificially resolved by critics committed to a tradition based upon synthesis and totalisation. But the contradiction is also less real than apparent, for it is preparing the ground for the cultural ultimatum – 'If a writer wants to promote a political revolution he must go out among the crowds as a *man*, go into action.'[122] He is not attempting to stifle writing, though he persistently urges the use of prose, of the language of the people, but merely to face up to what he sees as the limitations of its usefulness, which he sees as confined to the long term. Once again it is a little difficult to assess whether this revocation of a belief in literature's direct revolutionary potential is a natural development of his train of thought, or a consequence of self-censorship as he prepares himself mentally for return to South Africa.

There is no doubt, however, that whatever the degree of his subscription to revolutionary theory, whatever the Marxist characteristics of his cultural analysis, it is primarily as a nationalist, and not as a Marxist, that he identifies himself.

CONCLUSION

And once we have arrived at a conception of Mphahlele's ultimate self-identification, we have to ask what the function of his own criticism has been. What was he trying to achieve when he turned from short stories and autobiography to *The African Image* and *Voices in the Whirlwind*? We know that he had a recurrent pattern of turning to criticism during sterile periods in his creative work. Was it possible that he was attempting to siphon off into criticism the anger and protest he felt was fatal to his creative writing?

I began this chapter with the claim that Mphahlele's critical work constituted an intellectual autobiography: but it is important, in the context of the South African and the entire African cultural renaissance to sift out, as precisely as possible, how that criticism is operating as a cultural practice, both for the writer himself and for the audience for which, in his mind, despite the negation of banning, he wrote.

I have suggested earlier that Mphahlele's intended audience, in spite of all the obstacles used by the South African government and the entire mechanism of publication, are the writers producing poems, plays, novels and stories for the black people of South Africa. As he is also one of these writers, his personal project automatically becomes a surrogate project, directly for them, and indirectly for the masses for whom they write.

Mphahlele's critical enterprise was an act of intellectual self-creation. Through it he explored his cultural history and established the base for current cultural construction. Almost all the issues which confronted him in this operation were issues for which cultural resolution was required by the entire community. The most urgent was the question of whether to write or to act. Action was the logical imperative that arose from his intellectual acceptance of the need for revolution and the recognition that some degree of violence was an inevitable concomitant. His realism and honesty about his own limitations in this area help to provide a cultural framework in which others can take their own decisions.

His earlier efforts to deal with the problem of being white inside similarly gave others a field of operation, while his success in resolving some of the problems could not but give heart to others in similar straits: 'You have to survive. If you are more sensitive, you want to do more than survive. You want to create, to assert a presence.'[123] The fact that he was able to develop mechanisms and skills for survival, for overcoming the terrible deprivations not only of social context, but also of audience, enabled others to tackle the overwhelming difficulty of being wiped out of significant existence, not only physically but intellectually:

> We began as black writers in this land of false social values, unsure of ourselves. We used to mourn the loss of idyllic tribal life . . . We grabbed the tools education gave us . . . And now we are like banished prophets shouting in the wilderness but shouting all the same.[124]

His most important achievement, however, was his recognition of the need for the promulgation of the identification of culture with power, so that a discourse could be established within which the claim could be made and hands laid upon power. And it is to the enlargement and enrichment of this discourse that he directs his fellow scholars in their vital connection with their people. He sees writers as the ultimate reconcilers between past and present: 'Everywhere in Africa . . . we shall be the vehicle of communication between the two streams of consciousness as they exchange confidences, knowledge, wisdom and dreams.'[125] But more important is their transference of this power of repossession of their history to the people whose voice they are, so that the people may use it in their forward movement in the appropriation of power:

> They need to be told now who they are, and where they come from, and what they should be doing about these things that we're talking

about. That's where the scholar comes in; he must exploit that consciousness, the black consciousness, so as to probe deeper into the personality and move forward.[126]

In the course of his intellectual autobiography, Mphahlele has finally defined a role for the intellectual in the liberation struggle.

3 Autobiographical Writings

who am i
lost like this
broken like this
weary like this
who am i

Mongane Serote: *No Baby Must Weep*[1]

INTRODUCTION

The writings of the sixties autobiographies take us back from
Mphahlele's ultimate understanding of the connection between culture,
power and discourse to one of his much earlier stages, where the urge to
protest was interwoven with the urge towards self-discovery. Before
there can be an identification of discourse with power, writers have to
confront themselves and take the measure of their own identity, while
at the same time providing the structural framework for the reader, and
the community at large, to go through the same process. There can be
no analysis of the distribution and manipulation of power through
culture before the participators in the culture have deconstructed its
naturalising processes and reconstructed their alienated identities upon
which control and manipulation had originally depended.

For this reason, despite black South African writers' preoccupation
with dismantling the individualism of the western literary heritage, and
with establishing human solidarity, it is not surprising that one of the
most dominant features of their work is its autobiographical content.
Not only is there a large body of overt autobiographical writing, but
other genres are also strongly infiltrated with autobiographical
material to an extent that far surpasses the general dependence of

writers elsewhere on the material of their own life for their content.

Different writers resolve this need to work through autobiographical components in a variety of ways. While some writers, particularly those who went into exile in the late fifties and early sixties – the graduates of Sharpeville and the Treason Trial – embark on straightforward autobiography, such as Matshikiza in *Chocolates for my Wife*, Boetie in *Familiarity is the Kingdom of the Lost* or Hutchinson in *Road to Ghana*, others have adapted other literary forms to the same purpose – Serote incorporates his material in two long poems, *No Baby Must Weep* and *Behold Mama, Flowers*; Bessie Head draws on her own experience of racial prejudice for her novel *Maru* and on the traumas of her inner life for *A Question of Power*; Brutus puts his prison experiences into *Letters to Martha* and his feelings about exile into a series of short poems; Mphahlele uses a fictional autobiography; Manganyi and Nkosi use essays to embody their autobiographical fragments. Even Manganyi's biography of Mphahlele is cast in an autobiographical format. There are of course notable exceptions to this preoccupation with the self: Alex La Guma's stories have cut the umbilical cord and deal with materials and emotions that have been completely transmuted into literary materials and emotions; some of Kgositsile's poems achieve that standpoint of free response advocated by Sartre, and recent novels written in the eighties have begun to turn away from individual emotion and experience to group interaction – Sepamla's *A Ride on the Whirlwind*, Mzamane's *Children of Soweto*, Serote's *To Every Birth its Blood*. But apart from these exceptions, the majority of African writers in the last two decades have used themselves as mirrors, and their picture of society has depended on the reflections of themselves.

The form does seem in many ways peculiarly adapted to the needs of South African writers, absorbed as they are with their own and their people's search for identity, with the evolution of consciousness, with the attempt to make sense of their life and condition. Nevertheless we have to ask, having established the need for the writer in the revolutionary situation to create new forms or to radically adapt the old ones to new ends, whether autobiography is in fact fulfilling this need.

Yet any attempt to explore in depth exactly how autobiography is functioning in this particular context will inevitably be fraught with difficulties: throughout literary history autobiography has been an anomalous literary form, used for a great many different purposes and assuming a wide variety of guises. The various attempts made to categorise it have been no more successful than the attempt to capture soap bubbles – the bubble bursts as soon as it is touched. Northrop

Frye's identification of it as a confessional form (citing St Augustine, Rousseau and Newman as his examples)[2] seems to owe more to his urge to draw up a neat and all-inclusive schema for all types of prose writing than to a comprehensive consideration of the entire range of writing that passes under the name of autobiography.

One reaches a point, indeed, where one has to ask whether there is any such thing as an autobiographical form – whether it can, in truth, be classed among other such genres as poetry, the novel and drama, as literature, or whether, being a record of a life, it must be classed together with such factual categories as biography or history. And that in turn raises the more fundamental issue raised by Eagleton and others, of whether we should be confining ourselves to conventional literary categories in critical discourse, or whether we should be fabricating a much wider cultural discourse that covers, as rhetoric once did, the whole range of the written and spoken word, from poetry, philosophy and history to the mass media.

Autobiography is, of course, essentially an exploration of consciousness. I am not referring here to those records of a person's public life which well-known figures present to the general reader in order to give their version of the externals of their careers and the public events in which they have participated. It is the writer's self-examination with which I am concerned. And as our general consciousness of reality, since Einstein and Freud, has lost the fixity and composure of the mainstream nineteenth-century viewpoint:

> Objective reality has become fragmented, dispersed among a limitless number of conflicting subjectivities; it is no longer a solid substance, but the sum of our illusions.[3]

so the literary forms created by writers like Kafka, Joyce, T. S. Eliot and Virginia Woolf at the beginning of this century reflect this fragmentation of reality. And just as the apparent solidity of the outer world has disintegrated, so has individual consciousness:

> In the alienated worlds of Kafka, Musil, Joyce, Beckett, Camus, man is stripped of his history and has no reality beyond the self; character is dissolved to mental states, objective reality reduced to unintelligible chaos.[4]

Here we have the explanation for the increased popularity of autobiography in the twentieth century, and for the shifting, amorphous character of the form. And this shift in our view of the world in turn leads to a similar shift in our view of the operation of language:

> In every sphere our simple 'thingy' view of the world is being altered
> and often disintegrated at an unprecedented rate; and a crisis in our
> view of the operation of language is inevitable.[5]

Although South Africa, with its dependence on western culture, was
obviously exposed to this changed viewpoint almost as much as Europe
and America, it was exposed in rather different circumstances – and of
course South Africa has means of deadening the impact of outside
influences beyond the mere accidents of a country somewhat remote
from external cultural influences. Not only do ideas travel slowly from
the western world, but the censorship mechanism operates to ensure
that some of them never find an easy footing on South African soil.
Initially, however, it had no body of nineteenth-century realistic fiction
behind it, so it is hardly surprising that there was no emergence of a
Virginia Woolf or a James Joyce to give literary expression to the
changed world view. A *body* of literature, as opposed to isolated
literary works, has only begun to emerge in the twentieth century, and
fairly recently in the twentieth century at that. And it has been heavily
influenced by nineteenth-century European realistic fiction, undis-
turbed by the 'alienated worlds' of the Kafkas, the Joyces and the
Woolfs (at least until the 1970s). There are a variety of reasons for this.
Nadine Gordimer argues that African readers still have much to learn
about themselves and their feelings, and that it is the artist's job to
teach them – so that they are obliged to avoid the novel-in-depth for
'we are still at the stage of trying to read ourselves by outward signs. To
get at our souls it may still be necessary to find out how we do our
monthly accounts.'[6] And Manganyi dismisses the introspective nature
of western literature as incongruous to the African context:

> To ask and expect blacks to abandon this radical positivism for a
> sterile and unpromising metaphysics of a world they have not yet
> entered is like asking a semi-starved man to exchange his loaf of
> bread for a ticket to a concert of chamber music.[7]

Thus, if South African writers, until recently, have still been grappling
with the problems of embodying the 'simple "thingy" view of the
world', the effect of the ideas of the Einsteins and the Freuds of western
culture is not yet (though it is arguable that it is at the moment in the
process of becoming) as crucial an issue for its literature as it is for
English or French or German literature.

Nevertheless, there is a serious sense of fragmentation in South African literature; there is a feeling that objective reality has broken down, if not in quite the same way as for the European writer. It lies, of course, in the social fragmentation of the South African world: the physical, psychological and social barriers between races; the total lack of unified environment, so that a million people travel in from Soweto to Johannesburg daily for work and then return to the location feeling that the place where they have spent the daylight hours has nothing whatever to do with them. It is the foreign territory of Serote's 'City Johannesburg'; the macabre element of nightmare fantasy in everyday life where the processes of the law and justice have become a Kafka-like absurdity involving the regulation of the individual's private world – of movements and friendships and sexual relationships – by government statutes. The fact that both white and black have to apply for permits before they can enter each other's home ground reduces the operation to the level of buying tickets for the zoo, so that the two species may go and gape at each other to satisfy their curiosity without any danger of real intercourse of any kind. Thus South African writers' *content*, their actual external reality, as with western writers, is unavoidably fragmented, by law, and their knowledge of their material – people and their places – is severely limited, not by accident, or geography, or laziness, or lack of interest, as a European writer's might be, but by legal restrictions on physical movement and social interactions.

But all this is too simplistic an explanation of the kind of interference with objective reality to which South African writers and their readers are subjected. For this physical separation of the races can only be maintained by a top-heavy structure of laws, of policing, of social taboos, of group attitudes that can only further fragment the world of so-called 'objective' reality – a world where 'objective' reality in any case varies radically according to which particular ghetto you view it from – Afrikaner, English, 'Coloured', 'Indian' or 'Black'. For black people reality is a place where honest people become criminals because they have lost a piece of paper, or failed to leave or arrive at a certain place by a certain time (as Sizwe Bansi), or because they have sat on the beach, or asked for food in a restaurant:[8] a reality where Kafka's nightmares are not the literary reflections of a writer's insights into the breakdown behind the normality of everyday life, but the normality of everyday life itself. Fanon defines the trauma of such an existence: 'For a man whose only weapon is reason there is nothing more neurotic than contact with unreason.'[9] The contact with unreason is the staple of South African writers, and if they are black, then it permeates the whole structure – the people, the environment and the pattern of everyday life – of what they take for their content.

Under these circumstances, the creative intervention into the world of the artistic consciousness[10] is not quite such a straightforward concept as it might be in a society where there are no doctrinal or legal qualifications to a citizen's autonomy. It may be that the very best writers, in such circumstances, can rise above all the complications of their role – can free their consciousness of the conditioning to which it has been subjected from birth, can boldly ignore the consequences of speaking out (censorship, banning, exile, prison, 'accidental' death), can elevate themselves to a detached state of mind in which they can unemotionally overlook the limitations on their own and other people's freedom, can purge their work of that compulsive anger, hatred and didacticism evoked by what is happening around them all the time. But it would be foolish indeed to expect more than a very few writers to reach these heights. And even they are subjected to influences beyond the reach of their own will-power, to what Manganyi calls 'the censored imagination' – the more deadly, unconscious self-censorship that begins to operate automatically in the mind of the creative artist attempting to work under such conditions.

Manganyi sees the interference with artistic consciousness in South Africa as operating at two levels of the subconscious. The fact of censorship works unconsciously on the side of the censors when the writer's own subconscious does the censor's work without the writer even being aware that this is happening. He cites his own inability to continue with the fragment of *Mashangu's Reverie* when he returned from America to South Africa – his imagination dried up spontaneously – and James Matthews's inability to continue writing short stories after the end of the fifties.[11] Mphahlele reveals a similar failure of the creative urge in Manganyi's biography of him, *Exiles and Homecomings*. At a second level, the imaginative process is not merely dried up, but throttled at source: a kind of abortion of the imagination takes place. Assuming that genuine creation implies a need to 'create dangerously' and that creating dangerously is only possible when working under conditions of freedom if the writer is to confront 'the absurdity of life fully',[12] Manganyi argues that South African artists, lacking these essential conditions, are reduced from the heroic stature of artists giving a peculiarly personal gift to society, to the stature of ordinary people, whose gifts are necessarily preconditioned by their society: 'To "create dangerously" is the fate of the unfettered imagination. To "give the gift that society specifies in advance" is the tragic fate of the censored imagination.'[13] The mechanisms by which South Africa specifies the gift in advance are only too apparent.

Perhaps it is this fettering of the imagination which accounts, to some extent, for black writers' reliance on the autobiographical form. Physical and social conditions have, in the main, proved unconducive to the novel form; banning emasculated the short story: publishing problems have bedevilled poetry. Such impediments inevitably constrict the imagination, and it may be that, apart from all the other factors which attract black writers to autobiography, it is the single form which leaves them space, the form which society cannot entirely specify in advance.

It is not a literary form, however, that allows for the autonomy demanded of aesthetic form by latterday critics. (Though South African writers in any case reject autonomy as a criterion not merely irrelevant but actively pernicious within the South African cultural context.) Unlike the novel, even the autobiographical novel, the autobiography allows for no cutting of the navel strings between work and author. Autobiographers can never get outside their own person, any more than they can get inside any of the other characters in their work, in the way that novelists, from their omniscient standpoint, are able to. Nor can they manipulate situations, invent circumstances that will give full play to all the potential qualities of the hero in the way that novelists can (so that, for example, an autobiographical novel can come nearer to the truth of a person's nature than an autobiography by providing opportunities for behaviour or relationships which life itself might never afford.) Thus 'there are limits to the "truth" of an autobiography'[14] even for the free writer in the free society. When the limits are imposed, not merely by the nature of the genre upon the *presentation* of the life, but upon the living itself by the nature of the society in which the life has to be lived, then these limits become crucial indeed.

A QUESTION OF FUNCTION

Autobiography as a self-making process

But this intensification of limitations for the South African writer is balanced by a parallel intensification of function: whatever the autobiographical form performs for writers and readers in a free society, this pales into insignificance beside what it can perform for writers and readers working towards the removal of restrictions and restraints upon being. For writers the autobiography is the tool of their search for their 'inward moral being',[15] a means by which they can find the balance between themselves and the outside world and investigate that tension between subjective and objective that orders our whole life. It is through wrestling with images of their past life and resolving their relation to the self that exists at the time of writing that they are able to search out and assess their 'inner standing'[16] and thereby come to terms with reality – or with all that is not their own inner consciousness. It is, in fact, the ultimate means for writers to establish their identity, to work out, in their entirety, the dimensions and the significance of those dimensions, of their existence. And as Pascal so urgently has pointed out: 'the autobiography is not simply a statement of what a man was and is . . . It is an active contribution, not a closing of accounts.'[17] Above all, it is a tool by which man can most fully realise the existentialist demand that he make himself, and thereby assert his freedom. Pascal claims that in the autobiography, the autobiographer makes concrete Sartre's theoretical speculations: he lays bare the creation of his own life:

> Autobiographers however are nearer to the truth of experience than Sartre in that they establish the power of man not as an abstract or discontinuous freedom, but as a realisation of an inner self that is as much compulsion as it is freedom. It is not at all arbitrary, but presents itself to reflexion as a 'daemon' or 'persona' or 'life-illusion'. In every case, this dynamic creative element is as true as anything else about us, and is the driving force of a life as seen from inside by the man living it.[18]

The importance of these functions to South African writers is self-evident. In a society where individual identity is systematically denied and forcibly suppressed, subjected by the government to a variety of group identities – the tribe in the homeland, the candidate for Bantu Education, the tenant (number so-and-so) of a location house – where the right of individuals to move from place to place, have access to educational and cultural institutions, employment and housing, even to sexual and marital relationships are fixed by laws imposed by a government elected, not by them, but by a group of people with whom they have very little contact, these individuals can hardly be said to be participating in a 'self-making' process – their self is made for them from birth, through every stage of their life till death, by the laws of the state. Fugard's Sizwe Bansi, referred to in Chapter 1, shows us the anguish of this knowledge breaking in upon his consciousness when his only chance of staying outside prison and in the town where he can ea : enough to support his family is by assuming a total stranger's identity – 'How do I live as another man's ghost?'[19]

In this situation the writers' need to find their own individuality becomes a prerequisite to literary creation. And indeed, autobiography is the South African writers' answer to this interference with their consciousness – they use it to try to reverse the conditioning process in order to free themselves, through reassessment of their entire growth and development, of their mental subjugation, to remake their consciousness. Consequently, whatever genre they take up is likely to be used as a vehicle for this autobiographical search for the inner person. Writing becomes a request for reassurance that they in fact *have* an identity, that they have rescued the fragments and shards of a personality from the systematic official attempt to eradicate it.

Not that all these autobiographical writings are necessarily deeply self-analytical. For some writers such a confrontation in depth is still too traumatic an undertaking, and they side-step the issue by picaresque accounts of law-breaking adventures,[20] or by a humorous if schizophrenic series of apparently unrelated fast-moving sketches.[21] Though it is interesting that such autobiographies all pre-date the rise of the Black Consciousness Movement, after which such evasion mechanisms became impossible.

Yet some writers make an overt and sustained effort to analyse their own reactions, to sort out exactly what the system has done to them as human beings, exactly what areas of their humanity it has eroded. Bloke Modisane does this at great length in *Blame Me On History*. Others, like Noni Jabavu, while inspecting the damage, also pay attention to the healing processes contained within their own social backgrounds – but here she has an advantage limited to a very small highly-educated and self-conscious rural élite, from which the urban African, the class from which most African writers emerge, is totally cut off. But she not only examines herself as a black South African, or even as a westernised black South African coming back to her country, she also analyses herself as an African through her relations to East Africans in her own right as an expatriate wife, and as the family support of her younger sister in a difficult and finally broken marriage. Mphahlele does the same thing in *The Wanderers* when he explores his feelings and reactions in Nigeria and East Africa. Both find their failure to feel total harmony with the local population deeply disturbing, and this sharpens their sense of exile even though they are still in Africa and have grown up with a fixed belief in the oneness of all Africa.

The search for self becomes particularly poignant, of course, for those exiles for whom the cutting of the bond to the motherland (and circumstances ensure that it is a bond very prominent in the consciousness – a life spent attempting to assert rights of citizenship in the face of a battalion of laws denying it does not make for that subconscious, natural sense of belonging that the ordinary exile from other countries can comfortably carry from country to country) has redoubled the sense of denied identity, so that their need to understand their past becomes especially compelling.

The autobiographer as spokesman

Moreover, with the rise of black consciousness, black writers have become aware of a historical role of which they had hitherto been unaware, or at best only partially aware. Writers become spokesmen for millions who have no voice: in these autobiographies 'I' stands for all the people for whom the authors are the voice – that is, their own partitioned racial group. Serote explains it thus: 'I am looking at what has happened to me as a man in South Africa. I am trying to understand it and this is what I write about.'[22] In seeking their own identity they conduct the search on behalf of countless others, many of whom need to be made aware of the fact that they *have* an identity. Arturo Barea's claim: 'As I was one of them, I have attempted to be vocal on their behalf, not in the form of propaganda, but simply by giving my own truth.'[23] might be advanced by all writers who aim to foster black consciousness in their work.

Pascal attributes the development of autobiography in its present form, in part, to the emergence of a European middle class which sought to shake itself free of the values and forms traditional to aristocratic culture.[24] The parallel for South Africa is clear – where an entire race is attempting to shake itself free of the values and forms of a dominant minority, where the strongest current in contemporary literature is towards self-assertion and self-realisation.

Autobiography as an outlet for racial violence

However, the search for identity, the urge towards self-assertion, is not merely a question of battling with outside forces of suppression, as many South African writers have come to recognise. Outside pressures have brought about radical changes in personality, violent upheavals in the individual psyche, which sensitive writers realise they have to reckon with. A recurrent theme in Modisane's autobiography is the stifling effect upon his inner life of the compulsive hatred he has come to feel towards the white man.

He suggests that it is this suppressed violence, and this assumption of masks on both sides (a mask of arrogance and aggression on the part of the white man) which regulates the whole character of life and social relations in his country:

> South Africa was all around me, its attitudes were regulating my life, the violence of its hatred had forced upon me and those of my white friends a relationship of masks in which every response is carefully selected and rehearsed.[25]

It was this convention of masks that had made it so upsetting for him to be offered a personal kindness by the two Americans who wanted to sponsor him to the United States, for they thereby tore off the masks, both white and black, and forced him into confrontation with real people.

Manganyi takes the analysis one stage further. He explains that the dominant reason for writing *Mashangu's Reverie* was because he wanted, by self-analysis, to rid himself of disturbing impulses;[26] it was a way of coming to terms with the dreams of violence obsessing him. He too refers to the assumption of masks and attempts to trace the original causes for this in the education in repudiation given in the mission schools by which black people were not only enabled to read Milton or Shakespeare, but taught to repudiate their own culture and language and

> . . . everything which was native to us. Can you visualize that . . . each one of us carries a double . . . a kind of replica of self that is always in conflict with the mask that faces the world. To protect this mask from its double, one cherished an illusion and nourished it – the illusion that the future and prosperity of the mask depends upon a negation of the past both individual and collective.[27]

Both writers stress the accumulation of violence and hatred that builds up beneath the masks, because, in their view, it is this which provides the dynamic force of the African personality: 'hate was the single human emotion which held me together,'[28] insists Modisane as he states his preference for the prejudiced brutes of whites. His own attitude towards violence is one of extreme ambivalence. He hates it and yet

> I am saturated with violence, it was a piece of noise that was Sophiatown, of the feverish intensity of Sophiatown life, it was, and

is, the expression and clarification of our society. All of us, black and white, are committed to violence, it is the background of the complex attitudes of our dichotomous society, the relationships complicated and standardized by the permeability of skin colour; it is the quality of the group attitudes; we are born into it, we live with it and we die of it, each unto his own race, in the sweat house of our skins.[29]

He had worked out his own ambivalence as a youth, in his gang activities – a gang which purported to protect people from the violence of other groups:

It was a comforting morality adequately masking the violence in us, we were little giants with power complexes, filled with acts of cruelty, injustice and oppression. We cleansed ourselves with rationalizations . . .[30]

Manganyi shows himself here rejecting therapy as suited only to the Europeans with their neuroses: black people need to translate their suppressed violence into action or to sublimate it as writers, in their art. And just as one of Manganyi's characters is shown expressing her inner violence in her sexual taunts of white men, so Modisane tries to convey the strain of containing this volcano of hatred through repeated humiliations and insults:

I am on constant alert against anger, joy, love, getting drunk, becoming sick; I am afraid to vomit the accumulation in my stomach, the violence would be too great for me to control . . .[31]

Mphahlele shows how this hatred loses its impetus in exile, so that his reactions to white arrogance are slowed down, his senses no longer keyed up to violence as they had been in South Africa. And when whites walk into his house and address him as the gardener, he reproaches himself for allowing it, for not responding to them as he should have done 'because the embers (of hate, anger and awareness) had not been disturbed'.[32]

Yet not all of these writers transfer the blame for this situation between the races entirely onto the shoulders of the white population. Several of them attempt to analyse what it is in the African psyche which connives at the relationship. Reflecting on a fellow traveller's comment upon the arrogant behaviour of the ship's officer – 'The whites have forgotten that we are men',[33] Hutchinson pursues his train of thought relentlessly:

And in many ways they had forgotten. We had allowed the whites to relapse into a smug indifference, perhaps. And, being only human, they would continue in their smugness until they were shaken out of it. Hazel had said the same thing: she was sure the English or Germans would not stand it; would rather perish. Was it an all pervading streak of cowardice in the African? Was the much vaunted patience of the African just another name for cowardice? A baby whimpers and its mother gives it her tired breast . . . [34]

Nkosi suggests that it is not a difference in culture, or even smell, that causes blacks to be beaten by whites

but simply because powerless people invite contempt and deserve being beaten over the head. Most of us have been negroes long enough to understand that white people do not hate us so much because we are different as because we ask them to perform an extraordinary feat of self-restraint and self-denial . . . It is the context of power which changes behaviour and transmutes antipathy into sympathy. [35]

Manganyi lends his assent to such theories when he asserts that it is time now 'for black people to project new visions . . . The blackman must stop feeling victimized. He must stand out straight, tall and clearly.'[36]

There are other ambivalences in the relationship between the groups. Mphahlele uses his double narrator technique to try to give the friendly white man's reactions to this artificial situation:

Peculiar how skilfully, even cunningly, people on the other side of the colour line manipulate their relations with us whites . . . At first they put you to a test. They drag friendship and informality into business or official relationships. When they realize that you draw clear lines of distinction between areas of relationships, they do the same. And yet you will often feel you've been frozen out, that where you wanted to be treated as a friend you could not reach them. [37]

And then he quotes his co-narrator, Timi, on how he always lies to whites, because he has to keep accounting for himself to whites, never the other way round.

Nkosi relates at length the history of his contact with whites, almost non-existent before he began to work on *Drum*, and his gradual readjustment of attitudes: the loss of mystique when the distances were closed and whites 'became suddenly embarrassingly ordinary, even hopelessly undersized';[38] his shock at the appalling emptiness of lives that had seemed so immensely rich and beautiful as a consequence of all the privileges attached to them; his ultimate change from fear and envy to contempt – 'they were simply prisoners of a myth'.[39] Manganyi defies the myth, and the need of the white population for its promulgation: 'Euro-Africans are preoccupied with the creation of a mythological caucasian identity',[40] and he suggests that this obsession is what has caused the African's identity to be crushed out of existence.

Even those whites who attempt to dissociate themselves from this preoccupation with Caucasian identity present the African who might wish to relate to them with an insoluble problem. Nkosi confesses that intellectuals might naturally turn to fellow intellectuals in Europe and America for company rather than to the uneducated masses of their fellow countrymen. But he warns that it is an instinct to be repressed, since in the last resort, however liberal the whites may be, they will ultimately abandon their black friends to the prejudiced masses; it is those with whom he 'shares a community of suffering'[41] that he needs to identify with. And he writes with bitterness of the impact of this realisation:

> This very realization that he cannot mould his own identity, given whatever appetites he possesses, in such a way as to escape a gratuitous identity with any mass which happens to be black, is shattering . . . [42]

This question of identity is one of the leitmotifs of these autobiographical writings, for each writer is attempting to show the world the dilemma of black people in resolving their identity problem when all the forces of colonialism have been directed towards removing it, or at least perverting it. Nkosi summarises the problem with his usual succinctness – 'To be a black South African is . . . to live in perpetual exile from oneself.'[43] He shows how their destruction of their links with the past, the breaking of their tradition has left Africans without any way of relating dynamically to their past, and as a consequence unable to determine who they are today, the fragments of their own African culture having become impacted with imperfectly absorbed European culture. (Mphahlele, in his first version of *The African Image*, argues that this is in fact a benefit, that cross-pollination has enriched black South Africans rather than impoverished them, though his later version of the book shows rather less enthusiasm for European influence.) Noni Jabavu frequently refers to this question when comparing East African absorption of European culture with South African. However she tends to show how her own tribe, the Xhosa, have at least found a way of reconciling the two traditions, and there emerges from her book an impression of a much less harassed, more self-assured, and calm identity than we receive from writers who lack her settled academic, western-influenced background.

Nkosi perhaps gives the truer picture of general confusion and speaks more for the masses when he shows, in his essay on *A Question of Identity* the assault made on the African's self-image by the label non-white, its negativeness eroding any positive picture of themselves. He also outlines the wary path the educated African has to tread between over-identifying with a foreign *angst*[44] and wallowing in nostalgia for a '"lost Africa" . . . from the vantage point of the cafe in Paris, Rome or London'.[45] Richard Rive's point about the difficulty in establishing an identity in his youth (the situation has changed radically today) because he was denied empathy, by a thematically white literature, without any literary heroes (for of course the heroes were white),[46] is reinforced by Manganyi's call for the encouragement, or at least the tolerance, of a literature of the oppressed that might help the social scientists and the psychologists in their study of the problems of race. For Manganyi, too, is talking about a people's identity.

Humour as a defence mechanism

Not all autobiographers, however, are searching for their identity, and none are searching for it all the time. For some, autobiography serves as a forest to hide in: for those who cannot look into their trauma, for whom a confrontation with the issue of identity would be totally self-destructive, it provides, at least, a way of coping with the business of living: the pain can be so wrapped in humour that it cannot pierce the covers and penetrate the heart beneath. Boetie and Matshikiza use this method throughout their autobiographies. Both draw upon a style that emerged among a group of writers working for *Drum* magazine in the fifties:

> For a black man to live in South Africa in the second half of the twentieth century and at the same time preserve his sanity, he requires an enormous sense of humour and a surrealistic kind of brutal wit, for without a suicidal attack on Dr Verwoerd's armed forces, these qualities seem to provide the only means of defence against a spiritual chaos and confusion which would rob any man of his mental health.[47]

Drum, in the fifties at least, had provided some kind of harbour from this world, where writers could overhaul themselves and prepare their tackle. And it was on *Drum* that certain writers discussed in this chapter developed their 'cool sober prose in which they permitted themselves the luxury of a laugh'.[48] It was a style of living as much as a style of writing: reporters gloried in their tough image:

> A *Drum* man took sex and alcohol in his stride . . . considering it a mark of great honour to get into trouble with the authorities as often as possible while in pursuit of fact and photograph.[49]
> . . . Usually urbane, ironic, morally tough and detached: one's dedication was to be to a pure form of realism which would eliminate the thinnest traces of self-pity.[50]

Both writers draw on the slick, vibrant jazz style that emerged from this environment, and both put together books that flicker frenetically from incident to incident like the disconnected images of a film cut and jumbled and wrongly joined, flickering on the screen before a bewildered audience. Most of these incidents (for Boetie indeed, all the incidents) are satirically presented: it is the humour that most forcefully impresses the reader: the comedy of the actual incidents themselves, where the ludicrous is emphasised and the writer depends on the sharpness of the satire to make his point – a method which illuminates and veils at the same time, sharpening our appreciation of the harshness of the situation and the absurdities to which the black person is subjected, but at the same time completely removing the personal from the reckoning of accounts.

This is not quite so true of Matshikiza's *Chocolates for My Wife* as it is of Boetie's *Familiarity is the Kingdom of the Lost*. The latter gives such a highly coloured picture of the events in his life that the reader (the *white* reader is perhaps what I am saying) immediately identifies with the editor Barney Simon in his suspicion of the literal truthfulness of the narration. The black reader sees them for what they are – the reality of a people's life, Kafka-like absurdities as they are – related in the fantasy narrative mode of the nightly street-corner or shebeen story-swapping sessions. They are comic stories of the underdog outwitting authority: the tale of the thieves giving the illiterate white driver a written address and asking for his help, while their accomplices remove the goods from his lorry at their leisure, since he was too full of self-importance and patronising good-will to acknowledge his lack of literacy to a black man; Shambu's good-humoured humility and comic excuses for his overlarge overalls enabling him to carry bottle after bottle of liquor, unseen, out of the store he worked in.

Matshikiza's irony is more closely related to the effect he seeks to produce upon his audience, as in his act of dumb surprise at being treated as a human being in countries other than South Africa, which leads to a comparison of the two situations. His situations get more dangerously close to the eye of the whirlwind, the core of the hurt, than Boetie's do, dealing as they do with family homelessness (the exiled family unit seeking a home in London), with the racial one-upmanship even among so-called friends (the encounter with the South African play-white, Mabel), the total impossibility of the black man pursuing his career peacefully in Johannesburg, without having his deepest domestic sensibilities wounded (the coarse destruction of the gift of chocolates for his wife as he waited for the bus after the *King Kong* rehearsal). But Matshikiza also has learned his ironic technique, his energetic, shifting, fast-paced style, in the same school as Boetie.

Nostalgia and exile

For the exile, of course, autobiography inevitably serves as the outlet for nostalgia. It has been one of the most significant features of exile literature, from the earliest plaints of Odysseus, the Wanderer and the Seafarer: the longing for the homeland. And in this, at least, the South African writer is no special case. Whether it be Nkosi's instinctive flinch from the cold of his new home, or Noni Jabavu's rationalisation of the pleasure she takes in the Boer girl hostess's kindness:

> It is wonderful if you are a South African, when a South African of another 'colour' peeps through the prison bars of 'race' and you see another human being, warm, kind and nice . . . [51]

or Hutchinson's sentimental attachment to crowds, locations and mining landscapes in Johannesburg – they all display that hold South Africa has over them, despite all that they dislike about the country. For some, like Brutus, it is the land itself that holds them. For others, it is the way of life, or the people:

> I longed to see my fellow southerners again on their march forward to Westernization. With all its shortcomings, tiresome *tsotsi* boys, gangsters, this way of life seemed infinitely desirable. I wanted to go home and see once more how people sweat blood as they progress; how they gain experience in co-operation and cohesion as they pass

> through those steel-tempering ordeals of Treason accusations, women's anti-Pass campaigns, bus-boycotts, banishings . . . [52]

But beyond the official exile's nostalgia for his homeland, lies the nostalgia of the dispossessed for his birthplace – a nostalgia that is increased beyond the nostalgia of any victim of slum-clearance, in a situation where possession of land or homes is inhibited by law, and where movements of people are dictated by national policy. It is the nostalgia of protest that is manifested by Dugmore Boetie and Bloke Modisane for Sophiatown and by Serote for Alexandra. This yearning for old haunts is compounded with the bitter dregs of the apartheid cup: the devastation of the buildings is felt as a devastation of identity. The loss of those patches of earth and collections of hovels is seen in terms of a loss of integrity that can only be expressed by a metaphor of death – 'Something in me died, a piece of me died, with the dying of Sophiatown'[53] – and the failure of the fight to keep hold of them is seen in terms of total defeat of the man and his race:

> The pride of having grown up with Sophiatown shrivelled inside me; I had failed my children as my father and my forefathers and the ancestral gods of my fathers had failed me; they had lost a country, a continent, but I had failed to secure a patch of weeds.[54]

These autobiographers are writing of the interminable tragedy of dispossession long before they came to deal with the effects upon them of their sojourn outside South Africa's boundaries.

The emotion may perhaps seem too melodramatically portrayed: after all, they are writing about slum clearance – as Richard Rive points out in his autobiography. And slum clearance is hardly to be deplored, if it means better housing and the destruction of health hazards and eyesores. But of course, so often, slum clearance of African, Indian and 'Coloured' areas in South Africa does not mean better housing for more than the privileged few, and at the same time the homeless have to witness what was once their land being given to a section of the population that is hardly pressed for space, or else being left undeveloped and unwanted. It is these factors which make the loss of slum areas particularly poignant, so that they become a litany in the writings of South African authors.

Bearing witness

With such grudges as these, and with countless other humiliations and degradations that various communities are subjected to, it is not surprising that one of the primary functions of South African autobiography should be to bear witness. Even writers like Brutus, who in another context might have become writers of quite another kind, are automatically drawn into speaking for the people. The autobiographers use the record of their own troubles and humiliations to draw the reader's attention not so much to themselves as the suffering individual, but to themselves as type-figures, prototypes for their community. It is here that the key to the problem of inaccuracies and deliberate fictions lies. Boetie may well introduce fictitious escapades into his accounts (though no white has enough contact with township life to judge this), but they are there not because they have happened to the individual, the writer, but because they have happened to black people – perhaps to people he has known or known of. Biko asserts that it is a kind of miracle for a black man in South Africa to survive to an adult age,[55] so it is perhaps pedantic and irrelevant to waste time determining the degree of literal truthfulness or otherwise of the stories.

The use of personal history as an illustration of the troubles of an entire community is what transforms these autobiographies and autobiographical fragments into literature. It is here that the writer universalises (not in a romantic but in a socialist sense) his experience, where the 'I' of the memoir is transmuted into the universal 'I' of group identity; or even, as D. J. Enright suggests in his memoirs, where the 'I' bears the sense of 'eye'.[56] And it is here that South African writers might be said to be making their own original contribution by way of a new literary form. The development of the autobiography in almost all the conventional literary forms for the purpose of bearing witness to a common plight, of making the reader not only 'to know, but also to feel what it is like to be this kind of victim in this kind of situation'[57] is peculiar to South African literature. (Or perhaps it is really peculiar to the liberation struggle: Arturo Barea, the Spanish revolutionary, writes in a similar vein, as do certain Latin American poets and novelists).

Yet even in autobiographies, the least processed of literary endeavours, this can lead to didacticism. Boetie and Matshikiza present their experiences neat, unadulterated by any attempt to analyse their impact on themselves either as individuals or as members of a group. Hutchinson makes much more of an attempt to identify what has happened to him with what happens to all Africans, such as the fellow travellers and migrant workers he meets on his journey. Modisane, Jabavu, Mphahlele, Nkosi and Manganyi write much more reflective, analytical books; but I think for all of them the analysis stops short of proscription, though they all offer a picture of the chaotic lives of the urban African, whether middle-class and only pass-and-job harassed or destitute and in daily search of shelter.

THE SOUTH AFRICAN STRUGGLE WITH FORM

Introduction

During the period covered in this book many South African writers can be seen struggling towards some kind of autobiographical form, with varying degrees of success. Nowhere, in the straight autobiography at least, can anyone be said to have achieved perfect resolution of form and content. Though this is not a uniquely South African problem, the general problems for any writer anywhere become more painfully crucial for the writer in South Africa. So that a writer like Plomer, for example, one of the first of the South African autobiographers, writing of a period before many of the writers I am considering here were born, devotes a third of his autobiography to elaborating upon his antecedents in order to establish his English descent: there may be an element of snobbery here, but it is also an attempt to work through an identity crisis in much the same way as the black consciousness writers have to discover their roots and establish who they are as people.

Fragmented reality

The somewhat schizophrenic form of Matshikiza's *Chocolates For My Wife* reflects the breakdown of an ordered, stable reality in the world he is recording and in the mind of the recorder. His work is beset by two kinds of difficulties: he is trying to record the attempt to live as a normal human being in a paranoid society, and also to record the experience of a totally different society in England, with its share of racial prejudice, perhaps, but yet a prejudice not officially condoned and based upon apartheid.

As a consequence the book jumps frantically from incident to incident, starting with the plane flight then leaping back to the departure from South Africa and forward again to the arrival. The first few chapters skip from incident to incident in the new life in England, cutting back briefly to contrasting scenes in South Africa. The pace is nervy and skittish, and it is this which sets the mood of disconnection rather than the formal techniques of flashback and timeswitching.

In a curious way, the book does have an overall pattern: at least it has a beginning and an end. Its end comes on the first page as the family flies away from South Africa, and its beginning comes in the last few pages as Matshikiza records the final straw that tipped the balance in favour of exile: the crudity of the encounter with the police as he waited for the bus after the rehearsal of *King Kong*:

> 'Of all my night shifts I have never met a baboon like this one . . . The monkey's got cho'lates for his wife . . . The maid is now called wife, caw, caw, caw, and choc'lat's for her.'[58]

The nervous, dislocated style embodies the vexatious quality of the life that is lived, lacking all harmony and balance, without unity: it conveys not only the daily harassment of South African life, but also the frustrations of life as an exile.

Fame, in Matshikiza's case, makes for a see-saw both in South Africa and England: glittering parties and exciting meetings with celebrities; in South Africa the warmth of daily human contact with his fellows; in England the joyful reunions with fellow exiles. And all these contrast with the daily humiliations of encounters with South African bureaucracy or the depressions of fruitless searches for living space in England and the infuriating encounters with the bigoted Mr Fergusons of the show business world, who know all about South Africa and the ungrateful blacks there because they have taken an occasional show to the downtown Johannesburg theatres and no blacks came to see it.

Restructuring reality

While the form of Matshikiza's narrative clearly communicates the fragmentation of reality for the South African black, Boetie finds a different way of dealing with the chaotic flux of daily life. His work is also episodic and often unconnected, but he adopts a different overall approach to capturing the disjointed character of existence: he fabricates tales, elaborates adventures after the fashion of the picaresque English writers of the eighteenth century or the traditional African folk tales that always, in the end, demonstrate the quick wits of the hero and the gullibility of the victim: the escape from the reformatory; Sisinyana's framing of the policeman over the dozen bottles of brandy; the picking of the pockets of the whites preoccupied with defending 'good' African 'boys'; the tricking of the Greek shopowner and the policeman he called in over the stolen roll of notes; the 'job' at A. B. Bazaar that enabled him to steal full-time in the guise of a uniformed employee; the repair job kindly done by the police to the car that had broken down loaded with dagga.

Nevertheless, the prison sections and the tale of the wife who had remarried the same man wearing Boetie's own wedding suit, whether literally true or not, point to the despair underlying the satire. Yet the style remains unchanged, and the incidents are related with the same wry humour as the successful con-tricks against the whites or the system.

In his epilogue, Barney Simon, during the course of his own reminiscences of Boetie, goes at some length into the question of credibility. Yet somehow he misses the point, perhaps because he is unable to separate his own experiences of Boetie as the friend and con-man from the book. Human relationships, however close and warm and supportive, cannot but be affected by lies and betrayals of trust, whereas the self-revelatory literary form may not be invalidated by absence of truthfulness and trust, because that very absence tells as much about the person as the most scrupulous attempts at veracity. Moreover Boetie's book is an embodiment of many black South African attempts to come to terms with the irrational and anarchic confusion of their life.

Towards orthodox significant form

(a) *The broken form.* Not every writer, however, seeks to embody this breakdown of social and individual order in the phrenetic style of a Matshikiza or a Boetie, though all are aware of the literary problem involved here. Nkosi and Manganyi make no pretence at creating a whole out of the disrupted fragments that make up their life. They use a series of fragmentary essays to reflect the fragmentation of their existence. The essays themselves have often a coherent structure, but there is no attempt made to relate one essay to another.

Manganyi's publication, *Mashangu's Reverie and other essays* betrays its ambivalence in its very title. For 'Mashangu's Reverie' itself is hardly an essay: it is a fictional fragment, highly autobiographical in content but fictional in presentation. In his preface he explains that his reasons for writing it sprang from a need to resolve the violence within himself, of which he had become aware after arriving in America from South Africa. In his birthplace he had suppressed emotions too traumatic to face up to for the whole of his life; in America he felt 'free to be angry for the first time',[59] to come to terms with his fantasies of revenge:

> I started to write 'Mashangu's Reverie', which may be seen as a frivolous kind of 'self-analysis' and in this way started to rid myself of disturbing impulses . . .

There is a sense in which the fragments which formed themselves into the story in the first part of the book are autobiographical. Mind you, autobiographical not in the sense of factuality of events or situation but in the sense that the fragments are a free production of my consciousness including most that was unconscious but seeking recognition and expression.[60]

The 'Reverie' covers the events of a few days in the life of the South African academic, Mashangu, who is its hero: his sessions with his (white) psychotherapist; his journal entry in prose and verse; his conversation with his West African friend Chivuso and the meeting with the West African woman Okike and the history of their developing relationship, hampered by her guilt feelings toward her absent husband; the night out with the three South Africans – the politically-committed black refugee from Robben Island, the carefree black lawyer, the white liberal exploiter who runs a black newspaper – and the black woman who escalates the tensions in the group by the flagrant seduction of the white man; the memorial lecture and the meals with Okike; and finally, the evening at the Skeltons where the racial mix and sexual tensions are brought explosively to the surface. Throughout the story, the writer is exploring his own response to others, black and white, South Africans and other Africans, his sexual responses, and dragging into consciousness his suppressed emotions towards the whites he encounters: the psychotherapist, the South African business-man, the audience at the lecture, and the guests and hosts at the Skeltons. In all of these explorations it is the violence latent in himself and in others which obsesses him.

In his essay 'The Censored Imagination' in *Looking Through the Keyhole* Manganyi reveals a past ambition to develop the auto-biographical fragments into a full-length fiction – an ambition that was immediately quelled on his return to South Africa by the atmosphere that obtained there: an atmosphere which automatically subjects the writer to self-censorship:

> Once I had landed here from North America where the fragment was written, something snapped and froze inside. Had I attempted to extend the story of Mashangu at that stage it would have felt forced and unnatural, and would *have led to a lie*.[61] (Manganyi's emphasis)

The consequence as far as publication is concerned (there are much more far-reaching consequences for the future of the South African novel in general) is that this fragment is incorporated into a collection of general academic essays, most of which have some connection with violence, but none of which lend any continuity of tone to the title work. The essay that follows immediately upon 'Mashangu's Reverie' – 'The Violent Reverie: The Unconscious in Literature and Society' – does connect fairly closely in theme, though it is in fact a general examination of radical positivism in committed literature. And one of the essays in Part Two – 'The Baptism of Fire: South Africa's Black Majority after the Portuguese Coup' – in its examination of siege cultures and its consideration of the question of revolt and the eclipse of reason in South Africa, treats sociologically the questions he had raised psychologically in the earlier sections. Yet despite the connection through content, the overall impression the book leaves is one of disconnection: the broken form.

Lewis Nkosi's method of looking back at what has made him what he is, is somewhat similar. In *Home and Exile* he presents an assortment of essays ranging from memoirs to literary criticism (though he includes no fiction), and he, too, explains his motives for writing in his preface:

> In their very nature some of these essays are . . . a manner of proposing questions to myself and an attempt to render coherent some impressions and issues which are as yet only vaguely suggested to my mind.[62]

His first piece in the 'Home' section of the book, 'The Fabulous Decade', combines his memories of his personal life at that time, and of his initiation as a writer for *Drum* with a sketch of the political situation and social circumstances in Johannesburg at the time. He recalls the indignation with which his generation, in their youth, reacted to the liberal conservatism of their elders, who had, they felt, betrayed them by their pacific acceptance of oppression. (This youthful impatience with older generations is a leitmotif of the South African struggle, spotlighted in the 1976 uprising when young people set fire to beerhalls and attempted a massive moral reform and conscientisation of their parents' generation.) He shows how this was seen by the older generation as a rejection both of tribal values and of Christianity, and traces the lineaments of this rejection in their dismissal of Paton's *Cry the Beloved Country* with its Uncle Tom figure hero, Stephen Kumalo. He justifies the time he spends on the novel because its lack of any 'heroic' black character (that is, any figure to fill the *literary* role of protagonist) is symbolic of his generation's lack of literary heroes – a need which was more crucial for them, who reached their adulthood at a time when the entrenchment of apartheid was becoming an irrevocable reality, than it had been for their parents' generation, which had matured at a time when hopes were less desolate. Nkosi sees the fifties as a kind of culminating decade, when political ferment came to a head at the same time as the brutal repression of apartheid began to clamp down.

The question of literary heroes is carried into the next section of the essay where he relates his initiation as a naïve, earnest, ambitious and intently moral young man into the fast-living, quick-witted, hard-drinking life-style of *Drum* writers, and calls up the major figures and memorable exchanges and incidents by vivid sketches. The Johannesburg setting for these scenes is evoked, together with the characteristics of some of its racial groups and the insanity of its politics, in a prose that flits from lyrical description to sharp-edged narrative snippets, such as the mock trial held by ANC members in a shebeen that was ironically followed the next day by the real-life arrest of the play-prosecutor, and the subsequent trial that mimicked their prophetic improvisation.

His personal reminiscences are followed by a summary which takes the political and artistic temperature of the decade, and assorted recollections of inter-racial parties, *Drum* assignments, the visit of Louis Macneice and his experience of sexual relationships across the colour bar. The essay finishes on a nostalgic note, dwelling on the lost opportunities, on regret for the failure of the races to teach others their specific racial virtues while there was still some opportunity for inter-racial mixing.

The above summary will give some idea of the disconnected nature of the recollections: the sections are given some kind of loose link-up but the essay makes no pretence to a formal literary structure, hanging random reminiscences and reflections on the hook of its title. Nevertheless a very vivid impression of the decade is conveyed, and its atmosphere is convincingly summoned up.

In the following two essays, Nkosi sets out the black man's problems with his identity and his relationship to 'reality': 'Apartheid: A Daily Exercise in the Absurd' illustrates the thesis in its title by an account of his own arrest in Pretoria, while peacefully pursuing his lawful business there, by a policeman who then quite openly searched about for a charge. The incident serves as an introduction to reflections on the ambivalent relationship to the law experienced by all Africans in an apartheid society. The second essay, 'A Question of Identity', is a more generalised examination of the whole question of colonial interference with African identity and its consequences for art. Yet although, in contrast to the two previous pieces, this is on the whole an academic rather than a personal piece of writing, it is obvious that personal experience has prompted much of the cogitation: the nostalgic Africans haunting the cafés of Europe, anguishing over the 'lost Africa' are obviously acquaintances, and he confesses that the black identity problem surfaced, for him, not as intellectual speculation, but specifically on the day that he learned he was 'not only black but *non*-white'.[63]

Much of the 'Exile' section of the book is pure reminiscence. Here he takes certain very short periods of his life, such as the encounters with New York, or memories of certain powerful influences upon him at critical moments, such as that of Sheila Jordan, and encapsulates them in an essay.

This is a fragmentary approach to autobiography in itself, even when the individual essays are in themselves perfectly structured forms; yet, as I have mentioned above, this is not always the case with these pieces. Indeed, some of the essays' tenuously related episodes are thrown together in such a loose way that the reader brings away a confusion and dislocation in his grasp of the material which reflects the intellectual and emotional condition of many exiles. Such is the essay 'Out There on a Visit: American Notes', where the writer jumps from California to New York and back to the Californian coast in Tristram Shandy fashion, leaving the reader somewhat bewildered as to time sequences and order of events. The insecurity it betrays is touched on in a different context in 'Jazz in Exile' where Nkosi analyses the importance and indeed inevitability of jazz as a black South African form of artistic expression, where it serves both as therapy and vent, epitomising the yearning restlessness and frustration of black life. The theme is maintained in the following essay, 'Art Contra Apartheid: South African Writers in Exile', in which he explores the general need of a writer for roots, and the special relationship between writer and reader in South African society where there is a specific need for writers to focus mass feelings of resentment and exasperation since all normal political channels of self-expression are dammed. Here his own experience of the effects of exile – the blurring of moods and the fading of emotions once the navel cord is cut between writer and native land – is brought into play. In the course of the essay he also fumbles his way to his own role as a writer in exile:

> to preserve for the world the memory of millions I left behind in South Africa, those whom white facism attempted to strangle without success, whose continual survival is a reproach to our helplessness.[64]

This last essay is an interesting addition to the first essay of the book; obviously the passage of years since his first edition was written has brought him continued anguish over his function as an exiled South African writer.

Though Nkosi makes no claims to be attempting anything other than a collection of essays, the fact that the collection draws upon so much autobiographical material raises the question of why he did not attempt to incorporate them in a more extensive literary form. His literary production over the next twenty years has been confined to one volume of critical essays and his recently published novel *Mating Birds*, neither of which carries any significantly unresolved autobiographical content. It is idle to speculate on whether this is because the *Home and Exile* essays drained off the urge to take stock of himself when he left South Africa. But his case has interesting parallels with others who wrote a single autobiographical work and then lapsed into virtual silence – Hutchinson, Modisane, Matshikiza.

(b) *The partial form.* One of these writers, Hutchinson, together with Noni Jabavu, has however mastered the problem of turning a fragment into a significant literary form. And these two writers achieved this by deliberately limiting themselves to a specific period. Noni Jabavu begins her book *Drawn in Colour* with the funeral of her brother, and takes the reader up to the point where she returns to South Africa for healing – 'to be doctored after having been in foreign parts, to be cleansed by my own tribe'[65] after a period of living in Uganda.

It is not a chronological journal of the period: instead she confines herself to certain significant events or experiences. The thematic link is the family: the book opens with the family gathering for the funeral ceremonies of the beloved younger brother, killed by the tsotsis, or gangsters, as he was completing his medical degree. During her stay (she had returned to South Africa from England where she and her husband lived) she witnesses her father's second marriage to a wife chosen with the help of the entire extended family through protracted negotiations and discussions. She then goes on through Africa, by train to Rhodesia and from there by air to Entebbe, to visit her sister who was at that time married to an East African. There she participates in family councils to reconcile the parties in a marriage which had long been breaking down. The narrative then omits a few months and resumes at the point where she and her husband go to live in Uganda as expatriates on contract, so that she can be near her sister. This part of the book combines her reactions to living as an expatriate in an African country (to her horror she discovers herself assuming the role of the white settler in her unconscious reactions to the 'natives') with her witness of the eventual breakdown of attempts at reconciliation between her sister and brother-in-law, and finally her account of their divorce. Ultimately, overcome by the strain of life among a foreign tribe, she goes back to South Africa for three months to be healed by her family and tribe, of the psychological strains she had been enduring.

Each episode leads entirely naturally into the next – it seems as though life itself had fallen into a pattern without the autobiographer having to impose it (though this judgement may, of course, be a measure of the autobiographer's skill in naturalising the pattern), and the whole book, apart from an account of a safari, on her first visit to Uganda, and a section on her reaction to the country as an expatriate, is based on close-knitted episodes of family life; the communal grief at her brother's death establishes the healing force of the clan system; her visit to her sister is that of family representative to carry out the traditional rituals 'to bind her'[66]:

> Since she was not here to *see-for-herself*, you must go to her and act as if you had been her eyes. It is your duty to tell your mother's child everything word for word, enable her to re-live every phrase of our tragedy . . . Let it be as if she had partaken in the gatherings of consolation that families make at such crises. It will be only if you, eldest of the umbilical cord, properly fulfill your function that your sister will find the peace that we have found through these traditional rites.[67]

Once she has arrived, and has assessed the condition of her sister's marriage, she is drawn, as the representative of her sister's family, into the extended family discussions traditional all over Africa where such issues as marriage, death or marital breakdown are discussed, and in which the healing processes for soothing grief or effecting reconciliation are gone into.

Her move to Uganda some time later comes as a natural sequel to the previous section, and springs from her desire to give her sister more support. She herself however meets up with problems at this point in the story, in adjusting herself to expatriate life: her awareness of her own similarities to white settlers in other parts of Africa, including her motherland, when she comes to dealing with Ugandans, is compounded by the racial prejudice displayed towards Jabavu herself on account of her black skin, by the English in Uganda, despite her British nationality and white husband. And it is for these reasons that she has to return to her family in South Africa, for rest and healing, so that the autobiography comes full circle and ends where it began, at her father's home, the focal point of her extended family life.

With this very tightly structured pattern and dominating family theme, the book has greater perfection of form than any of the autobiographies hitherto considered, and there are many possible reasons for this achievement. The intact family structure of which Noni Jabavu is a part belongs to a tiny handful of families of great intellectual distinction and secure income living in a secluded rural retreat near Fort Hare University. These families have survived the damaging disruption and fragmentation to which urban families are subjected by law in the big townships (of course individual family members, though they retained this secure rural base, were exposed to the disintegration of township life, as her brother's murder demonstrates so tellingly). Hence Noni Jabavu grew up with a security, a shelter from the worst brutalities of apartheid existence experienced by none of her urban compatriots. Psychologically she is in a better position to tackle the problem of form.

Along with the family structure comes a strong sense of tribal identity as a Xhosa. Moreover, living in England, married to an Englishman, she has an established footing in a country free from the stresses of apartheid life. For all these reasons she is better equipped than the majority of contemporary black South African writers to devote herself to questions of literary structure.

Hutchinson, writing *Road to Ghana*, lacked these background advantages, coming from an urban environment and growing up on that shady borderline between African and coloured (eventually his father and brother were reclassified as coloured, and Hutchinson fled before the issue of his own classification was entirely resolved). He had none of Noni Jabavu's long sense of family and tribal continuity, or her deep roots in a fairly tranquil environment. And indeed it is this rootlessness and permanent sense of wandering which he treats symbolically in *Road to Ghana*, an account not only of his own long journey into exile, but of the ceaseless wandering of an entire people – batches of migrant workers for white farms, factories and mines, waiting like flocks of patient sheep on both sides of the railway line to move down to and back from South Africa as contract labour. It is the story of the subjection not only of South Africans but of all the African peoples living within reach of South Africa's greedy materialism, so that a migratory existence is the predicament not only of those like Hutchinson, caught up in specific political trouble, but of the ordinary person in the street as far north as Nyasaland.

Thus the choice of the journey itself as the formal structure of the autobiography is highly significant; it is no mere traveller's account of a train ride through Africa; it is not even the story of the exile, showing through his own hardships and difficulties, the trauma that besets the black South African who decides to leave his country: it is the odyssey of all the peoples of Southern Africa whose daily lives, whose families, whose life-styles, ethics and livelihood, are all affected by white South Africa's need for cheap labour.

The book opens dramatically with the closing of the first phase of the Treason Trial, and the insecure freedom granted to the defendants who expect at any moment to be rearrested, and whose celebratory party is raided by the Special Branch. In the confusion about whether they are free or on bail, his white girlfriend, Hazel, urges him strongly to escape immediately. Once the decision has been taken, during the necessary pause for the collection of false papers and money, Hutchinson is once again exposed to the terrifying illogicality of the South African police system in the two arrests for not carrying a pass (which, as a 'coloured' he is not in any case obliged to do) – the second arrest ludicrously occurring immediately after the first for which he is already on bail. The muddles and confusion, the friction between the ordinary police and the Special Branch, the strained efforts of friends and relatives to find a way through the maze to achieve bail are all very typical South African stories. But Hutchinson's vivid economy conveys better than most the swift schizophrenic changes from elation to despair, the impossibility of living to any settled routine, and the hourly interference with the process of existence to which black people are subjected so severely that it often reduces them to apathy and inertia.

The effect of this approach to law and justice is brilliantly conveyed in the short sharp dialogue-style reports he gives of the cases that precede his on the day of the trial: so perfunctory is each 'trial', so unconcerned is the magistrate with any real attempt to sift through degrees of innocence and guilt (indeed every trial begins with the practical assumption that the prisoner is guilty, whatever the theoretical assumptions of the law), and so absorbed are all the court officials in getting through the cases that the mockery of the law has no need of comment from the author to assist its impact on the mind of the reader.[68]

After the failure of the prosecution to establish that Hutchinson is a 'native' and therefore cannot be found guilty of not carrying a pass, Hutchinson sets out on his second attempt to reach Ghana. In the persona of Alfred Phiri, a Nyasa contract worker carrying his supply of fish and chips and bread to sustain him on the journey, he joins the community of the train on their uncomfortable trek north, entering into their conversations and preoccupations, some of which were to last as long as the train journey itself.

At Mafeking a noisy violent encounter takes place between the migrant miners returning home and the band of recruits going to the mines, and the effect of such conditions on the human being is reflected in Hutchinson's despair at their behaviour. At Bulawayo, the band of a hundred young boys recruited from Northern Rhodesia for the white farms around Salisbury re-emphasises the social disruption that had been so evident among the group of miners, though apathy and fear are their way of expressing this rather than violence and vulgarity.

The journey, with its frequent stops, where there are utterly inadequate or non-existent waiting quarters and where food is sometimes difficult to come by and usually impossible to cook (the antelope meat is riddled with maggots before they have a chance to cook it, and the hen that accompanies him on the latter part of the journey lives on as a gift to the small boy who had taken charge of it), is documented so thoroughly that it begins to seem as endless to the reader as to the travellers. The problems of acquiring the right documents, of finding a way through the corruption (the need to buy at the Machado Store in Salisbury in order to acquire a pass from the Portuguese is ironically set beside Hutchinson's naïve establishment frame of mind in which he goes about asking for Nyasa House), of checking that he is on the right train, of avoiding the notice of the ruthless customs officials who ruin the travellers' precious hard-won acquisitions, and the endless halts – in Blantyre to wait for Hazel and to arrange the onward journey to Tanganyika, in Dar-es-Salaam to meet Nyerere and arrange a visa to enter the Sudan and to enjoy the hospitality of the prison service while charged with illegal entry: all these convey to the reader the seeming eternity of the journey and the ever-present uncertainty about how to go on, how to find the money, acquire the necessary papers, meet up with the people he is supposed to be meeting, about whether the people on whom he has to depend can be relied on, all the endless harassments of unofficial exile.

The discomfort and slowness of the overland journey to Tanganyika is not only demonstrated by the detailed account and the amount of actual space in the story devoted to the telling of it, but also by the speed and suddenness of the flight to Ghana at the end of the book, just as the harassed mental condition in which he fights through the train and steamer trip is heightened by the high spirits and light-heartedness bestowed on him by the two telegrams ensuring his plane fare and the end of his travel problems.

Hutchinson makes no attempt to take the reader back into his childhood or forward into his period of exile. So that the book neither performs the function of stock-taking as he starts off his new life, nor arranges his existence into a pattern he can take hold of, that he may begin to own his life. The book, after all, only covers the short months between October and December 1958, from when he left South Africa, shortly after the first acquittal in the Treason Trial and his arrival in Accra, a little late, for the All-Africa People's Conference, as the ANC representative. So, although it is about a significant period in Hutchinson's life, it can hardly be classified as a regular auto-biography. This period, however, is one of overwhelming consequence, not only for Hutchinson personally, but also for the liberation struggle in South Africa, and the journey he is compelled to undertake is so identified with the endless wandering of the deprived and poverty-stricken Africans in all the countries surrounding South Africa, that Hutchinson fulfills the most stringent requirements of later black African critics writing in the black consciousness period: he is speaking for his people, awakening the consciousness of his readers to the injustices suffered by a nation, and bringing alive the whole process of victimisation. The limits he places on his material enable him to forge a tight-knit structure that gives the account of the journey much of its impact – the literary device enabling the reader to undergo the experience vicariously in a way that a looser, more digressive form could never have achieved.

Autobiography as novel: the hybrid form

For a form which allows for a more extended period of time and yet maintains a tight pattern we have to turn to the novel. Two writers have used the novel form to embody autobiography, and it is interesting to examine how their use of the form succeeds. Bessie Head used it twice: once indirectly autobiographically in *Maru*, where she draws upon a life-time of experience of prejudice against 'coloured' South Africans to create the story of a Basarwa girl, and again in *A Question of Power*, more directly, when she charts her own mental breakdown in the story of Elizabeth, the heroine.

The first novel has more of an autonomous existence than the second, for the author's own experience in *Maru* is not central to the plot as it is in *A Question of Power*. The shorter novel concentrates mainly on the battle for the younger Margaret Cadmore between the two most important men in the village, Maru and Moleka, close friends, fellow royals in the tribal structure and rivals in love. The book is a passionate plea on behalf of the San tribe, long denigrated in Botswana and other parts of Southern Africa as 'bushmen', and reviled for their backwardness and their refusal to accept the impositions of so-called western civilisation. But the instances of prejudice which the writer draws upon are experiences of her own, as another kind of outcast in African society – a 'coloured'. In South Africa the 'coloured', the child of African and white, for all the disadvantages this brings in an apartheid society, at least belongs to a group and has a place. In Botswana, where tribes survive more or less intact, the 'coloured' is the despised outsider, only a little higher in the social scale than the San or Basarwa. Thus the younger Margaret Cadmore's experiences as a child, a student and a young teacher mirror the author's own.

She, too, had a special relationship with a white teacher, who encouraged her as Margaret Cadmore encouraged the adopted Masarwa child; she, too, had this mixed reception from strangers who knew of her white connections and accorded her a little more respect as a result; she too had had to face the reactions of an inbred Setswana village to her alien presence, as the young teacher did on her first appointment to Dilepe.

Unlike Margaret Cadmore, Bessie Head was not carried off by a chief who gave up his chieftancy for love – though perhaps this fantasy performs the same therapeutic function as autobiography in allowing the novelist to work through the trauma of racism; indeed the novel gives her greater scope, for she can devise an ending which re-instates the victim – an example of the novel's capacity for exploring the unrealised potential of the protagonist not afforded by the auto-biography. Certainly the fantasy ending of *Maru* mirrors the fantasy everyone indulges in real life – seeking alternative endings to humiliating life-experiences.

In *A Question of Power*, however, the autobiographical element is worked through in actuality rather than in fantasy. For although the writer casts the material in novel form, and although indeed much of the detail is fictional, the central issue, the mental breakdown of Elizabeth, is avowedly based upon the author's own experience of a mental breakdown,[69] and the village setting is recognisably Serowe, the author's adopted home village in central Botswana. A straightforward comparison with *Maru* is hardly possible, for in *Maru* the content element based on the author's own experience is drawn from real life *situations* whereas in *A Question of Power* it is drawn from the author's emotional and mental life.

Thus the fact that *A Question of Power* lacks the technically impressive resolution of form possessed by *Maru* cannot be accounted for simply by its greater reliance upon untransformed autobiographical material. Moreover, given that the subject of the novel is a mental breakdown, a confusion of form is perhaps an expected by-product of content, perhaps even a deliberate mirroring of content. (Though this is not necessarily always the case – witness Sylvia Plath's *The Bell Jar* where the form has the elegant structure of a crystal, despite the hysterical confusion of the protagonist's mind.)

The novel's official structure divides it ostensibly into two parts: the first 'Sello' and the second 'Dan'. And indeed the content does fall principally into these two sections, though the character Dan is present in the 'Sello' section, and the character Sello in the 'Dan' section. This division conveniently underlines the curious battle between the two men. It is reminiscent of the contest between Maru and Moleka for Margaret Cadmore, only that was an open, situational competition whereas the *Question of Power* struggle takes place only in the overwrought mind of the heroine, though each man has a real existence, unconnected with Elizabeth, in the village in which she lives. The divided structure also marks the major division in the battlefield of Elizabeth's mind, though there is no simplistic division of good and evil between the two men, even while there is an overall identification of Sello with good and Dan with evil.

Within this formal division into sections, however, rage the contradictions and confusions characteristic of the most placid human relationships and dominant in the paranoia of mental breakdown, with Sello personifying evil though his principal role is to personify good, and Dan showing kindness and tenderness amidst all his wickedness.

At the beginning of the novel there is a strong sense of authorial control of the material: Sello, for all he is, for most of the time, a figment of Elizabeth's tormented imagination, is lucidly, if strangely presented, and Elizabeth's early life is rationally summarised and its significance for her current experiences effectively analysed. However, as the writer delves deeper into her own mental turmoil the material takes over and the reader is plunged into a mass of unresolved symbolism and only partially articulated visions. A full supporting cast enters into these visions: the Asian men, the poor of Africa, Medusa, the monk, Buddha, the concubines, the homosexual Coloured men, the Father, Miss Sewing Machine, Miss Wriggly Bottom, Pelican Beak, the cesspit filled with dead bodies, the sailing panties in various colours, and all are mixed up with the emotional and inexplicable encounters with Dan and Sello. And yet, through it all the structure of the book does not totally disintegrate. Bessie Head tethers the madness to an on-going reality by sustaining throughout it the daily life of the village

– the hospital, the school, the garden project – and the people of the village – neighbours, teachers, her small son and his friends, fellow workers in the garden, arrogant expatriate experts and charming voluntary workers. All these are integrated into the hysterical upheaval of Elizabeth's mental chaos. So that when, at the end of the novel, she emerges strong enough to begin reading once again, Elizabeth can feel contained in peace by the external life that has run like a thread through the course of her journeys into insanity.

The weakest link in the structure is of course the treatment of the nervous breakdown itself, where the protagonist's loss of grip upon her sanity is paralleled by the author's loss of grip on her material. Bessie Head has said[70] that this book was the straightforward setting down of her own breakdown, and the naming of the heroine is no doubt an indication of the degree of identification between author and protagonist. Much of the setting and all the characters in the novel are taken from life too, but they are subtly fictionalised – they have undergone the transformation from life to literature. Perhaps the problem with the inner experiences is that the author has not yet had time to separate herself from them in her mind – to recollect them in tranquillity. It is one thing to attain artistic detachment about other people and a village setting and quite another to achieve this mastery of an extremity of personal pain. Nevertheless, whatever the book's shortcomings (and they are insignificant compared with its merits), by adopting the novel form she has been able to structure her autobiographical material more stringently than some other South African writers who have written before coming to terms with the problem of intention and form.

Mphahlele, in *The Wanderers*, tackles the same problem of incorporating autobiographical content into the novel form, and resolves it with perhaps less success. Part of the reason for this is his attempt to cover a much more diffuse period of his life, and to bring together too much incompatible material. Thus he tries to shelter between the covers of a single novel a long section on his investigation of the prison farms in South Africa, his life in Nigeria and Kenya, and a section on a white *Drum* writer's nanny fixation and marriage to a black South African. It is easy to see why he wanted to do this: the book, after all, is about wandering, about exile. Yet in order to transform the material into significant form, he would have had to resolve the selection and structural problems with greater refinement.

For example, the only inherent link between the three sections is that they happened to be parts of Mphahlele's life, or rather the life of his fictional hero, Timi. It is true that Naledi – a fairly prominent figure in the first section in which the journalist Timi investigates the circumstances in which her husband disappeared on a prison farm – figures also in the second section when she is wooed by the white journalist Stephen Cartwright. But this is a structural device rather than a structural necessity: both Stephen and Naledi are irrelevant to the development of the novel.

Perhaps the problem is that at the point of writing Mphahlele had not yet arrived at the perception of a pattern, so that even the step of adopting the more formal structure of the novel did not compel order (artistic or otherwise) or significant form from the as yet undigested life-experiences. (One thinks here of the thirty years Virginia Woolf allowed to elapse between the death of her mother and her attempt to deal with her parents in a novel in *To the Lighthouse* – South African literature lacks the leisure of such a necessary time-scale by the very political conditions that motivate it.) Many writers do in fact write an autobiography in order to seek a shape in their own lives, in order to perceive a pattern: thus it is not essential to have the pattern present in the mind before beginning to write. But perhaps what is not essential for an autobiography is essential for a novel. For by selecting the novel form writers are making a statement about their intentions and committing themselves to a specific art-form; they cannot offer up their raw experiences as they can (though by no means always do) if they confine themselves to autobiography. And though I would argue that autobiography also involves artistic form, the form is inevitably more amorphous: it allows the writers greater latitude in that they have an almost infinite variety of options, and the fact that the work is openly based on actual life reduces the necessity to commit themselves to a specific kind of artistic formula.

Of course this whole argument collapses if one admits that all literary forms are the product of the literary institution, and accepts, as I do in a previous chapter, that experiment with form, and indeed a refusal to be bound by the conventional forms of the western literary tradition is the *sine qua non* of black writing in South Africa. And yet it would be specious to accept this as a vindication of *The Wanderers'* weak artistic impact, since Mphahlele, until very recently indeed, was in fact working, in his creative writing, in the mainstream of the western literary tradition, notwithstanding the South African slant he gives to his work through its language, setting and presentation of relationships within the individual stories, novels or autobiographical works.

The failure to achieve formal resolution in the novel cannot be attributed to any single factor: the lack of emotional distance from the material contributes to it, but then one has to seek the reason for this. Mphahlele has repeatedly worked over his life, in the form of autobiography, novel and short story, and more recently he has allowed Manganyi to work over it again in his biography (which, interestingly enough, Manganyi has chosen to write in the first person as though it were autobiography – another instance of the dominance of the autobiographical form in South African writing). Manganyi, in his introduction to the biography, questions the reason for this 'confessional streak . . . together with his willingness to have another version of the story of his life',[71] and admits that this was something he had constantly to re-examine:

> The readiness with which Es'kia Mphahlele agreed to have the work done has never ceased to tease my professional interest. And the reason for this hesitation on my part is not difficult to find. As a psychotherapist I have come to know that too great a willingness for self-disclosure is in some instances a defence against self-revelation. It is a psychological manoeuvre that pre-empts scrutiny . . .[72]

And it is true that in *The Wanderers* there is detectable an urge towards self-justification, especially with regard to relations with his son, which manifests itself in all later accounts of his life, and also in his letters.

This need to justify is a dominant thread in many, perhaps in most, autobiographies. And perhaps if *The Wanderers* had been cast in autobiographical form, there would not be this nagging worry about artistic resolution: it is an element in writing which is absorbable by autobiography but not by a novel. For it prevents the novel from cutting itself free of the author and taking on its own existence as an artefact – a necessity which is irrelevant to autobiography. It prevents *The Wanderers*, that is, from achieving artistic autonomy, just as Bessie Head's continuing involvement in the anguish of her mental breakdown prevented *A Question of Power* from doing so.

Another problem with the book is one that has dogged Mphahlele, as he is the first to admit, ever since he exiled himself from South Africa. The first and largest section of the book, set in his motherland, has a vibrancy, dynamism and immediacy which is completely lacking in the sections set in Nigeria and Kenya. For Mphahlele was never able to achieve that emotional consummation with any of his adopted countries of exile that he had had with his own land. There is an intellectual involvement with Nigeria's problems of government, but never an emotional integration into the community, he was always the stranger looking in through the lighted windows of the family homes, and prevented by his own with-holding of himself, as much as by the glass, from entering into the warmth and kinship of the families within.

Thus the South African section depicts community life from the inside, whereas the following sections confine themselves to the family, or the small circle of friends (all of whom for some reason – either because they are exiles themselves, or because they have foreign spouses – are outsiders themselves). As a consequence there is a lifelessness about the later sections, which is also depictable in Mphahlele's other novel, written in exile, *Chirundu*.

Life entire as autobiographical form

Thus both Mphahlele and Bessie Head run into difficulties when they attempt to use the novel form for predominantly autobiographical material which, at the time of writing, remained unresolved; though where the autobiographical content was not central to the plot, as with *Maru*, this presented no problem.

Where writers seek to focus on themselves, however, it seems to set up fewer tensions between reader and author, to minimise the conflict of avowed and unadmitted (perhaps subconscious) intentions, if they adopt a straightforward autobiographical form. In this way they can tell the story of their life, search out the significance of the pattern of events, attempt to come to terms with the person they have become, uninhibited by external and foreign formal restrictions, and in so doing, curiously enough, the work (or should I say the author?) often achieves a formal resolution of its own, which grows naturally out of the content of the work.

Down Second Avenue, Mphahlele's account of his childhood and life up to the point of exile from South Africa, in this way attains a crystalline clarity of form combined with a warmth and vitality of tone to be found nowhere else in his longer works. *Chirundu* is perfectly structured but is completely dead; some of his short stories hint at the powers evident in *Down Second Avenue* but do not give room for them to be tested out, and *The Wanderers* has vitality in only one section and fails to achieve any kind of form.

In his autobiography, Mphahlele gathers up the chronological story of his childhood, education and early adulthood, marriage and family into chapters that cluster memories around specific places or people. Thus the book opens with a powerful evocation of the setting of his early childhood – Maupaneng – where he cowered under the glowering mountain and harsh, dour grandmother, spending his time, clad in lice-ridden rags, tending goats, playing truant, fighting on the river sands in the moonlight, gathering round the men's communal fireplace to be educated in the tribal traditions by the old men of the tribe. The skill of the description lies in the holistic nature of the evocation of Maupaneng. There is none of the romantic landscape description one might find in a western writer, and yet the physical setting and its dynamic impact on the people who inhabited it is presented as a part of their activities: nature, in Mphahlele's writings, always has a human context – the moonlight on the white river sands illuminates the fighting boys, the solitude of the bush is where they tend their goats and sour the milk to escape a beating for their short measures, the mountain is a terrifying figure in the nightmares of a small boy. And this skill for evoking place through the people who inhabit it is even more evident in the sections on the Marabastad location, scene of his later childhood. Its dusty streets filled with dongas and rubbish and the faeces of children and animals are brought to life for the reader through the daily lives of the inhabitants – the street gangs of young boys, of which he was a member, of Rebone, the beauty he courted, of his Aunt Dora, Ma Lebona, Ma Bottles, the old women who dominated the location community with their vigorous personalities. Because these people and places are so deep-rooted in Mphahlele's consciousness that they have become a part of his psyche, his re-creations have a vibrancy peculiar to his evocations of his Southern African background, and unshared by any of his attempts to evoke the settings of his various places of exile (a point I have already noted with regard to his presentation of Nigeria and Kenya in *The Wanderers* and of Zambia in *Chirundu*).

As with the Maupaneng section, a vivid picture of location life emerges apparently accidentally in the course of remembered encounters with people: the exhaustion of grandmother and Aunt Dora as they struggled in the yard with the unending bundles of white people's washing; the children's daily round of cooking and cleaning for their money-earning adult relatives; the work and the hasty concealments necessitated by the beer-brewing and selling by which the women made enough to raise their families, and brought on themselves the police raids, the fines and imprisonment if they were not quick enough to hide their pots; the stinking overflowing lavatory buckets filled by the weekend customers; the horses and carts of the hawkers; the quarrels between neighbours; the location school, churches, street-gangs and dance-hall.

The location dominates most of the book, throwing into the shade by the vitality of its portrayal the later accounts of St Peter's School or Adams College, his marriage, his period working for *Drum* or his dealings with the ANC. And yet these are no mere pedestrian narrative efforts, documenting as they do Mphahlele's growth towards maturity and his encounters with the adult world of apartheid. Perhaps

Mphahlele is really sharing a common problem with most other autobiographers: the especial vividness and clarity of childhood memories printed on an imagination as yet unattenuated by the stress and tedious monotony of adult life – a factor which accounts for the large number of autobiographical accounts that end with childhood.

Down Second Avenue, therefore, though it takes us right up to Mphahlele's exit from South African life when he took up a teaching post in Nigeria aged thirty-seven, devotes most of its space and detail to his childhood and early youth – a fact which raises the question of why he chose to take the autobiography past the childhood years. The answers are obvious: it is the setting down of a record before taking up a new life in exile – an attempt to take hold of all that has happened to him before this momentous change that has come upon him. And although, at this stage in his life, it is the earlier memories he is eager to capture, the analysis of the childhood years which he is more psychologically prepared to face, he nevertheless also recognises, in those scanty later chapters, that the years from twenty to thirty-seven also need to be reckoned with.

However, it is not from the chronology of his life that *Down Second Avenue* gains the backbone of its formal structure, but from the five 'Interludes' which interrupt the narrative, bringing the past forward into the present by the imaginative reconstruction of reverie. Mphahlele becomes once again the child or the youth or the young adult that he was at the time he chronicles, and broods in the present tense on the preoccupations of the moment. The first 'Interlude' concentrates on the thoughts of the young boy on a sleepless Saturday night in Marabastad, as he lies crowded with his relatives on the floor of his maternal grandmother's house. In the second, the schoolboy struggles with his bible passage homework on a Saturday afternoon he would rather spend at the cinema. In the third, after the break with the navel-string of Marabastad as a young worker at Ezenzeleni, he reflects on the world's perpetual Marabastads, and the many more second avenues 'with dirty water and flies and children with traces of urine running down the legs and chickens pecking at children's stools'.[73] The fourth 'Interlude' takes the shape of a night walk in Basutoland, whose breath-taking beauty only inflames his sense of bitterness and frustration. The fifth reverie occurs to him as he looks out on the Saturday night lights of Johannesburg, on the point of leaving the land, and is unhinged once again by the combination of the beauty he looks out on and the desolation of the life within him as an individual and without him among the black community of which he is a part and a representative.

The 'Interludes' are evenly spaced throughout the protagonist's life, though not evenly spaced through the book. By the device of bringing into collision time past and time present, of leaping out of the chronological narrative to establish mood and sustain it across the passage of years, Mphahlele constructs his unique autobiographical form, perfectly tailored to his material – a form that is significant not only in traditional literary critical terms, but also in terms of the social context out of which and on behalf of which it was generated, and of the community to which it is principally addressed.

Modisane in *Blame Me On History* has no such formal structural device to contain the disparate fragments of his life. Or rather the formal structure he attempts to impose fails to carry the book and disintegrates in the mind of the reader, as well as in the course of the narrative as the book progresses. He begins by attempting to contain his memories within the framework of a walk around the shell of Sophiatown in 1958, after all the removals and official destruction. It is a good image to choose, for the ghetto had contained his growing up and all the important events of his life, and the desolate emptied suburb symbolises the hollowness of his own life, just after resigning from his post on *The Golden City Post*, and shortly before he was to flee the country as an exile. The parallel hardly needs to be laboured.

Yet it soon proves too limited a device to carry the weight of the entire autobiography, and Modisane quietly drops it in acknowledgement of this. Thereafter, though he hunts for a substitution – there is a half-hearted attempt to contain chapters nine to sixteen within a sketchy dream framework between two cups of tea brought to his Sophiatown room by his sister after his wife has left, which is barely noticeable – the book is left to its own momentum. And, curiously enough, this is sufficient. The book leaves the reader with a powerful impression of the breadth and depth of his analysis both of his own personality and of the social repercussions of apartheid. And yet it is difficult to analyse exactly how it achieves this impact.

The book's time-scale is roughly, but certainly not consistently, chronological. That is, it tends to cover childhood memories on the whole, before moving on to memories of his working life. But it jumps forward, early on in the narrative, to the breakdown of his marriage and back to the street-gangs of his adolescence, then forward again to the birth of his daughter before going back to his first job. These jumps are neither obviously planned, in the manner of Mphahlele's 'Interludes', nor do they serve so definite a purpose. Mphahlele's reveries infuse the past with the present; Modisane seems to be erratically filling in the gaps in the story as they occur to him, or to be unable to prevent himself from moving forward to a particularly urgent memory.

The beginning and the end of the book give it a small degree of cohesion: it begins in the middle of 1958 (he had originally applied to leave South Africa in January 1958) and ends with his actual leave-taking in March 1959. Like the majority of South African autobiographies, Modisane's is the exile's stock-taking as he embarks on his new life, so it is not unnatural that he, like Hutchinson, should begin and end his life-story with the period of the leave-taking. Yet while Hutchinson limited himself carefully to the events immediately preceding his departure and the journey itself, Modisane cheerfully embraces all that life has been and meant for him and for the community of which he is a part.

The book does not gain its effectiveness, either, by its thematic unity. The writer is haunted by certain subjects and ideas throughout the book – his father's death and his own nameplate on the coffin, his broken marriage and his promiscuous sexuality, his daughter, the violence in himself and in those among whom he lives in the black community, his intensely ambivalent feelings towards whites, and his repetitive efforts to escape his own situation into culture, or married bliss, or orgies, or work or exile. Yet persistent as they are, none of them, any more than the recurrent figures in the book – Fiki, Ma Bloke, Daisy – provide structural leitmotifs for the autobiography. None of them are used systematically as the string on which to thread his memories or analyses. Yet they do provide dynamic focuses for the welter of emotions and memories.

There is in fact a rough division of chapters in the book: chapters 1 to 6 deal primarily with Modisane's life-history; chapters 7 to 12 cover the history of apartheid, its social effects and the responses of the black community over the years; chapters 13 to 15 deal with certain of his personal frustrations, and chapter 16 completes the story of his life up to the point of exile. Although none of these sections are in any way exclusive – indeed the mixture of personal experience and social history is the main strength of the book – they do suggest the dominant material of the groups of chapters, though here again it would be stretching a point to argue that they amount to a structural pattern.

It might be useful at this point to look at what the book does achieve rather than labour the ways in which it falls short of formal structural pattern. It gives a series of vivid glimpses into his upbringing and his childhood world. Like Mphahlele he brings the urban setting to life for the readers and enables them to see for themselves the squalid yards, their dynamic or apathetic, vigorous or pitiful inhabitants, the beer-brewing and selling by which many women like his mother (like Mphahlele's grandmother and aunts) strove to earn enough money to rear their children, the street-corner-gangs of boys and the menacing gangs of violent youths that ruled the streets, took tithes and killed and raped at whim (as indeed they still do in the townships). One retains, long after reading the book, a sense almost of having participated in the riot of living and destroying, in the good times and the terror that was the daily life of Sophiatown.

There is always a withering honesty in his self-analysis rare among writers of autobiography. His failings are neither omitted nor palliated. His self-pity at the breakdown of his marriage is not allowed to obfuscate the reasons for it – his own failure to shoulder the adult responsibilities of family and home and steady life, his promiscuity, his lust for white friendship and white flesh. Modisane never seems to have that fear of alienating the reader that keeps lesser writers silent about their more repulsive qualities: thus his purchase, at the cost of a week's wages, of caviare and smoked salmon, for a single meal to impress white guests (and amaze the shop assistant) is relentlessly set beside the admission that he had recently stood by while his sister's child died of malnutrition. His need for white friends, white women and white culture is analysed exhaustively in the clear hard light of his own disapproval. The self-revelation is a necessary step in his demonstration of the degrading effects of apartheid upon the human psyche.

The book also provides, well within the framework of the individual development it sets out to trace, one of the most readable, informative and comprehensive short guides to the history of apartheid, and of black opposition up to 1959, that is to be found. Although this account takes up a large portion of the book, it never seems intrusive or laboured and carries the reader with it quite easily and naturally. One reason for this is because it follows on quite spontaneously from Modisane's own political development: having watched the young 'situation' reluctantly face up to the necessity for political commitment and political action, the reader is naturally curious, as the young Modisane was, about the roots of it all and the possibilities for intelligent opposition.

Thus the facts he gives about black poverty and malnutrition, about poll-tax and restrictions, about the ANC and the PAC, are all necessary answers to questions that have been raised in the minds of readers as they follow the protagonist through the maze of adult black life. Thus without any pretence at 'objectivity' or 'impartiality' Modisane succeeds in putting across the black man's point of view – his gruesome daily humiliations and the emotions of rage and shame, hatred and violence that these experiences arouse in him; the political choice that faces him between apathetic, passive acceptance and the militant political action – without, curiously enough, ever seeming didactic or stridently self-assertive. This is a rare achievement in any literature, and ensures a special place for his work, whatever critical standards are being applied in the assessment.

If Modisane had been writing later, at the time of the Black Consciousness Movement, it might be that I would be arguing now that he had achieved a new literary form: one which has cast aside the formal restraints imposed by western literary tradition and which was uniquely suited to his role as a black consciousness writer. But the truth is that Modisane was influenced by western literary tradition as much as, if not more than most writers of his generation (unlike later writers whom Bantu Education deprived of any real familarity with literary writing from England) and I am sure that, at this point in time, he was making no conscious effort towards establishing a revolutionary black South African tradition. So my use of such western literary critical terms as 'theme', 'form', 'structure', 'time-scheme' are not as inappropriate in his case as they often are in the case of later writers.

And yet, without fulfilling any of the formal criteria of western literary genres, Modisane has written a book which has made its mark in the West as well as in South Africa. I think perhaps the key to it all lies in his integration of personal history and analysis with community history and analysis. The absence of any obvious structure in fact makes it impossible to detach the writer's life-history from the history of his people, or his personal emotions from their communal emotions, since they are all generated by the overwhelming effect of apartheid upon their consciousness. In analysing the destructive effects of apartheid upon his own character, he is explaining the weaknesses of a whole people, and in his unconscious demonstration of the strengths he has retained despite this assault upon his humanity, he is illuminating their common strength.

Moreover, by a partial fragmentation of form, Modisane gives us an insight into the fragmentation of reality in South Africa – a fragmentation that would be masked by perfection of literary structure which would be in contradiction with the content, in the way that Hutchinson's and Jabavu's works evidence such a conflict, for the orderliness of the books' shapes is out of kilter with the appalling displacement and alienation they record – the murdered brother, the exiles and broken marriages, the mass of people blindly wandering the Southern half of the continent at the whim of white employers and at the mercy of any petty official who seeks to vent his spleen upon them. But although, in

Blame Me On History, the passages back and forth in time and in subject matter work out, situationally, this fragmentation, the book somehow yet maintains an encapsulating wholeness over its sixteen chapters and epilogue. Modisane shows us the truth about his fragmented reality in such a way that our intellects and emotions can gather up its overall significance. Emotionally we are able to identify with (though he may at times repel us) the broken individual who searches for himself through writing, and intellectually we grasp the implications of his situation and that of the people he speaks for when we learn of the historical context in which they exist (or should one say despite which they exist).

In this way, *Blame Me On History* is a genuine search for meaning – that ultimate criterion of autobiographical form. Modisane has set out on his journey without a map: the startling honesty and brutal self-revelation of his record spring, to a great extent, from his refusal to predetermine his form. For planned structure is an autobiographer's chief tool in the evasion of total self-revelation. And it is the courage of this refusal to draw the map before he begins the journey which accounts for the book's power – for as a result the reader is able to accompany the writer *genuinely*, not apparently, by virtue of some clever literary device, on the search for identity: the book is a voyage of discovery for them both. Only thus can he reflect his being authentically, and liberate the consciousness of the reader as successfully as he liberates his own. (Though of course, such a venture in the hands of a lesser writer may well have involved foundering on the rocks, or missing the way.) Modisane thus provides for South African autobiography what autobiographers still seek wherever such personal histories are written: a viable autobiographical form.

4 The Poetry of Mongane Serote

no is not a word but an act – remember that.

Mongane Serote[1]

The role of an artist in an oppressed place is to sensitize the oppressed to their oppressive surroundings, sharpen their consciousness and shape the mode of their response.

Mandlankosi Langa: Review of *No Baby Must Weep*[2]

INTRODUCTION

The corpus of Mongane Serote's poetry, published between 1972 and 1982, is in effect the autobiography of a writer coming to terms with an entirely new function for literature, and the personal record of a man moving from the anguished bewilderment of a sensitive youth attempting to reconcile an overwhelming faith in humankind with the implacable brutality of an apartheid regime, to the serenity of a mature and dedicated worker for the creation of a new society: a worker who has recognised that such a society has to be paid for in blood, as the old society has been, and still is being, paid for in blood. Throughout his entire writing life Serote has sought his significance as a writer within a particular historical context, and used his raw nerve endings as the sensor mechanism for a vulnerable, victimised, but ultimately staunchly enduring populace.

Mongane Serote grew up at a time when the South African government's racial attitudes were hardening as it began to pass the accumulation of laws that entrenched apartheid in the country's legal system, as it was already entrenched in social arrangements and attitudes. During his childhood legislation was passed to prevent any kind of racial mixing (The Prohibition of Mixed Marriages Act in 1949, The Group Areas Act – an act to ensure total segregation of residential areas – and the Immorality Act in 1950), to control the movement of black people in accordance with the needs of the labour market (The Population Registration Act in 1950, The Native Laws Amendment Act and The Natives (Abolition of Pass and Co-ordination of Documents) Act in 1952 – the latter an ironically named act to extend the pass system), to eradicate any form of opposition by making it illegal (The Suppression of Communism Act in 1950 – an act which defined opposition to apartheid as communism) and to condemn black people to an inferior education deliberately constructed to prepare them for servitude (The Bantu Education Act in 1953). As black discontent focused itself into two political organisations – the African National Congress which articulated its beliefs about a just society in the well-known Freedom Charter, and the Pan African Congress – and active opposition began to manifest itself in the form of strikes, demonstrations and pass burning, the South African government became increasingly ruthless in attempting to suppress it, banning the political organisations and declaring a State of Emergency in 1960, after the Sharpeville demonstrations and killings, and introducing powers for detention without trial for increasingly long periods, imprisoning and banning individual dissidents and halting the distribution not only of all political propaganda but even of literature by black writers under the Publications and Entertainment Act of 1963.

Of course these acts did not directly affect the township environment of Serote's childhood – Mphahlele had witnessed the same conditions of squalor, poverty, hardship, violence and despair twenty or thirty years earlier as he grew up. What they did alter was the shape of the world he had to encounter as an adult – the white city life of Johannesburg – and they narrowed the already extremely constricted range of options open to a young black writer. But Serote was very deeply affected in his earliest years by the political climate of Alexandra, the township in which he grew up, by the political activism of his grandfather within the community, by the bus boycotts, the Defiance Campaign and the Bantu Education boycott. After he left school he became involved with the South African Students' Organisation (SASO), the black student body which broke away from the multi-racial National Union of South African Students, and which initiated the Black Consciousness Movement; Serote was in the

Publications Unit of SASO until he left South Africa.[3]

His poetry was published in four collections and one selection between 1972 and 1983, spanning the years of the rise of the Black Consciousness Movement and the Soweto uprising in the life-history of his country, and, in his personal history, a sojourn of just over three years in America while completing a degree course, and six years of exile in Botswana (which still continues) upon return to the African continent. His first two volumes of short poems, *Yakhal'inkomo* (1972) and *Tsetlo* (1974), and his first long autobiographical poem *No Baby Must Weep* (1975) were written while he was still in South Africa; his second long autobiographical poem was written while travelling around the United States to New Orleans and Washington D.C. in 1975, and published together with a collection of shorter poems dedicated to other exiles under the title of the long poem *Behold Mama, Flowers* on his return to Southern Africa in 1978. In 1983 Ad Donker felt that it was time to bring out a volume of selections from all his previous publications, and at the end of it several new poems, or excerpts from new poems written since Serote began to live in Botswana, were included. It is significant to note that Donker turned down some poems instigated by the Soweto uprising and the brutal suppression of it – an illustration of some of the difficulties faced by black poets seeking publication in South Africa, even when they are as well established as Serote. His last collection marks Serote's response to such editorial censorship, for it is published by Medu Arts Ensemble in Gaborone – the community of artists of all kinds from South Africa and Botswana of which he was a member. This way his work will not be as well distributed, but at least the writer is not confined by commercial and political censorship. This collection, *The Night Keeps Winking*, was published in 1983.

It is tempting in assessing the corpus of Serote's work to evolve a neat theory about his poetic development from a highly sensitive and sometimes violently angry young individual seeking his identity and attempting to come to terms with the damage apartheid has done to him, through a middle period of awakening consciousness of the whole community of black people under the auspices of the Black Consciousness Movement, to a final total commitment to the liberation struggle and an assimilation into the corporate identity of the group. Such a line of development is undoubtedly present in his work, and can be traced in a number of its features: in the gradual change of mood from one of frustration and despair to one of confident optimism; in the three stage evolution of form, from short, often personal poems with a lyrical quality to long autobiographical poems and finally to poems between five and ten pages long, with specific pedagogical intentions – a form unique to Serote which he appears to have devised for his own particular purpose and directed specifically at an audience involved in the struggle for liberation. There is also a progressive dominance of the historical perspective in the poems, and a move from youthful fascination with stylistic techniques to a very deliberate design to allow content and intent to shape the simplicity of his utterance.

But such a theory would be a gross over-simplification of the processes at work in the development both of Serote's consciousness and of his literary work, and a distortion of its temporal character, which is not merely linear. The later poems do not entirely dispense with technical virtuosity, and the earliest of his poems often manifest a simplicity of style which makes them available to the least educated of his audience. Serote was aware of the importance of history's role in South Africa from the beginning of his writing career, though his grasp of the implications of this has grown stronger and clearer with time. The formal development from short lyric through autobiography to communal and didactic forms is a general rather than an absolute one. And finally, there is a note of optimism present in many of his earliest poems, though it is true that the despair of the early seventies has almost entirely disappeared by the eighties, or rather it has been transformed from a paralysing to an activating force.

However, as it is impossible to analyse five volumes of poetry without recourse to some kind of structural framework, I propose to attempt to conduct my examination of the poems on three levels simultaneously: the chronological (i.e. the chronology of the poems and of the development of the author's consciousness), the formal and the historical levels, in the hope that this will yield a fairly comprehensive understanding of his work. But I must ask the reader to bear in mind the fact that, for the South African writer it is content which is the most important issue, and that any such scheme as I propose will inevitably distort what it seeks to explicate by smoothing out confusions and eradicating contradictions.

'I WANT TO LOOK AT WHAT HAPPENED'

Individual development

Serote has exploited his inherent over-intense sensitivity in order to voice the collective suffering of his people, and in doing so he has been compelled continuously to re-examine both his philosophical stance as the common voice, and the literary methods he can most effectively employ to engage in his role.

Mbulelo Mzamane identifies the poem 'Ofay-Watcher Looks Back' in Serote's first collection, as his most important statement of poetic intent.[4] The thematic line used as a leitmotif – 'I want to look at what happened'[5] – encapsulates the poet's motivating force throughout his writing career, and explains the aim, not only of all his poetry, but also of his novel. His writing can be seen as a continuous re-working of the past – at first to come to terms with his own and his community's pain and anger, then to analyse the history of his people's struggle against oppression, and finally to act as a dynamic force, propelling the liberation movement. It is one of the constants holding together the entire body of Serote's work as a coherent totality.

Within this framework each of the first three collections communicates a different mood. The first collection, *Yakhal'inkomo*, has a gentler tone than the next two collections, and many of his poems constitute a kind of appeal: an appeal to black youths to have a thought for the mothers and women whose suffering they cause; an appeal to whites, not for sympathy, which he rightly scorns, but for a realistic approach to dialogue before it is too late; an appeal to humanity to reify the humanity of South Africa's black people. The second collection, *Tsetlo*, has a more violent, more aggressive thrust consequent upon Serote's growing recognition that neither protest nor appeal would be heeded in the state in which he was trapped. *No Baby Must Weep*, the autobiographical account of his childhood and growth and of their geographical context, explores at length the personal emotions, social conditions and community relations which had been raised in a brief and preliminary way in the shorter poems, which provided a kind of dress rehearsal for the autobiographical poem, identifying areas for exploration.

All of these three early collections constitute a search for identity, but it is important to recognise at the outset that with Serote it is impossible to separate out the personal from the communal experience, the individual from the group emotion. For the poet always takes up the private experience and examines it within a historical context as the inevitable consequence of a series of historical circumstances: he reaches out from his own emotion, using it to identify with the common fate – in Jungian fashion he transforms his sensibility into the litmus paper of his community, using it to test the reactions of a people to a social and historical experience. There is a complete absence of self-engrossment from the record of even his most private reflections in that it is never his fate as individual but as representative with which he is concerned. And the representative quality of his search for identity is substantiated by the findings of black psychology to be found in writers like Fanon, Manganyi and Biko. He uses his own search as data to help him analyse the black person's role in South Africa. It is not only for Serote that 'the sea of identity is tears'[6] but for an entire population whose national as well as individual history has been one of alienation and oppression.

(a) *The effect of environment.*   This identification with the group and the concomitant absence of western-style individualism, for all the dominance of the first person narrator and the apparent confessional nature of the confidences made by this persona, is evident from the paramount role played by the environment in his work. By environment I do not mean a mere setting, a lively backdrop to his internal anguishings, but an active participant in his consciousness. The African township is very much a human circumjacence rather than mere scenery: the inhabitants wear their hovels and backyards like old clothes that are almost self-identical with the wearer. The physical geography of the place has no existence apart from the people who live in it. This is ironically symbolised in the materials out of which the backyard rooms and the shanty towns are constructed: the peeling, crumbling bricks, the corrugated iron strips, the stones that attempt to hold down the zinc roofs, and in the worst cases, the flattened cardboard boxes and hammered-out oil cans. Nothing endures, nothing is permanent: even the matchbox houses set down in regulation rows on the veld in the new townships merely perch on the dust until something better comes along. So that although Serote can burn with anger and indignation that people should be reduced to such utterly inadequate makeshifts by want of a home, he is nevertheless intensely aware of how these houses and these dirt roads, with their muddy pools and dongas, have shaped the people who have constructed them.

It is no surprise that his poetry should manifest such a strong physical consciousness of place, and identification with 'my comic houses and people, my dongas and my ever-whirling dust'.[7] There is no compromise in the image he offers, no softening with sentimentality or reminiscence: the affection and the awareness of the warmth and companionship fostered by overcrowded slum conditions are rooted deep in realism, not only about physical squalor but also about the moral squalor to which it inevitably leads. It is not the swinging shebeen-life of the *Drum* writer that he presents, but the gruelling daily treadmill of the overworked women, the uneducated children and the unoccupied old people:

> these streets are dirty
> i said these streets are dusty
> yes, these streets are bloody muddy[8]

His anger is sparked by what he sees, but it is the human destruction that lies beyond it that is the real nourishment of his wrath:

> these streets go nowhere
> they've woven the children of this town into their dust . . .
> the children died baked in mud
> washed by dirty water
> these streets stink like apartheid
> these streets are traps
> hold my hand my mother let's look at them
> these squeaking blood-stained hungry-rat battlegrounds
> where children pick the idea of making children
> here
> only whores know how to breathe in the dust
> and only murderers live long.[9]

An image he frequently uses of the township streets is that of the pit – the abyss of despair out of which it is impossible to climb, and inside which people are sunk in a mire of apathy. Deprivation and degradation go hand in hand and reduce the entire community to a state of passive dejection. In one of his ofay-watcher poems (Mzamane defines ofay-watcher as 'an Afro-American expression used by advocates of Black Power in the 1960s' to describe 'someone who has set himself up as the watchdog of his community')[10] Serote records the social consequences of a system which condemns people to such conditions, and emphasises by repetition his identification with what he examines:

> I come from there,
> The children have no toys, they play with mud,
> The boys and girls have nothing to do,
> Their minds are laboratories and their bodies apparatus;
> I come from down there
> The parents there are children of other men and women,
> There the old just sit and wait for death
> Like people wait for a train.
> I come from down there below,
> My friends are tender people who look old.

> They are wild,
> Like rats living in an empty room,
> They are meek like sheep following the other blindly.
> They and I come from down there below
> Down there below the bottom.[11]

He captures the effect of the cycle of deprivation on the entire life-span, from the toyless infancy, through the educationless youth to the pointless old age that waits for death with the same patient resignation that can be seen on an African station platform. What he misses out, of course, are the middle years, for black people who are fit are absent from the locations during these years, always during the day and often all the time, using their health and strength in white-owned factories and houses, gardens, farms and mines. An adult life of self-alienating labour (labour in which the process of alienation of consciousness has been translated into physical alienation from home and family as well) leaves them devoid of resources in old age, in the places 'below the bottom' that provide the structural framework for their lives.

(b) *Alexandra.*   Despite his remorselessly clear perception of all the unsavoury and damaging aspects of the township, the navel cord that binds him to Alexandra, the township where he grew up, remains uncut. Not only does he make frequent reference to it in many of his poems, but several poems, which have come to be known as the Alexandra poems, focus on it entirely. The distinctive image in which he embodies his relationship with the township is that of the mother – a relationship he did not choose, with an entity that frightens him by her cruelty and yet holds his love secure in spite of the fact that, instead of nourishment, her breasts 'ooze the dirty waters of her dongas' and give him dust, not milk. The bond between the two of them is inherently physical – 'you throb in my inside silences' – and the town exercises over him the hold that a mother has over a rebellious, wandering child:

> I know
> When all these worlds became funny to me,
> I silently waded back to you.[12]

And in this poem, called simply 'Alexandra' he once again emphasises the effect – the dehumanising effect – of environment upon consciousness:

> What have you done to me?
> I have seen people but I feel like I'm not one,
> Alexandra what are you doing to me?
> I feel I have sunk to such meekness.
> I lie flat while others walk on me to far places.[13]

The total lack of stimulus, from birth to the grave, yields the hopeless apathy that contributes to the oppression it endures: the township not only shelters its inhabitants, but alienates them from humanity.

The two poems in his second collection, 'Amen! Alexandra' and 'Another Alexandra', were written after the process of resettlement and destruction had begun in order to make room for the erection of barracks to house single migrant workers from the bantustans. The whole process is symbolic of the fragmentation of reality that is the consequence of apartheid for the black community: the break-up of the township is reflected in the break-up of the country into bantustans (or the ironically named homelands of the English) and families are moved out of their township homes to their unknown homelands to make space for the refugees of the system – the migrant contract workers separated from their families and their homes, who are to be housed in the comfortless, communal hostels. So the inhabitants of Alexandra, who in their lives have 'nodded for worse moments', have to nod at the obliteration of their homes. In 'Amen! Alexandra' the township is again addressed as a woman, a woman who was once firm on her feet, her back 'soaking the chilly winds and rains', sheltering her children; and those children must now look on while they weep at her destruction.

The second poem, 'Another Alexandra', examines in more detail the changes that have been wrought as a consequence of this bureaucratic decision. The poet shows the broken streets left empty and silent as the process of removals and destruction rolls inexorably on: 'the screams are mute' and 'the mothers now depart'.[14] As always, it is in terms of people and their reactions that he visualises the scene – the dazed little girl, the blank-faced man, the women who sweat and yet can smile; and again, his own bonding to the broken township is expressed in physical terms:

> Alexandra
> if love is pain
> this i have carried inside my loins
> as i walked . . .[15]

And the ghost town he walks around is peopled with actors of past events, memories of 'concubines conspiring in secret with husbands' and 'murder declared while we sat on a broken sofa, drinking', whores screaming and a man weeping as he pleaded for his life: all the intense miniature sequences into which he regularly crams the life of his people and their places. His final image is drawn from the source which provides all his most forceful incarnation of pain and despoilment: the woman lying ransacked by birth (or is it rape?):

> i cannot look
> for your legs are chained apart
> and your dirty petticoat is soaked in blood
> blood from your ravaged wounds.[16]

(c) *The downward gyre: deprivation and degradation.* The effect of such an environment is not limited to the individual anguish of the poet who records it: it saps the moral fibre of the inhabitants – the girlchild robbed of her innocence, who nurses her own infant in a bewildered daze; the men sunk into apathy; the whores and murderers and their terrified victims. The degraded surroundings produce degraded human beings, and even their degradation is victimised in the programme of destruction. (This needs to be read in the historical context of the early seventies, since which time there has been a change in tone in both Serote's work and that of most black writers.) In 'Ode to Somebody' he hopelessly asks someone to pray for the community's despair:

> everything is broken
> even people don't look any more,
> their eyes are broken; and empty; and shut,
> everybody's back is facing the future[17]

People's only refuge is to refuse to face the reality that confronts them and such a refusal involves loss of contact even with each other, lest their eyes should betray their consciousness of their state. The demoralisation even contaminates the animals and the helpless refrain 'somebody say a prayer' reiterates the collective refusal not merely to take responsibility, but even to make acknowledgement. It is left instead to the unidentifiable, absent, faceless 'somebody'.

Inevitably, such communal demoralisation leads to violence among the disaffected youth in the locations. Gangs of tsotsis seek outlets for the assertion of their humiliated egos and compensation for the sense of emasculation instilled in them by an apartheid system that denies them adult responsibility and subjects them to intimidating harassment by subjecting those they do not fear – that is their own womenfolk and elders – to similar harassment in the form of mugging, rape and murder. This in turn creates an additional and perhaps the least bearable pressure for the ordinary man in the street: fear of his own young ones joins his inherent fear of white authority, and together the two emasculate him. This fear is transformed with great vividness and intensity into the night fears of a child in 'Streetlights and houses', where the boy-child narrator begs his grandmother for stories as protection and reassurance, and chatters on innocently about the threatening characteristic of everyday objects after dark. The language is perfect transliteration of childish speech, but the allegorical content soon becomes apparent: the child's fear is the terror each grown man and woman is subjected to by location existence, and each image has its own story to tell:

> And the walls have holes, *wounds* of windows and doors[18]
> (my emphasis)

The presence of physical violence surrounds them, as do the spies and traitors who gather information for the police:

> Are those windows and doors
> Or are they eyes and noses?[19]

while government relocation policies evict whole communities and dismantle entire townships:

> And why do the houses look like deserted spiderwebs?
> Did the spider eat the people?[20]

The small child's natural fear of imaginary terrors in the dark has become the grown man's unnatural fear of death by violence:

> Grandmama, please grandmama
> Tell me stories
> Why, when I walk, there are noises,
> Why, when I come, the shadows move,
> Why does the light look at me?[21]

Such nervous imaginings of the very young are turned by government policy into solid fact – the followers in the night, the searchlight, and then, of course, the pursuit, the man-hunt, in the context of a society that, unlike the adults to whom the child appeals, has no care:

> In my chest there're drums, their boom is so loud, and my
> ribs shake,
> And the street-light doesn't care, and the houses look dead
> And the street-light is like a big eye
> And grandmama, please grandmama
> Those dusty barbed wires like eye-lashes
> Those dongas like running tears,
> And the noise of footsteps before me . . .
> They sound loud and hasty . . . [22]

The tone of the poem gets increasingly breathless, words tumbling over each other as the chase closes in and finally the fall comes and the furrows of the street come up to meet the stricken victim.

The nightmare of pursuit (whether by police or by tsotsi murderers) is a recurrent theme: it is dealt with again in the account of a nightmare in 'Death Survey'. Here again a simple narrative allows him to expose whole areas of destruction wrought by apartheid: his friend, in his dream, is viciously wounded by the tsotsis, themselves the victims of their social conditions. His own immediate response – fear and the getaway rather than courageous opposition – is a consequence of a life-time's exposure to street violence. His escape is hindered by a gang of Zulus blocking the way as they beat a frightened child – a gang formed by the government's policy of separating tribes and fostering inter-tribal rivalries and even warfare under the leadership of such chiefs as Gatsha Buthelezi who hold 'some meeting with the old leg of the past'.[23] The terrified narrator makes for the shelter of Frank's house only to find that his place of safety has been eradicated in the bulldozing of homes and uprooting of families in one of the relocation schemes by planners who are guided by statistics rather than human understanding. In a brilliant cameo, personifying the bulldozer to bring out the cruelty of the programme, Serote uses a rubble of words to encompass the destruction not only of the fabric of the building, but of all the daily human life it contained:

> this bloody bulldozer had done a good job and its teeth
> dripped blood;
> bricks-pillars-hunks-of-concrete-zincs-broken-steps-doors-
>   broken-glasses-crooked window-panes-broken-flowers-
>   pots-planks-twisted-shoes

> lay all over the show
> like a complete story[24]

And, with the end of the narrative, Serote completes the story of the human cost of an apartheid policy.

Yet the cost has to be measured not only in social terms but also in terms of individual consciousness. It is not possible for a man to be subjected to daily onslaughts of such fear, and a prey to regular nightmares of this kind without incredible damage to his psyche, which has to take daily account of his cowardice. There is a malicious irony in the way that a man not only has to lose his self-esteem as a result of daily exposure to such real threats to his physical integrity so that fear becomes his shadow rather than a rare nervous spasm, but also has to become subject to the contempt of his womenfolk. Thus the man in 'A Poem' (*Tsetlo*, p. 17) has to endure not only the physical agony of his wound, but also the disdain of his cold-hearted wife who, having long 'packed her dresses and petticoats neat in her heart', now allowed her 'long-hidden manhood' to emerge. The humiliations of a man who is given a child's place in society – forbidden decisions and responsibilities and subjected to continual chastisement – are stressed in Serote's poetry by his repeated use of the phrase 'blackmanchild' and the contrast between his size and his status:

> We, the huge men that we are,
> Are just like small boys.[25]

> I am no big blackman
> I am a blackmanchild.[26]

The bitterness of this self-recognition inevitably brings in its train moods of self-disgust and despair. In the effort to come to grips with a consciousness fragmented by such onslaughts on self-esteem and confidence, Serote works through the feelings of insecurity, alienation and loss that afflict the black man, making of this consciousness a negation or absence that is effectively a denial of identity:

> i can say
> i come from nowhere
> ask any white person you meet
> they will tell you, while they shake their heads
> we grow our kaffirs bigger than that[27]

It is possible to trace, in his work, the cycle of this rejection in the black man's life, starting from his birth. In 'Mother Dada and Company'[28] the baby is born knowing 'nothing of love or life' right from its first entrance into the world. And its upbringing among a people whose 'hearts and minds are torn out' leaves the growing child asking 'who am i?' as it faces the confusion of adolescence made intolerable by the violence that surrounds him. A passage in *No Baby Must Weep* elaborates this theme: 'you grew a hollow and named it me'.[29] The usual strain between parent and child is exacerbated by the special accusation that the child brings against the mother who has inflicted this life upon him. The hopeless despair he notes in the eyes of his grandmother sitting on the stoep 'like a dry twig in a flowerpot' weighs upon the child. He sees those eyes as

> . . . a passage
> dim like the sky without the sun –
> empty like a barren womb[30]

As the child passes through adolescence he also grows into his consciousness of his own lack of place in the world. As the three sons wound their mothers in the poem 'The Three Mothers' with their failure to communicate, they affirm:

> Tomorrow we know,
> We shall be homeless, just that.[31]

The trivialising of this crucial issue with the cursory 'just that' only serves to underline its magnitude.

The cycle of rejection, however, is not restricted to the rejection of black people by white people, but the poison spreads into their relationships with each other, making murder and rape regular forms of social interaction. The whole issue is queried in 'Ofay-Watcher Looks Back' in a series of apparently naïve questions: is there always smoke or dust above houses? What has gone wrong when after seeing the houses you need to ask whether people who are alive can really live there? What has gone wrong when people spend their time knifing each other:

> I look at what happened
> When jails are becoming necessary homes for people[32]

The ironic use of the word 'home' here epitomises the issues at stake:

that people should be reduced to regarding such inadequate shelters as permanent homes, and that crime and violence should be the inevitable fruits of that kind of environment.

Dispossessed of their homes, the people are left without any sense of direction: without purpose in life, they are the passive victims of fate:

> Where can the ants go
> without the earth, without their molehills[33]

And for all his passionate support of their case, he shows impatience at their acquiescence under affliction, and he openly discusses the damage such an attitude does to their cause:

> we've shut our eyes
> we've smashed the ears
> we've peeled the flesh[34]

with the inevitable consequence that the baby must weep, for he is 'lost alone in this deep sea this fathomless sea'.[35]

Worse than the loss of a sense of direction is the loss of a sense of identity. So rootless have these dispossessed people become that they have finally lost any sense of who they are – a situation that the Black Consciousness Movement set itself to remedy. Serote expresses this trauma in 'Heat and Sweat' by portraying time and history, the present moment, as being surprised and shocked by their continual existence:

> lost as we are
> torn and bewildered by the sounds of our names[36]

The total effect of this manifold deprivation of roots, homes, traditions and identities is a stunting of the human personality, a loss of self-assurance and confidence. He writes of the loss of ease, the loss of the ability to laugh and smile: 'they are all hesitant like a man walking within shadows'.[37] He speaks for a people forced into so radical a change that it affects the way they speak and the way they walk. Their gait has to show the humility of a subject people, and it has come to show their lack of confidence in themselves as human beings too. And their mother tongue has had to be replaced by the official languages brought from another continent. Old ways must be set aside, old prides forgotten, old words forgotten:

> remember how our home
> our fathers and mothers were taken away by a howling
> and were again taught speech and how to walk[38]

Reduced to the status of children, they were also compelled to relearn their life-skills.

And their lives were robbed of all value and significance, so that the disappearance of the exiled, the imprisoned, the dead becomes a thing of no moment:

> Those who have dropped
> Just died like plants
> And the pulse beats on.[39]

This, for a people who had always attained godhead as they became ancestors. And for those lost in this way 'their lives like a faraway note fade away'.[40] Their ends become as meaningless as their lives have been: 'does it matter where i die?'[41] and they leave no memory behind them: 'your footprints have been taken away by the wind',[42] whatever power they might once have held. He recalls their fathers, spilling blood as they tamed a bull, and the image of the bull brings out by contrast the powerless present of these vanishing people, who now spend their days hiding in shadows, wearing their footsteps in foreign lands, speaking in 'broken tongues'.[43]

So much of a people's identity is bound up in their language that the South African government's interference in this area, and their downgrading of the mother tongues (together with their compulsory education policies in this area – using mother tongue education to produce inferiority) is a particularly sore point with Serote. He impresses on the reader the significance of exiling people not only from places, but from language itself.

And he is anxious to make people realise, too, that all the damage that has been done is irreparable. When the eye is poked out, he says, only a hole remains, and he asks how they learn

> that this assaulted space
> will never be the same again
> that the hole remains like a womb
> it throbs and throbs with memory[44]

As always, Serote sees the issue in universal rather than particular terms and he sums up the core of the business by means of a brilliant contradiction:

> this homeless
> fatherless
> motherless child of your loins[45]

And the only defence he can offer his people against the pain of losing a home, identity and loved ones is that of indifference and the immunity of death:

> what is there to cry about
> beyond death who can still touch us[46]

Historical consciousness

Serote did not acquire historical consciousness at a particular stage in his poetic career. The seeds of historical awareness are present in his earliest poems, though it is comparatively unformulated and lacks the coherence that integrates his latest writing into social praxis as a potent social and historical force. Nevertheless, even in his first collection, his reflections on the black man, on himself and his fellows, and on their condition show him groping towards an understanding of all the factors which have brought this about, and draw back from the simplistic accusations and panegyrics that characterise the mass of fledgling poets whose poems, stimulated by the Black Consciousness Movement and its aftermath, fill the pages of magazines such as *Staffrider*. His comprehension of the interaction of political environments and people's moral reserves has enabled him to develop a kind of poetry capable of fostering the conditions for the regrowth of moral energy by confronting people with the real issues and with their own habitual evasion of them.

Thus, while he has no doubt about where the primary responsibilities for the condition of black South Africa lie, he does not allow this to overwhelm his judgement of black individuals or groups. In response to the murders and violence that comprise the most salient area of township consciousness he attempts to enable the young tsotsis or gangsters to understand the social forces which have produced them and to persuade them to a greater sense of social responsibility towards their victims. In 'My Brothers in the Streets' neither the possessive adjective of the title announcing his identification with those he chastises, nor the thorough-going analysis of the pressures to which they are subjected who

> . . . holiday in jails,
> Who rest in hospitals,
> Who smile at insults,
> Who fear the whites[47]

and of the degradations – violence, drink, music, sex, theft – in which they find refuge detract from Serote's estimate of the damage they do to others and to themselves. Yet in 'Motivated to Death' he ascribes the ultimate responsibility both for the murdered and for the murderers with uncompromising force to the government:

> The R.S.A. condemned him
> Not Alex – where he died, where his killers exist.
> No!
> His crime? (Thanks he's beyond this now).
> He had no pass. Didn't work, had nowhere to stay.
> His meals? He shared beer with friends.[48]

Victims and victimisers are equally pawns of the system while the legal apparatus of the state condemns both executed and executors to a cycle of violence and depravity that drags down family and community into its maw:

> Widows' memories that will be erased by death
> Weeping mothers who'll be wonderstruck till death,
> Frightened little fathers whose eyes never leave the ground,
> Sons whose hands have tasted blood,
> Sons whose eyes are bloodshot like your dawn,
> Sons who play at death as a game
> Your urchin children who rode on tyreless bicycles.
> Oh you bloody brothers,
> Listen to the many many sobbings of mothers,
> Look at the weeping faces of mothers
> Who tore sons and daughters out of their flesh,
> And you tear them out of their hands
> To dust.[49]

Another aspect of the historical condition which Serote sees as directly affecting the relationship between governors and governed, oppressors and oppressed, is the apathy to which the mass of the black population (including himself) had been reduced by brutal repression and confinement. Certain of his poems in this first collection treat the ineffectiveness of the apathetic subject either directly or symbolically, as in 'Burning Cigarette':

> This little black boy
> Is drawn like a cigarette from its box,
> Lit.
> He looks at his smoke hopes
> That twirl, spiral, curl
> To nothing.
> He grows like cigarette ashes
> As docile, as harmless;
> Is smothered.[50]

The deceptive calmness of tone and the apparent naïvety of the image mask an embittered encapsulation of an entire life-cycle of shattered hopes, despair, impotence and death. The casual brevity and simplicity of the language, and the pauses inflicted upon the otherwise gently meandering rhythm by the brutal conciseness of the third, sixth and ninth lines which shatter both form and content by their rhythmic harshness, enables Serote's comment upon the implacably destructive life open to black South African youth, and their resultant inertia, to work upon the consciousness of the reader far more radically than any amount of passionate protest.

A direct charge of apathy is laid in 'What's Wrong With People', where another terse statement presents the drama of a murder victim's death and ends with the cryptic accusation:

> People stood to look,
> I was among them.[51]

with which he confronts his own conscience as much as his community's. And it is towards the cracking of this condition of mind – this tendency towards humble acceptance and passivity, that much of his early poetry is written. His first move is to create awareness of their own estate in the minds of his readers:

> We draw carts like horses do
> And we do not move from here to there in our minds,
> We only think we do.[52]

Self-analysis is the only effective preparation for a change of attitude, and by the time he comes to write the poems collected in the second publication, *Tsetlo*, the consciousness of apathy has fermented and produced the indignation requisite for revolt. 'I have been put in the world backyard too long'[53] is the opening shout of 'Anonymous Throbs + A Dream'. In the course of the poem he rebukes not only himself (Every Black Man) for his cringing humility and affectionate pleading like the dog that wags its tail and fawns even when kicked, but the callous whites who responded to his plight with shallow amusement:

> How can you laugh . . .
> When you see me come
> dressed in rags which I picked up from your rubbish bin.[54]

And the righteous anger of the opening rebuke of 'Throb II' removes all traces of self-pity from the ensuing portrait of degradation while at the same time preparing the reader psychologically for the full impact of the nihilistic despair of the father unable to face the responsibilities of fatherhood imaged in his inability to look (in the Sartrean sense) at his children:

> . . . my children holler 'Papa Papa Papa'
> and I just look away as if to count my toes.[55]

Serote reinforces the message with image after image – his own dog's look saying please as he ran away with his tail between his legs after being kicked; the woman's look and her shouted command that he should look between his thighs to discover whether he has any manhood left; the look at the sister being raped by a white man – and all are summed up in the protracted pun on 'eye' which encapsulates the pith of the self-confrontation in 'Throb VIII':

> I
> eye me
> why because I
> is a cruel memory[56]

Moreover, this 'look', this confrontation with the truth of his own presence, does not take place in a vacuum, but in the context of a common frustration, a common instinctive impulse towards reaction:

> I fear to see the stars at night
> why because the brothers charge my life
> the brothers are bloody restless
> why because they are wounded bulls[57]

And in the final throb we reach the dream of the title and Serote sets this growing consciousness in its historical content, revealing the links not only between the acted-out past and the acted-out present, but between the dreams of the past and the dreams of the present: the chain is not merely a chain of events but also a chain of consciousness:

> when he was dying
> tshaka had a dream
> that's why black brothers must not fuckaround[58]

Poems such as these operate by eliminating the possibility of evading unpalatable truths. By forcing into consciousness the functioning of his own repressions –

> Skies of truth are now scenes
> At the mercy of my curtain eyes,
> I wink often more often
> To draw the curtains
> To cut and forget the skies.[59]

– he makes it impossible for any reader to regress to the former state of unconsciousness. The dawning of a formerly repressed consciousness is a recurrent theme, and one which he always treats with the ambivalence due to it, never underestimating the contradictions involved in the process. Although 'Waking Up. The Sun. The Body' ends up on a positive note with the line that provides its title, embodying the hope that pumped on somewhere in the poet's being, the body of the poem is punctuated with the discomfort of greyness, shadows, exposure, coldness as the poet is forced into facing the day, the cessation of sleep, the 'things he hides exposed to' him as he dresses. And along with the reckoning he has to make with his own body in the act of undressing and dressing, goes the reckoning he has to make with his emotions in his recognition of his own inability to hate despite the incentive of the situation and the power it could bring to motivate action:

> This is a waking deep as the distance of the sun,
> Mind-defying as the knowledge of God.[60]

The thematic metaphor draws together the confusion and self-absorption that characterises the dawning of consciousness, whether physical or political, while suggesting in the narrator's final action – putting on his jacket and facing the day – that he speaks for a people no longer totally submerged by their own fears or wilful ignorance.

But it is not merely with the dawning of individual, or even corporate consciousness that Serote is concerned. Just as the dawn that wakes the poet brings 'thoughts of past days'[61] so, in 'The Face of a Happening' he attempts to harness developing consciousness to its historical context. There is a persistent striving to capture the significance of experience out of the contradictions inherent in the event, its social and historical context and his own response:

> And like I have just woken up,
> Things unfold themselves but I stop them.
> And I sit and look through the gap between the curtains
> And I feel like saying this is not the way to look at the world.
> Where's the world? How do you look at it?
> Its like you are trying to put the wind into bed.
> You write, you talk, you think, you . . .
> And you experience an anguish
> For things can turn out to be a reality –
> The people:
> Maybe that's what the world is . . . [62]

The poem figures or images the hesitation and confusion of his mental processes, yet latches on firmly to his two eurekas: the perception that the significance of a happening is locked into the people, and the recognition of the historical momentum of their experience of oppression that breaks through while he is asking how long

> Are we sunk into a pit
> And roofed in a misty mirror
> Where we watch the face of a happening?
> A wink is a century, the noises cry
> And we who watch the sun rise, the sun set,
> Are folding and unfolding in creation
> Like the womb of a woman.[63]

Though this does not diminish the devastation of the moment, or mitigate the 'dreadful page of his people's daily life', the horror, the hatred and the squalor, where men, like boys bored with a book

> . . . rage at each other,
> Tearing pages of our flesh where God wrote with our blood[64]

nor does it obviate the need for present action, it does provide, in
its grimly realist vision, a rope for people to hold on to through
periods of defeat. It enables them to view the struggle as a war
rather than a battle, in which defeats are as much a part of the
process as victories.

Serote's self-appointment as 'ofay-watcher' (community watchdog)
in his first collection gives us some idea of his conception of his role as
writer. And throughout the early poetry, very specific concern for
specific groups emerges – for old people, women, children, youthful
tsotsis or gangsters – concerns which in his later poems will be merged
into his over-riding preoccupation with group action. (Though it is also
perhaps a consequence of his exile from the Alexandra community.)
The role of guardian of the social group is one which ties in very closely
with his deliberate programme of consciousness-raising, bringing
together as it does his instinctive and detailed empathetic social
response with his need for close observation of the readership whose
consciousness he seeks to raise at the same time as he is raising his own.
The participatory nature of the process – the inward-looking as well as
the outward-focusing of his analysis – dilutes the didacticism of his
intent: the poetry functions as joint exploration rather than either
individual self-absorption or community exhortation.

He is not only able therefore to concentrate on community rather
than personal issues, but he is also able to monitor historical process.
He can chart the movement of the times and estimate the progress of
the black people. The poem 'What's in this black "shit"?' is no mere
shock tactic to release his own aggressive bitterness into the mind of the
reader: it charts very precisely the degree of progress achieved over the
generations. His father, faced by white aggression and obstructiveness,
contained his swearing. Serote's generation has advanced a step in
courage:

> When I went to get employment,
> The officer there endorsed me to Middleburg,
> So I said, hard and with all my might, 'Shit!'
> I felt a little better;
>
> But what's good is, I said it in his face,
> A thing my father wouldn't dare do.
> That's what's in this black 'Shit'.[65]

But this is no simple narrative of an incident: the swear word is employed as a symbol of all that is wrong with black existence, from the appalling physical conditions imposed upon them, to the psychic humiliations and the destructive effect of such stresses upon family relationships. Analysis raises the whole issue into consciousness and provides the necessary base for active reaction rather than passive acceptance. A swearword addressed to an official hardly amounts to revolution, but it signifies the beginning of rebellion and the hardening demand. Consciousness also brings patience in its train:

> And now I know,
> Having been so flooded and so dry,
> I wait.[66]

It is not the immature rashness of adolescence that prompts rebellion, but a clear-eyed stock-taking combined with a reluctant acceptance of the need to take action, not only against white oppressors, but against the entire social and governmental edifice which necessarily includes white friends:

> If you crowd me I'll retreat from you,
> If you still crowd me I'll think a bit,
> Not about crowding you but about your right to crowd me;
> If you still crowd me, I will not, but I will be thinking
> About crowding you.[67]

The context – of growth and pruning to foster better growth – is however the very positive one most characteristic of his vision of liberation. A similar tone is conveyed in 'Hell, Well, Heaven' where in an easy blues rhythm that admits to the confusion he still feels about the past and his own responses to it, he nevertheless affirms with genial optimism his certainties about the future in his repeated calls:

> But Brother,
> I know I'm coming[68]

Yet the ease is not based on an evasion of the violence involved – there is a harsh realism in his acceptance of all this:

> Hell, my mind throbs like a heart beat, there's no peace;
> And my body of wounds – when will they be scars? –
> Yet I can still walk and work and still smile.[69]

Nor is there any false modesty about his own response: his coming is visualised in terms of tides or storms over the veld, both natural forces that build up to great power over a period of time with their Janus faces of patience and ultimate violence.

Whether the storm is conceived of as destructive force or nurturer of growth depends very much on the poet's mood of the moment, though he rarely rejects conciliation out of hand. He veers from ironical appeasement linked to genuine lack of aggression –

> I am just polite . . .
> I am calm[70]

– apologising for wanting to shout, so much does he long for the time when there is no need to write about people dying in the streets – to surges of anger that make him feel justified in doing anything when he considers the family figures destroyed by the system: the grandmother who forgot how to laugh, the grandfather whose hope froze on his lips when he died, the niece whose survival beyond her precarious nine months is in question, and the sad mickey mouse figure of the father. Analysis brings him to question the point of existence on such terms, yet the survival instinct is indestructible:

> but I keep on, I want corn
> for I can make milk in some woman
> for somebody to suck[71]

There is no humble pleading in the poem 'I want corn' – the alliance of his pressing need to succeed as provider, and the confidence, nurtured by black consciousness, to stand up and assert his rights as a man produces the reasonable demand and the firm insistence that it should be met.

Several poems evince this greater political maturity that has resulted from the free discussion of ideas and a growing community consciousness, and manifest it in a ripening of tone that shows confidence in the inevitability of concerted community action. This is often articulated by the form of the poem as much as by its content. In 'Movement, Moulding, Moment' (a title which epitomises his conception of historical process) he uses the repetition of short lines to break up the flow of the poem (as he does in 'Burning Cigarette') and to convey its dominant theme – twice by punctuating paragraphs with the abrupt line:

> Of darkness

and once, at the end, with the line:

>   Of dawn[72]

The poem conveys, in quiet, controlled lines, the protective effect of the darkness, subduing fears, and allowing a new impetus to form slowly in peace:

>   Something is breathing
>   There is a silent life walking to the horizon.[73]

until the poem closes with a sense of impending doom.

Another thematic image of the natural process is that of the turning tide in 'During Thoughts After Ofay-Watching', and he exploits the symbol of the tidal river to its utmost to capture the apparently erratic but actually inevitable movement of revolution: the depressing ebb tide with its bubbles of bloody memories; the agonising stagnation of initiative between ebb and flow, and then the slow-mounting pressure of the rising tide. The image provides a very precise parallel to all the aspects of the revolutionary movement that he wishes to convey – the slow gathering force, the set-backs, the coming-to-naught of certain individual contributions, even individual lives:

>   We are caught up in a turning tide,
>   Slow; taking its pace, slow;
>   Throbbing like the pulse of one dying,
>   The turning tide, we are caught up there
>   Where the waves break before they ripen,
>   Many will break there,
>   Many will not become waves, they will peep and perish
>   There at the turning tide.[74]

But it is the historical movement that is important, the submergence of the individual in the group and the corporate action and the acceptance of the individual tolls that have to be paid in this collective effort:

>   One day we'll wake up,
>   And on the rocky cheeks of the bank there'll be huge droplets flowing
>   And the reeds of the river will be dry like skeleton bones:
>   And the river shall be heard
>   Flowing, flowing on, and on.

> The route will be long and straight
> The bubble will burst, like eyes looking back,
> But the river shall flow like the song of birds.[75]

It is easy to see why Serote returns again and again to the image of the river, the river flowing into the sea – an image peculiarly poignant in a land where, for most of the year, the river beds are dry while the people pray for rain.

Another favourite image of historical continuity is the growth of plants, and his most serene and confident early poem 'The Seed and the Saints' uses it to sing of assurance. After all the tribulations of the past – the winter wind that has blown the trees' leaves and scattered them, the drying up of the sap of the heart, the freezing of the blood – a time of fruition and ripeness has come upon the people: they have emerged from their suffering with strength and maturity, to face the future:

> I'm the seed of this earth
> ready with my roots to spread deep into reality'[76]

– a seed that has been nurtured by all the black saints and prophets of the past, not only in South Africa, but also in America and elsewhere:

> I'm the fruit of this earth, this time
> when I become ripe my beloved,
> let me be food for the children[77]

The strong sense of community and continuity is embodied in the concept of the handing on of nourishment from the past to the present to the future. The bitterness has been worked through and the energy released for growth.

Out of such achieved serenity and security he can offer comfort to a banned friend, Don Mattera, without in any way underestimating the effect of the banning on the victim: 'It is a dry white season' he ironically reassures his friend, but despite everything 'seasons come to pass'. His image encapsulates the sterility and deadliness of a regime that causes such destruction:

> dark leaves don't last, their brief lives dry out
> and with a broken heart they dive down gently headed for
> the earth.[78]

(André Brink paid tribute to his skill in gathering up a whole history in a single brilliant image when he took it over for the title of his novel *A Dry White Season*.) And the sense of 'pass away' that inheres in the biblical phrase 'come to pass' is typical of Serote's many-stranded significations, catching up the idea of sacrificial death, the end of oppression and the coming about of liberation in a single phrase.

The serenity of this sense of common destiny, however, does not in any way mean that he underestimates the cost of any liberation struggle. We have already seen, in the tidal river image, his rationale for accepting the cost to his own community in lives that have been lost (broken like waves) and lives that have never even known the gathering strength of the wave but petered out to nothing before achieving anything in terms of action. In one of the early poems in *Yakhal'inkomo*, 'The Three Mothers', he counts the cost of the rebellion of the community's youth to their mothers, who are most deeply wounded by their inability to protect their young. In 'Won't You Cross Over' he counts the cost to himself of the commitment he has been asked for, and the cost to all the young of any action they take for the cause:

> i know little boys who are going to dirty their hands and
> may have to
> clean them on their bosoms[79]

He is open about his abhorrence of violence, however firmly he accepts the necessity for it. This combination of moral abomination and dedication to struggle and to hope comes out most forcefully in 'Sunset', towards the end of *Tsetlo*: he acknowledges the need to focus not on the monstrosity of the situation, but on its positive aspects:

> I
> I shall hold my palm over my eyes
> to shade the horror away
> to look at a brand new hope . . .
> For
> I shall have harnessed my loins
> it will be a brand new destination,
> that night,
> black child's laughter will ring in the dark sky
> only
> I wonder where I'll cleanse my hands.[80]

These are not the misgivings of the doubter, but the very real concern of one who has made up his mind and accepted the consequences without being able to divest himself of concern for the victim. Because he is never able to imitate the white government and turn human beings into types – the very quality that distinguishes his poetry from straightforward polemic – he has therefore to pay the continuous emotional toll himself.

Formal resolution

The question of appropriate form is not one confined to black South African writers. Indeed it is one that has become especially crucial for all writers everywhere since the breakdown of the great certainties on which nineteenth-century realism was based. Yet not only is there a more pressing urgency to find an answer in a revolutionary situation where there is a need for direct communication with a mass audience not generally susceptible to literary influences, but black writers have to confront this necessity at the same time as they are learning to write in an alien language unassisted by a supportive literary tradition and the confidence born of a lifetime's use of a mother tongue.

Serote himself has always been acutely conscious of these factors. He was among the first generation victims of Bantu Education – a system which turned out 'frustrated semi-literate adults' – and claims that he really began to learn English after leaving school while he was trying to learn how to write.[81] Thus while he was struggling with the correct use of language he was at the same time confronting the whole question of what poetry was, and whether it had any significance for him, in his social context:

> There was the queen's language. It was a problem. There was the idea that I was writing poetry, which is what? I struggled through.[82]

And then, the most important issue of all:

> Who are you writing for when you write in English? So maybe I have never written in English.[83]

He was wrestling with the two-pronged torture of having to master an alien tongue, and then having to use that tongue to convey feelings and ideas which the language was inadequate, for cultural reasons, to embody. At the same time he had to deal with the sense of inferiority and alienation that all this entailed. Serote perceived early in life the power of the word: speech not only gives relief to overcharged emotions by allowing people to shout out to the world what is happening to them, it also bestows to some extent the power to prevent such infringements of their human rights. No wonder that a lament for his 'broken tongues' is threaded through his work: subjugation has entailed the rape of his mother tongue and a forced marriage to two new ones. In fact his home language is a mixture of Zulu and Tswana (mixed languages are common features of most Southern African homes owing to the dispersal of tribes under white settlement in South Africa), to which the colonists have added English and Afrikaans:

> now i speak in many, many broken tongues
> while i seek Africa[84]

Biko, in his evidence in the SASO/BPC trial explored at length this peculiarly effective invasion of a man's soul by an interference with his use of his mother tongue. And Serote himself, at a Writer's Workshop at the University of Botswana in January 1978, recounted a curiously moving trial he attended as a court reporter where the defendant refused the services of an interpreter and insisted on defending himself in his own language, regardless of the fact that the judge and jury could not understand him and would inevitably be more severe upon him as a consequence, so vital was it to him to speak out exactly what was in his own mind, unhampered by the distortions of a foreign and unfamiliar tongue or by another man's interpretations of his ideas.

In *No Baby Must Weep* Serote evokes the damage caused by words, the pollution and decay they have imposed on life, so that the only hope of redemption lies in new ones:

> so our broken tongues
> and long-soiled lips
> can grope for new words because old ones have broken
> this earth to pieces[85]

Thus the broken tongues and the words they give rise to interact to destroy not only the man who speaks them, but also the world he inhabits, and the poet's task is to forge language anew for his message, and in doing so recreate this broken earth – a task Eliot discussed in 'East Coker':

> And so each venture
> Is a new beginning, a raid on the inarticulate

> With shabby equipment always deteriorating . . . [86]

Their function as a causer of pain and distress is something that engrosses Serote: he tries to show the purely private cost of words:

> . . . words
> Make pain
> Like poverty can make pain[87]

He frequently envisages the pain words cause in absolute physical terms, showing them bleeding like limbs and bodies:

> what do we want
> screaming wounds that throttle the whistle of the wind
> of words which bleed as if they were crying[88]

And in his vision, ink becomes blood, as in 'Prelude' where his crimson heart oozes into the ink and the pus of his soul defaces the paper, or when he tells Bra-Kippi:

> i write you a letter
> by dipping a finger into my blood, or is it already pus[89]

and later he writes of his blood speaking – something more than a casual literary figure in the circumstances.[90]

His poems are progressive stages in his private struggle with words. That it *is* a struggle is witnessed by the ferocity of 'Black Bells' where he calls words 'elusive', claims that they trip him, that Whitey uses them to trap him (this concept of the colonialist's use of words as an offensive weapon is important to the understanding of Serote's whole attitude to language); and as his struggle progresses in the poem, his words dissolve into nonsense syllables symbolic of the losing battle he fights to escape their trap.[91]

He deliberately uses disgusting images in his references to words, as though the pollution he is attempting to describe has infected his own relationship with his medium so that:

> i sit here
> bursting words between my wringing fingers
> like ripe boils
> sometimes they deflate and hide their roots
> bury the pain for tomorrow

> yesterday the pus spurted out and the smell clung to my
> nostrils
> i sat back and saw the typewriter staring
> and the whores were still screaming in the night[92]

The squalor of the comparisons he has chosen – 'ripe boils' that burst
or else deflate, burying the pain for a later day – all emphasise the
sordid struggle that coming to grips with words means for him, and the
sordid state of affairs that he so urgently needs words to describe.

By such images of disease, of the distortion of the body's balance,
Serote attempts to convey the fragmentation of reality – of warped
social order and overturned personal stability – experienced by him and
by all his compatriots. And it was there that he encountered his first
major struggle with form. Serote found himself in a double bind where
form was concerned, for his struggle to master the literary skills and
forms necessarily ran parallel to the development of his philosophy: he
had to experiment with forms from an alien tradition before he was able
to discard them, and he was discovering that certain forms were
inappropriate at the same time as he was learning to use them. The first
two collections, *Yakhal'inkomo* and *Tsetlo* record the progress of his
struggle, and reveal the poet as a skilful manipulator of the traditional
western poetic forms that he later rejects: he experiments with word-play
and rhythm, indulges his inherent preoccupation with imagery and
explores rhythmic mechanisms that might embody his content.

Several poems use ruptured rhythm – as 'The Burning Cigarette' –
or rhythmic anarchy – as with the description of Frank's place in
'Death Survey' – to convey the total social disorientation produced by
apartheid. In 'Mode of Broken Pieces'[93] he attempts to give formal
shape to this disintegration at some length. The poem deals simultaneously with his own restless wandering from place to place in South
Africa (all 'black spots') – Alexandra, near Johannesburg, District Six
and Langa near Cape Town, Chatworth, Durban, Swaziland – in
search of his own wholeness, and with the internal fragmentation of the
townships he visits: Alexandra's head has been chopped off and the tail
remains, wagging awkwardly in his guts. The other places clutch at
him, pulling him in different directions. Langa, the place on the Cape
Flats to which the District Six inhabitants were banished, lies like a
dead reptile on the sands. The partially evacuated District Six is imaged
as a derelict old man who chews on his gums after losing his teeth, or as
a dump heap 'where white people throw refuse thought about us'[94]
(note the psychic pun on 'refuse thought'). And throughout his
peregrination of all these broken places are scattered:

> . . . the pie
> ces
> of my bro-
> ken hea
> rt[95]

which the poet vainly attempts to gather. And here we come to the core of the poem's form, which by disruptive, staccato rhythm and visual and oral breaking up of actual words, attempts to act out fragmentation rather than discuss it.

The repetition of this stanza is characteristic of his style and springs from the most important of his formal influences: the traditional African praise poem. It is perhaps ironic thus to ascribe an influence when Serote himself has admitted to only a sketchy acquaintance with traditional praise poetry. But, as Mzamane has shown, many elements of the praise poem have filtered into daily speech patterns and the general culture of urban Africans: the use of praise names (for footballers for example), the habit of circumlocution, repetition (very apparent in songs of all kinds, traditional and modern, in everyday use). So that all Southern Africans, whether conscious of it or not, grow up heir to fragments of their ancient cultural traditions.

The way repetition is used in the praise poem is very different from the way it is used in western culture, where there has to be a direction, an element of accumulation and growth in the repetition if it is to be accepted by the literary institution as a valuable literary technique (i.e. the critic has to prove that it is not *mere* repetition, but serves some other purpose). In African tradition, repetition is much more like the 'cut' in Afro-American culture[96] – a point of return, effecting reassurance and consolidation rather than a structural impulse effecting progression. For this reason it often seems monotonous and a sign of paucity of poetic imagination to the western critic. And indeed, Mzamane, himself an African critic sharply aware of his own cultural inheritance, has been so imbued with the values of the western critical tradition as to fault Serote on these grounds instead of examining what it is about his own (Mzamane's) literary training that induces him to appraise the effect of repetition in this way.

But the traditional African heritage is not the only source of Serote's (or indeed any black South African poet's) reliance on repetition. Jazz music has proved a powerful influence on black South African writing for many decades, and this uses repetition in a similar kind of way. Serote is less influenced by jazz than a poet like Sepamla, yet a poem like 'Hell, Well, Heaven', with its refrain:

> I do not know where I have been
> But Brother,
> I know I'm coming[97]

uses jazz rhythm and the language of jazz songs to establish its basic
form. The fact that this is an isolated example of the use of jazz form
supports the theory that in these first two volumes Serote was
experimenting with a variety of forms in order to find out which best
embodied his poetic purposes.

One point on which Serote was clear from the beginning, and which
required no experiment to establish, was his choice of voice. From his
earliest days, even when he was indulging his passion for image and
word-play, seizing morsels from western tradition to play with, his
poems were directed at his people, and it is their language, the
embodiment of their everyday life, that serves him as his voice. For this
reason it is pointless to begin examining his poetry for grammatical
errors or logical non-sequiturs. Though occasionally drawn by his
lyrical impulse into literary indulgences, it is the words of Alexandra,
Soweto, Sharpeville from which he forges his poems. These words are
drawn from a multitude of languages – South African conversation
passes fluidly from Tswana to Venda to Zulu to English to Afrikaans,
drawing words and phrases from any source at need. Even when an
exchange is primarily in a single language, the speaker will casually
borrow expressions and explanations from any of the others as they
find they need them to clarify their meaning. So poets writing in
English out of such a background of necessity rely heavily on
transliteration if they wish to speak directly to their compatriots. I am
using the word 'transliteration' here to mean setting down township
speech exactly as it is spoken. Sometimes this involves translation, at
other times not. It almost *never* involves correcting the grammar or
clarifying the meaning for the reader. (South African writers aim their
work at fellow South Africans and use their common language; they
argue that if Westerners wish to read it they must make the effort to
understand it.)

e.g.   (a) 'Oh you black boys,
            Who spill blood as easy as saying "Voetsek" ' (*Yak*. p. 19)
       (b) 'I smiled when we met, she said snap me a picture,
            I said "Yy's laat!" (*Yak*. p. 6)
       (c) 'Hell my mind throbs like a heart beat there's no peace' (*Yak*.
            p. 16)
       (d) 'the dark and the beer house where whores are made
            eat people' (*Tsetlo* p. 39)

And the idiomatic character of the vernaculars and Afrikaans render their transliterations richer and more vibrant than any attempt at correct English could be (and any such attempt would of course alienate his chosen audience). A western critic has to be careful when examining the language and imagery of poets like Serote to distinguish individual literary skill from the characteristic idioms of local vernaculars.

'I WEAVE MY FOOTSTEPS IN MANY FOREIGN LANDS'

From individual development to group consciousness

There is no point at which Serote turns from concentration on self-awareness to the consideration of wider groups. As is evident from the preceding section, not only is Serote, as an African, much more instinctively community-oriented than the majority of western writers, but from the very beginning he has been drawn to consider the needs and to analyse the problems and to seek to raise the consciousness of his people.

However, as a young poet he necessarily had to come to terms with powerful emotions of rage, frustration, humiliation and yearning, before his full energies could be released to look outward at the world. The long autobiographical poem *No Baby Must Weep* provided the arena for just such a process, but it is a search firmly based in the community, an analysis that makes no division between self and social group.

It takes the form of a confessional walk around the township with his 'black mother', in which he recalls his growing up and talks through his adult dilemmas with his real yet symbolic mother. This figure that merges Serote's real mother (recognisable from the intimacies of the township and the specific nature of the memories) with all black mothers, and indeed with mother Africa, is typical of Serote's use of people in his poetry: in the way of all writers, he unites the characteristics of several people to produce a fictional character, but above and beyond this he uses the character symbolically, often, as in this poem, on two levels, a communal, human level and a geographic/ metaphysical level. Such economy provides him with a powerful literary device that enables him to unify large masses of material. Thus *No Baby Must Weep* opens with a very realistic image of an actual mother, with hands ruined by hard work and sweating in the heat:

>   let me hold your hand
>   black mother let me hold your hand and walk with you[98]

and closes with the same image turned symbol:

>   ah
>   africa
>   is this not your child come home[99]

The walk around the township streets that make up the narrator's
kingdom gives a sharp picture of the environment that robs the black
child of his childhood while ironically forcing upon him the truth that
he will remain a child all his life in the whiteman's world of South
Africa: the yards and fences, the wrecked cars that provide a setting for
the gropings that take the place of romance, and the stoeps of the
decrepit shops where he used to gather with the other boys to joke and
swap dirty stories. He recalls the struggles with his parents who wanted
him to be educated while he wanted to earn money as a caddie or a
garden boy, and his curious mixture of love, respect and judgement
with which he regards the father who was unable to communicate with
him. He remembers the train journey, when he saw from the window
the herd boy starved as the twigs and stones he sat among. As he drifts
from memory to memory – all so similar to the scenes and memories
recorded in prose by Mphahlele and Hutchinson – the reader realises
that, along with the personal reminiscences of girls and fraternal
comradeship, along with the self-disgust that regularly punctuates the
verse (the soiled fingers that break and batter and stain the flower
petals as he touches them) he is writing the history of his time and of his
people. He is, like the old testament prophet, chastising them for their
depravity:

>   these less than dogs
>   drunkards
>   smoking pipes
>   cigarettes
>   dagga
>   benzine
>   petrol . . .
>   who dirtied their paws
>   and licked them[100]

in yielding weakly to temptation and compromising themselves by their complicity, though he does not fail to point out that the ultimate responsibility for the state of affairs lies with

> the gods of destruction
> who know nothing about songs
> who are more petty than birds
> who can't even listen
> or be moved
> by the sight of machine-gunned children[101]

As a member of a community subjected to external and internal destructive forces, haunted by a sense of defilement, he struggles to incorporate his feelings in images of decay and putrefaction: words are ripe boils spurting pus, exuding smell, and whores scream in the night.[102] The feelings reach a climax as he bends over Tiro's coffin and reaches out gently to touch the half face that is left after the explosion of the petrol bomb that killed the black consciousness leader in exile in Botswana. His shattered body symbolises the ravages of the oppressive social system to which they are subjected, and the extermination of the hope and strength of those who attempt to oppose it.

Yet the candle of hope can only be snuffed temporarily: eventually Serote, and those he represents, slowly rekindle their determination. Finally the pain and the immolation have to be survived:

> i see that i am the one who has to build this world out of dust
> i have to clutch the wound of the trees and birds
> tame the snakes and make a path[103]

The wounds themselves, that nearly destroyed them, have to be made into a source of strength to go on:

> i emerge a wound in my gut
> using broken tongues and a bleeding heart . . .[104]

and out of suffering he has to compose a chant of defiance to the oppressors:

> i am the man you will never defeat
> i will be the one to plague you
> your children are cursed
> if you walk this earth, where i too walk

and you tear my clothes and reach for my flesh
and tear my flesh to reach my blood
and you spill my blood to reach my bones
and you smash my bones and hope for my soul[105]

Serote is too much of a realist, too wise in the ways of the human heart, to use this point in the poem to pivot its content from despair to determination. There are still regressions where the narrator turns child again, pleading for mother-love and reassurance. Tears and memories still beset him; his consciousness of the squalid hopelessness of the township streets persists: their dirt and dust, the fact that they lead nowhere, like the lives of those who dwell in them and that only whores and murderers can survive them, for children are broken by them – looking for water and bread and finding none till 'this thirst begins to burn our throats'.[106] Yet he recognises that the thirst for freedom has now grown to such a pitch that the time for action has come – 'let my hand go now my mama'[107] – the child is now ready to leave the shelter and stand alone, 'motherless/fatherless/ . . . lost in a wilderness of woven curses/homeless,'[108] exposed, unprotected, to his destiny. And it is out of this moment of resolution that the hope for the narrator, for his people and for Africa, can come: the dominant image – of the river, of waters gathering, of rivers flowing into the sea, of floods – captures this sense of feelings reaching a bursting point, of a whole people's resolution coming to a head and forging a common optimism and a common destiny:

> i can say
> one day the word will break
>
> i can say
> one day the laughter will break
>
> i can say
> one day the sky will weep
> i can say one day
> this flower
> will stand in the bright bright sun[109]

While *No Baby Must Weep* was in the hands of the publishers, Serote went to New York to begin his degree course, and his experiences in America – experiences of another culture, of exile, of the formal educational system – activated another phase in his emotional growth and political development. The poem *Behold Mama, Flowers*, according to Mzamane, was written as he travelled around America, to New Orleans and Washington DC in 1975.[110] And whereas the dominant image in *No Baby Must Weep* is the river, that in *Behold Mama, Flowers* is the road: the road of self-discovery, of political consciousness, of communal aspirations on which the writer is travelling.

There is still the same acknowledgement of bewilderment, of confusion about directions, that had beleaguered the narrator of *No Baby Must Weep*:

> . . . i have never known where to go
> on the road of days to come . . . [111]

But whereas in *No Baby Must Weep* the search took place within a South African context which offered familiar footholds and the shelter of a supportive community, in *Behold Mama, Flowers* he is exposed, as he was prepared to be at the end of the former poem, to the bleak inhospitableness of a foreign land. He now has to contend, not only with his fits of despair about his personal and communal destination:

> i hope roads lead somewhere, nowhere leads to dreams
> about nightmares
> i walk
> i hide in shadows
> and i am always looking for a hole[112]

and with the anguish of specific memories – Phaladi bleeding to death in the street; the wife bewildered by her husband's imprisonment; the old man weeping alone in his cell[113] – but also with the inability of people to communicate in their distress:

> what will happen then
> when we no longer look at each other
> how can we talk
> if we don't see each other . . . [114]

Faced with such unsought and undeserved inflictions of pain, death and injustice, he can only reiterate the question: 'how can i forgive?'[115] He is haunted by corporate memories of power in the land – great-grandfathers spilling blood as they tamed the bull that used to sprawl across the green kingdom – memories that have disintegrated into nothing:

> that memory is now sprawled
> like a thrown-away jacket[116]

and he is taunted by his lust for an ordinary, carefree existence in which he can 'walk with ease, laugh and kiss with a giggle in my heart'[117] instead of which he is subjected to the apocalyptic voice 'blood-stained as the ears of the trees'[118] reminding him of the martyrs of the recent past – Luthuli, Sobukwe, and all of the blood that has been shed.

His concept of the struggle in South Africa is enlarged by his acquaintance with racialism in America, so that Jonathan Jackson's death is seen in perspective alongside Tiro's and those of the other South African victims. Living in the West has also served to convince him of its irrelevance to his own destiny and that of his compatriots:

> my brother
> what do we want
> now that we have left the smell of our sweat in foreign nights
> and longed to go back home
> now that we have twisted our tongue into harvard and oxford hisses
> and begun to wonder what our old people used to talk about[119]

And his personal sense of exile from South Africa is blended into his corporate sense of the African's displacement that has resulted from colonialism and settlement:

> my brother how long must we wonder whether we will have a home
> how long my brother
> must our eyes graze the earth like reptiles
> how far is the road, where are the paths
> ah
> africa, every moment, like an alcoholic
> walks back to its death.[120]

His own search for his destiny is a part of a people's search for their own common destiny, and an entire continent's attempt to shake off the death throes and the apathy and move forward. At the moment all are hampered by memory 'like chains' embracing the feet, by mud, by fear of eagles and hawks that watch for their shadows, poised to swoop and destroy. He agonises over the squalor of his people's self-betrayals and self-inflicted violence, and yet, though he walks in fear, hiding in shadows, pursued by the memory of his people's condition – the father's bleeding wings, the grandmother's frozen sight, the mother's timid walk like a rat at point of death – he recognises the inevitability of painful parturition, of the time for positive action, with all the gruesome sacrifices it entails, arriving.

Historical consciousness

His poem has a much more wide-reaching content than his previous long poem: the concept of Africa is now placed in the context of capitalist hegemony: 'you own nothing'[121] – and the threat of nuclear annihilation, the slaughter of comrades and the bland lies over the radio about progress, democracy and change. The sense of determination comes over much more forcefully at this stage in his poetic career, in the image of the road and the footprints that are pools of blood – the blood of those who have trodden the road and lost their lives for their efforts and in the image of the hill that the narrator is resolved to mount, whatever the pain involved.

There is no glib passing over the destruction involved in such a decision; and yet, he reminds the reader, the initial demands were so reasonable: 'all i needed was to have a home and sing my songs'.[122] And he points to the suffering of his generation, and the memory of the suffering of former generations that have brought about his moment of rebellion, the storm and the nightmare of birth, in the continent that dropped, by accident, into savage chaos, out of god's back pocket, in the continent where sirens scream and the children can't smile any more. Yet his urge to explain, to justify, the difficulty with which he has reached his acceptance of violence, the regret that overtakes him – none of these sap the firmness of the resolution:

> now again time has come
> the hour
> it breaks my heart and leaves me tearless
> the hour is here
> if we can't have a home nobody must have a home
> the hour even burdens the sun.[123]

The significance of this point of decision is marked in the poem by an interesting grammatical feature. Serote begins here to use 'we' instead of 'i', and retains the form almost exclusively in his later poems. The 'i' was never an exclusively personal, individualist persona – it was always representative, symbolic of a whole nation of people like himself. But by the time he comes to write *Behold Mama, Flowers* the transition is beginning to be made to a corporate identity, he is merging with the liberation movement, a group with a common goal and devoted, communally, to a common task. The change of pronoun marks a change of outlook, a positive commitment from which, hitherto, he had been withheld by his own prejudice against violence whatever the provocation or the need. A frequent theme in his earlier poems had been his inability to hate despite the justice or even the indispensability of such an emotion. As he looks at the wider world outside South Africa and measures the global power of the opposition, the hidden supports of capitalism and philosophies about defence propping up the oppressive South African regime, he is brought to the point of decision, made to get down from his humanist fence and accept the inevitability of armed struggle. At the same time he begins to learn that hatred need not necessarily be the motivating force; black consciousness and the working through of his anger, humiliation and frustration, the concentration on raising the morals of his own people instead of giving voice to their negative complaints – all these have made him realise that hatred, rage and the enemy themselves are best forgotten; that what needs to be concentrated upon is the urge towards justice, equality and freedom; that what he has to foster in his poetry is the resolve not to be demoralised, not to give up the struggle and not to allow the forces ranged against them to sap the strength of their will-power; that what can uphold his people in their common efforts is a vision of a humane and just society, where there is a place for dignity and brotherhood and human trust and love.

The end of this second long poem summarises the collective experiences of his people, not obscuring the shame of defeat or the indignity of suffering: the slaughter of the cattle urged by Nongqause that heralded the defeat of the Xhosa near Fish River; the fall of Dingaan and the death of Tshaka on ' . . . the day when the future turned its back on you'.[124] Years of shame when

> . . . we could not look at the women
> because we knew now that the storm had taken our
> houses[125]

followed these defeats, when apathy reduced them to a helpless submission to their conditions:

> we know of songs made by chains
> we have heard while we sat on stones our heads buried in
> our palms.[126]

Yet now, the narrator reminds his listeners, the time has come for the storms of the future, when the defeated people can begin to take the initiative, when they must choose between resistance and victory or death:

> i can say
> your dignity is locked tight in the resting places
> in the places where you shall drink water
> around the fire where you shall laugh with your children
> i can say otherwise
> your dignity is held tight in the sweating cold hands of death
> . . .
> i will say again
> behold the flowers, they begin to bloom.[127]

The global perspective that Serote has struggled for in this poem has brought, together with the grim acknowledgement of the necessity for recurrent defeat, the invincible conviction that, ultimately, history is on their side: the struggle will finally be won, the flowers will bloom.

Formal resolution

The fact that Serote chose the extended poetic autobiographical form for *No Baby Must Weep* and *Behold Mama, Flowers* indicates his dissatisfaction with what I shall call, for want of a better name, the short lyric. And the fact that he abandoned lengthy autobiography after the second poem seems to indicate that such a form fulfilled a passing need but proved unsuitable to his long-term poetic aims (aims which indeed became clearer to him in the course of writing these two poems). Serote himself admitted, in an informal interview in 1980, that he had felt confined by the brevity of the form he had been using in his first two collections, and wished to explore at greater length and with greater freedom issues which had become particularly crucial to him at that time. And certainly neither of the two long poems submits to any conventional formal constraints: they are genuine explorations, both in content and form, making no claims through adherence to a specific genre, to a place in the traditional western literary hierarchy. And indeed both poems have been condemned by the majority of western-trained critics (I include in this African critics, since only in the last few years have students begun to benefit from a literary training that exposes them to ideas of traditions and standards and values other than those of the western literary establishment – all of which were applied, in the early days, to the study of vernaculars themselves and the indigenous literatures) for faults heinous according to established standards of judgement and accepted values: discursiveness, repetition, lack of direction and lack of specific form.

While not attempting to justify either poem as a literary masterpiece, and while having to admit that, to my western-trained mind, these characteristics detract from the poems' effectiveness for me, I think it is necessary to examine whether some of these criticisms are in fact relevant to the poems' intended readership, and if not, whether effective function is a valid criterion of effective form.

Both poems are logical evolutions of their author's own personal, social and political development. After examining various aspects of his own emotional reactions and various facets of the social structure of which he was a part, Serote was ready for a more leisurely, detailed and untrammelled exploration of his own community's consciousness. The walk around the township which provides a loose framework for this may have been unconsciously modelled on the framework Modisane sets out to use in *Blame Me On History*: but it is essential for any true representation of autobiographical detail, to find some way of conveying the role of the township in the creation of identity.[128] The poem is essentially a search, as indeed are all autobiographies. But it differs from western autobiographical writing in that it is a search for the self-within-the-community.

Behold Mama, Flowers, on the other hand, is a search for the self-in-the-world. Transposed from the security of his own community and the familiarity of his own land, Serote is compelled in this poem to confront himself unsupported by his life-time human context (a confrontation more traumatic for an African even than it is for a European who has had to forge his identity without such close community bonding). But at the some time he also finds this confrontation impinged upon by a great many other issues and conflicts which he was not directly exposed to within the South African environment, and which lead him to take into account world political forces in working out his own political position. While *No Baby Must Weep* could be roughly categorised as personal autobiography, *Behold*

Mama, Flowers has more of the flavour of a political autobiography (i.e. a record of political *development*, not a record of political *action*).

To acknowledge that the two poems are both genuine searches is, in fact, to recognise the impossibility of finished form. Form can only be given when a search has been concluded: it is the writer's answer, not his question. The shaping of material into a coherent pattern is basically a verdict – the embodiment of a writer's conclusions on an issue. At this stage in his poetic growth, Serote was seeking deeper ways of asking questions and evading sophisticated but superficial answers that sometimes emerge too easily from his earlier lyrics. Thus while discursiveness may be irritating to a western reader conditioned even by the mythic freedom from structure of the modernists to look for a pattern and distinctive shape, to lay bare the skeletal structure of the work of art, it has an essential liberatory function in the poems. Yet certain devices that Serote uses in the poems not only underline the search but also serve to hold each poem together in ways that could be (mis)interpreted as structural, were the critic inclined to construct such a justification: namely the imagery and the repetition.

These features are interlinked insofar as each poem has a thematic image which recurs at intervals in lyrical passages that are often repetitive in character. Thus in *No Baby Must Weep*, where the central image is the river, among the many other repetitions in various passages of the poem, this kind of leitmotif keeps alive in the reader's mind the sense of flow and mystery and inevitability:

> the river was dark and hiding its depth
> the river was dark, hiding its depth and coiling its flow
> the river was dark[129]

Very slight changes in the basic line or the addition of an extra phrase such as 'coiling its flow' involving the transposition of 'and' in the second line separate out Serote's use of the technique from simple choral repetition as we know it in the West. A few lines later the same idea is reworked with additional details:

> the river was dark and hiding its depth
> its movement was coiled deep into its gut . . .
> the river was dark the horizon was dark . . . [130]

Later in the poem he extends the metaphorical base of the image, incorporating the 'i' who has provided most of the content of the poem into it:

> i am the wound of this earth
> which will turn the river red
> and the river is dark
> and nobody wants to take a look
> the river was dark, the river was deep
> this dust and this mud and this dirt
> are my witnesses.[131]

But it is not always the case that the lines are changed and extended in scope: sometimes there is a straightforward repetition of the words in which the only variation is a slight change in the rhythm consequent upon a change in the way the words are divided into lines.

There is however a point of progression towards the end of the poem where the river blends into the sea and the image is used as a straightforward metaphor for the absorption of individual efforts into the anonymity of the mass struggle:

> the river flows
> the river is dark the river is deep the river flows
> the river whistles
> flows
> the river reaches out the river stretches
> groans
> whispers
> the river breaks into screams echoes in the mountains
> the river flows
> the river is silent like a resting body
> if we see we have seen
> if we hear we have heard
> when the river broke and died into the sea
> the sea is dark the sea is deep the blue sea is vast
> the sea purrs like a sleeping cat bathed in the heat
> of the sun
> like we die and leave bones behind
> the sea dies and leaves rocks behind
> the sea is deep
> deep
> the sea stretches and stretches
> the sea reaches and touches
> the sea touches to the end of the world
> the sea struggles
> the sea builds and breaks and builds and breaks[132]

It is necessary to quote at such length to demonstrate the slow way in which Serote builds up his ideas through repetition of the images. One reason for this is the oral poet's traditional reason that an uneducated audience without a text before it requires the repetition of a point in order to absorb it; but another reason for it is that the poet here is concerned with attempting to act out rather than explain or describe. The rhythmic monotony of the chant has a physiological effect upon the audience, promoting an absorption that is triggered by emotion and physical response. I have watched this take effect upon a Batswana audience when a similar passage from this poem was included in a workshop play created by the actors and Serote. Most of the play was didactic explanation and exhortation of the significance of the battle of Isandlwana, and the passage from the poem was included at some point in the middle. When the actors came to the passage, the audience, which up to that point, in typical Southern African fashion had conversed, moved around the hall visiting friends and eating and drinking, were suddenly lulled into utter stillness and concentration by the lyrical chanting of the lines by completely static actors making no other efforts at this point to command attention.

This gradual extension of the image and build-up of ideas finally allows Serote to work the content and theme of the poem into a confident climax that articulated the fundamental optimism that underlies all his passing despair:

> i can say
> i
> i have gone beyond the flood now
> i left the word on the flood
> it echoes
> in the depth the width
> i am beyond the flood
>
> i can say
> these eyes
> this water this river this flood
> washed me
> i can say
> one day the word will break[133]

The autobiography ends with the self absorbed into the flood, the poem's thematic image of water come to a crisis point.

The principal image of *Behold Mama, Flowers* – the road, footsteps, the path – is less omnipresent and used in a less unifying way than the leitmotif of the previous poem. It is difficult to say whether this is a formal issue – that Serote was beginning to make less use of repetition – or a content issue – that this poem covers a much wider spectrum, geographically, socially and politically, focusing beyond self and South Africa, on America, global racism, the pull of economic forces and political systems. Africa, perceived from another continent, becomes a much more complex organic force than the segment seen hitherto which gave him birth and nurtured him in bitterness. Perhaps all this serves to illustrate the irrelevance of western distinctions between form and content in the consideration of African writers.

Whatever the reason, the recurrences of the image are briefer and less developed. After the initial introduction

> how can i forget
> that i have never known where to go
> on the road of days to come[134]

there are often merely brief passing references to 'these journeys, long journeys'[135] or to 'footsteps'. Occasionally however he develops his theme:

> i can say
> while i watched
> while i heard
> i have had to walk so the road can whisper wisdom to me
> i can say
> i hope roads lead somewhere, nowhere leads to dreams
> about nightmares
> i walk
> i hide in shadows
> and i am always looking for a hole[136]

The psychological pressures of the black man's journey are brought out through the repetition of the walking, the hiding in shadows, the lack of a hole – all of which press home the restless wandering of the exile and the desolate sense of loss of protection and security. Yet it is the pressure of the environment that produced him, not the exile itself, which prevents him from walking with ease, forces him to walk like a man within shadows.[137] The fear in which they all live affects their very gait, twisting and distorting it into a death pose.[138]

In customary style Serote gives his images an independent existence through personification. Thus the footsteps themselves take on an identity and learn 'the sound of the thunder'[139] and the implications of the personification are extended from writer and subject to reader: 'walk the days we have left for you',[140] he urges the reader, and see for yourself. Though, like a western poet, Serote often draws his image from nature or the works of man, he humanises it, saturates it with people in a very un-western fashion: thus the road becomes footsteps, people walking and panicking and laughing:

> the road
> split and running into so many ways
> this road
> whose rhythmic air limps into a million frantic footsteps
> and broken wet laughters[141]

And Africa itself is seen to be walking:

> how far is the road, where are the paths
> ah
> africa, every moment, like an alcoholic
> walks back to its death[142]

Yet more often the continent is the security figure – the mother he has walked away from, whose hand he has clutched when lost and insecure:

> why have i walked many foreign plains and streets
> while my desires for you were tortuous
> i have seen many terrible nights come and go
> i have clutched your hand many times when i was lost in the
> streets whose names
> i could not pronounce
> africa
> i have had no choice but to walk from between your
> thighs[143]

And the image, extended, serves to account for the fear he is subject to – fear caused by the thought of his brothers erased by the system: they are the shadows he hides in and from:

> i walk
> i hide in shadows of erased faces
> i walk
> i hide in moving shadows

> and i have lost my hole
> here on the road[144]

Indeed, as the poem progresses the road is crowded with sacrifices
made in the long journey of the struggle:

> ah
> on the road, my brother
> shadows and shadows and shadows
> ah, moving shadows
> i can say
> to die is to leave or live when nothing is acceptable
> like you say, my brother
> that is another journey, those are blood-stained mile-
> stones[145]

The footsteps of those who have gone before are erased, their
bloodstains lost in the dust and yet 'hills are milestones'[146] and the
difficulties, though they cost dear, mark progress:

> for paths are made by time
> on the road
> in the mud whose earth was baked in napalm
> that is my present, your future[147]

Since the day Dingaan fell and Tshaka fell, his people have been
walking on the paths, leaving their bloodstains on the mountaintops
and trees, knowing the dregs of despair but secure in the knowledge
that the flowers, eventually, will bloom.

POEMS OF THE STRUGGLE

'If the we is the most of us'[148]

The point at which Serote began to substitute 'we' for 'i' as his most
commonly used pronoun is the point at which he grasped the need for a
common strategy, closely worked out and adhered to with discipline if
the liberation struggle was to become effective. And it is also the point
at which optimism takes over as the dominant note of the poetry –
which is not to say that despair and the old pessimistic images that
conveyed it suddenly disappear: the change is gradual, beginning

perhaps when a note of pessimistic determination creeps in:

> remember
> you ride the hour like death rides life[149]

he reminds his musician colleague and friend Jonas Gongwa, a fellow
exile with whom he shares common memories.

   In the process of this change from despair to optimism memory also
changes its function: originally that function was entirely destructive,
rendering Serote's subject (himself: the Black Man) impotent through
rage and frustration at all he and his race had to endure. He recalls its
destructive force in 'Exile' in his last collection, *The Night Keeps
Winking*, written in the quiet of exile in Botswana:

> here, the bad things I once said about memory
> come back
> memory is a thin red-hot membrane on the brain
> it vibrates all the time
> makes sounds
> rings and chimes
> and once
> when over-used, can shrivel like burning plastic[150]

By the time he comes to write 'Notes for a Fighter', however, a poem
dedicated to the sculptor Dumile Feni in 1975, he has recognised that
memory has the power not only to wound but also to fuel resolve.
Memories of specific incidents, particular failures, of waiting for
news that never came, have now become a people's strength, for in
spite of the fact that every footstep leaves a fresh wound, still 'we
move'[151] – a phrase that provides a persistent refrain – and all the
memories that remain provide the impetus for that movement. There
is a whole-hearted acceptance of all that the past entails: as he points
out in 'Shadows in Motion', written for Bra Zeke Mphahlele, the
damage, once done, can never be undone – when an eye is poked
out, all that is left is a hole that will never be the same again, a hole
that 'throbs and throbs with memory'.[152] Yet despite deformity, the
wounded body persists with its struggle against the oppressor: 'one
with one foot must move must still move'.[153] He brings out the
endurance that can survive even the worst damage when he reassures
prisoners in the South African jails in 'When Lights Go Out' that
'one day hope begins to walk again'.[154] He can speak from authority, having during his nine months of imprisonment without charge

under the Terrorism Act in 1968–9 experienced himself the

> ... heavy weight of every minute come followed by another
> and nothing
> even everything written in blood
> says nothing about how we could wake up tomorrow and
> build a day[155]

There is an inside knowledge here of the endless pressure of time and empty lives and the desolation and bitter memories that obsess the empty mind; and also of how hope slowly begins to grow at the nadir, when you are at your most hopeless:

> it is when there is no hope, that hope begins to walk
> again[156]

Historical consciousness

Many of his most recent poems are written in this vein, their main purpose and common theme being to encourage his comrades in the struggle: and the encouragement he gives never makes light of the suffering and despair already lived through, merely emphasises the power in all of them to endure, to outlive disaster and survive. In 'Heat and Sweat', written specifically for sisters and brothers who may be weary this message comes across especially powerfully:

> the present is surprised at our songs
> it is shocked that we still walk the streets the way we do
> lost as we are
> torn and bewildered by the sounds of our names
> and though the gait of our shadows seems to limp
> we still put brick on brick and tell our children stories[157]

The stories, the bricks out of which the struggle is built, are of course important: they enshrine the common memory and pass it down the generations – a vital historical process in any well-grounded liberation struggle.

While Serote understands the depth of their prostration, he strives to reassure them that it is still possible to carry on in spite of it:

> don't you hear the songs
> they can live in the present if we let them[158]

Here we touch on the essential function of art within a liberation struggle – and one is reminded of the flautists and singers on the Chinese Long March, playing and singing in the snow on the mountain tops to give heart to their comrades still climbing. And the poet attempts to infuse their weakness with the tenacity of determination:

> child
> feel the wall while you walk and hold, hold
> glue your eye into the distance and keep walking
> move, child, move
> if we don't get there
> nobody must . . . [159]

In that last line, 'nobody must', is detectable the gradual hardening of the heart against the oppressors, the determination to reach the goal whatever the cost, that accompanies the unconditional acceptance of the terms of the liberation struggle.

In 'There Will Be a Better Time' this hardening of the heart towards black betrayers and white oppressors – liars and 'those who take and take and take from others . . . for themselves alone', summarised in the line 'time has run out for those who ride on others'[160] – emerges as one of the two dominant themes of the poem. The other is the power of the group, the strength of the community even in the face of totalitarian power – a concept which he sees as being as important as the function of memory within the historical process, and which consequently he attempts to impress upon his reader with all the emphasis within his power:

> if the we is the most of us
> and the most of us is the will
> the will to say no . . .
> there will be a better time[161]

Together, the community can take charge of the historical process and become the instigators rather than the victims of fate: they can

> learn to carry the past
> like we do with dirty clothes
> carry them to the washing place and wash them[162]

The command of the historical process cannot however be achieved by corporate memory and co-operation between individuals alone: it needs to be founded upon accurate analysis of the situation that covers all its historical and political ramifications. In 'The Breezing Dawn of the New Day', such is his urge to clarify, explain and expand that he resorts on three occasions to prose, interrupting the flow of the verse for the sake of clarity of analysis. The imagery of the prose sections however maintains continuity with the verse sections – images of milestones (Isandlwana, Bulhoek, Sharpeville, Soweto) on the revolutionary road, of junctions at which those who know the way cannot be diverted but walk straight on. The range of his images throughout the poem – 'we keep the record', the road, the song, the building, brick on brick – all voice his historical perspective and reify liberation both in poetic and everyday-life terms, as a continuous process suffering from frequent setbacks but with a momentum of its own which renders its gradual progress inevitable. The poem also serves to define the past, themselves, the perimeters of the situation they inhabit, the struggle in which they are involved, the allies they must seek and the strategies they must maintain:

> we keep in our hands, as if a fresh hot coal from the fire
> our memory
> this is when we keep choosing the weapons
> and like a storm
> keeping calm before it emerges
> we gather force
> we *are* here
> betrayed by everything else but ourselves
> and our best ally is clarity about who we are
> where we come from
> who our enemy is
> where we want to go to
> and those begin to define our natural allies
> as we gather force
> as we create the storm[163]

Serote accepts very earnestly, in his later poems, his role as the mentor whose responsibility it is to ensure that his people, especially the young, know their history and accept the necessity of acting upon that knowledge: any evasion, either through frivolity or weakness, is unmasked as far more sinister than mere ignorance:

> on this earth in this time
> where politics is rules for a game called genocide

> my brother
> it is evil to be ignorant
> it is evil to walk without looking back
> we must know we have only one life
> it cannot be wasted in thirst, or death can be a way of saying
> things[164]

Events of the past are seen as links in the chain of struggle, and the young are reassured that 'like fathers and mothers we can build a day'.[165] Past traumas, by the mere fact of having been survived, provide them with confidence and identity:

> us
> a people with a long history of resistance[166]

And the gist of their lesson is that

> we did learn from terror that it is us who will seize history[167]

– a lesson re-iterated in 'There Will Be a Better Time', where he points out that they learn from bad times how to make time better.[168] Nowhere is there a more concise statement of Serote's political convictions about the twofold interlocking impact of time on people and of people on time, the inter-relationship between history and the group. Once this lesson has been absorbed, terror can no longer leave people paralysed into passivity like a sheep in the mouth of a crocodile,[169] for now 'we know that we will move'.

Formal resolution

As Serote becomes increasingly clear in his poetic aims, so do the formal and stylistic methods he employs to achieve them. In this latest group of poems published at the end of *Selected Poems* and in *The Night Keeps Winking* – all of which were written during his exile in Botswana – there is a parallel between the shift in focus (from the black individual in South Africa and the victim of global racism and oppression to the issues of the South African liberation struggle) and the change in form. The earlier forms, suited to self-expression (the short lyric) and self-examination (the long autobiographical poems) are exchanged for the didactic exhortatory form specifically addressed to black South African youth participating in the struggle. Undoubtedly a major factor in this change was the uprising by the youth of Soweto in 1976 – after which these young people came to be seen by Serote and many of his peers as the major thrust of the movement. In these poems he speaks as teacher, expounding lessons as important for himself as for his readers – hence the pronoun 'we' indicative of his non-hierarchical stance. Mzamane refers to these poems collectively as the Soweto poems, but I do not think this is a limiting code, rather it views Soweto as a generative function, not a single historical event.

The imagery Serote draws on in these later poems upholds his object of instilling determination and maintaining hope and strength of purpose. This is achieved not by a change of source but by a complete recreation of signification: the natural world – always a major source of images – is no longer saturated, as it was in the early poems with the guilt of the oppressors, no longer a participator in the process of victimisation, universalising both action and reaction, but has now become an ally, a participator in the struggle: the night, previously always a place and a time of terror for the lost and alienated individual, now gives shelter and protection to the guerrilla groups that are working for the 'better time'; the sun, the moon, the stars, the earth, the water, the trees and the mountains throw off the stains of their guilt and affirm instead the justice of the people's cause. Growth, seasons and tides provide his ideology of resistance with its foundation stones. The symbols remain constant but their referents have changed.

And through his initial forays and his extensive explorations, Serote has finally reached the point where he can force words to carry the burden of his message, to make them communicate to his readers those truths that have burnt themselves into his bones about living and being black in South Africa.

For him, the word, both spoken and written, has had such crucial importance, has carried such power, has caused such pain, that the poet, the writer, the man of words has become a literal creator in the pattern of world history:

> i am the one who has to build this world out of dust
> i have to clutch the wound of the trees and birds
> tame the snakes and make a path . . . [170]

he had declared in *No Baby Must Weep*. Through words, the poet creates the world all over again; through words the legislators can destroy it – 'the word of a merciless civilisation'.[171] Without words a person is powerless, a whole people are powerless – they have no way to prevent the misinterpretation of their silence, no way of making their protest. Such people go as ' . . . lumumba went, the way of speechless people'.[172] Yet, through it all, he has maintained a faith in his own and his people's power, finally, to attain the power of the word (in the sense of St John's 'logos'):

> i left the word on the flood
> it echoes . . .
> one day the word will break[173]

he had prophesied in *No Baby Must Weep*, and when he comes to the poems in his final collection, he has discovered the ultimate power of the word:

> we did amazing things to say simple things
> we are human and this is our land[174]

And the power of the word is one with the power of silence – the silence that has waited, conceded, till the time when the seed must pierce the earth. Word and act have become one: poetic form resolves itself in historical action – 'no more is not a word but an act, remember that.'[175]

Serote has finally solved Sartre's life-long puzzle, and located the poet and the word in the eye of the storm. Two lines in 'Time Has Run Out' indicate his vision of the place of poetry within culture, and the place of culture within history: in expressing his poetic creed he summarises his beliefs about all the subject matter of his writing:

> we must now claim our land, even if we die in the process,
> Our history is a culture of resistance.[176]

5 The Literature of Combat

INTRODUCTION

One of the products of the Black Consciousness Movement, in addition to its establishment of a black identity in South Africa, was a consciousness of the ideological function of literature in maintaining the hegemony of the ruling group in the society – a consciousness, that is, not among professional critics and theorists, but among the writers themselves. Black writers, by their questionings and experiments with form and genre, were able to lay bare the naturalising processes at work in accepted literary forms and genres (usually of western derivation) which contributed to their people's subjugation, and to establish a search for alternatives that would counteract the cultural onslaught of white domination and serve the evolution of an ideology geared to the needs and aims of a black proletariat and rural population.

We have seen in an earlier chapter how poetry has become a vehicle for this ideology, but in recent years black writers, some of them established poets, have felt the need to develop an extended prose genre that would relate the narrative of their people's struggle. Their efforts have resulted in a new kind of novel which I have loosely termed the literature of combat. For it is a narrative form that aims not merely at historical and social documentation, but also at bringing about a movement towards commitment on the part of the readers. I have used the term 'autobiography' to describe it, despite the inappropriateness of 'auto', for it remains the most precise classification available. 'The writing of one's own history; the story of one's life written by himself' is the Oxford Dictionary's definition of autobiography. And indeed these novels are the history or the life of a people, written by themselves. They are part of the process of conscientisation in which black South Africans seize hold of their history and make it their own. The books differ from autobiographies only in that they document the development of a group, and the search for identity of the whole body of the people, rather than the individualistic struggle for self-realisation that has characterised western literary autobiography and its fictional extension, the autobiographical novel.

Miriam Tlali in *Amandla* (1980), Sipho Sepamla in *A Ride on the Whirlwind* (1981), Mongane Serote in *To Every Birth Its Blood* (1981) and Mbulelo Mzamane in *The Children of Soweto* (1982) have all attempted to give form to the escalation of the liberation movement in the seventies, and to convey to their readers the dynamics of the corporate effort involved.

THE EARLY PROTEST NOVELS

In order to assess the degree to which these four novelists have succeeded in the tasks they set themselves, it is necessary first to look briefly at earlier writers adhering to the more conventional western literary forms. For the novelists of the eighties are not the first South African writers to deal with themes of struggle and revolution. Peter Abrahams in *A Wreath for Udomo* (1956), Richard Rive in *Emergency* (1964) and Alex La Guma in *In the Fog of the Season's End* (1972) had each taken this as their subject matter in earlier decades. But the traditional novel form they adopted tended to impede their message and limit the transformation of consciousness of their readership.

In Abrahams' *A Wreath for Udomo* the central action takes place in a fictional neighbouring country where independence from colonial rule is sought and gained, whereas direct concern with the South African situation is confined to the support given to David Mhendi in his establishment of a base camp on the borders of Pluralia (South Africa) and the forays of Mhendi's guerrillas into the country – together with Udomo's ultimate politically-motivated betrayal of his old friend and the cause Mhendi serves. But the approach to revolution and political change characteristic of Udomo in his country may be taken as manifesting Abrahams' general political attitudes and may go some way to explain his abortive relationship with the South African Communist Party. For his political apprehension is essentially liberal and élitist. His African political leaders in exile in London are all intellectuals, separated by culture and interests as much as by geography and exile from the masses in their respective countries. They have been isolated from the African working classes and the peasants and rural workers by their western education and by the cultural set which this has given them. They are not only divorced from their fellow countrymen by the language they speak, the ideas that engross them and the values they have internalised, but they have reached a stage where they are unable to communicate with them except from the platform of a political meeting: any natural interaction with ordinary people has been forestalled. This is very apparent in the absence of any representatives of the mass of the population from the novel, except as a shouting mob providing crowd scenes for the personality cult. Udomo is conceived of as an old style Great Leader after the fashion of Napoleon or Hitler (I write of *styles* of leadership, not politics here) or Stalin, manipulating the masses in the interests of individual political strategies, and facing moral crises on an individual scale as one man striving to maintain his own integrity rather than as a member of an entire population attempting to establish a common identity and to reach a common goal.

Although Abrahams makes his own comment on this route to revolution in the sad, cynical ending to the novel – Udomo's death at the hands of his political enemies despite the sacrifice of his own integrity earlier in the novel to try to secure the economic survival of his country – the novel nevertheless subscribes to the bourgeois ethic it criticises. For it makes the criticism within the framework of the ideology it manifests (an ideology which indeed encourages the expression of such criticism as a way of containing it), in the genre (the realistic novel) which was developed out of that ideology, and which the novel helps in turn to perpetrate through its style and the values it propounds. Udomo is a typical hero of the novel form developed out of the ideological framework of capitalism: the title of the book establishes his pre-eminence; his country and its struggle for liberation is part of the fabric of his quest for identity; his personal relationships – with Lois, his lover, and with his friends, Mhendi, Adebhoy and Selina – dominate the novel, so it is with personal fates that the reader identifies, and with individual moral crises. The character weaknesses of Udomo are expressed in terms of a love relationship, and those of Adebhoy and Selina in terms of friendship. Thus individual fates, far from being subordinated to the struggle, ultimately dominate it entirely. And just as the form of the novel is worked out in terms of one man's struggle to balance political imperatives against personal integrity, so the style is the straightforward lucid narrative of critical realism developed by nineteenth-century English novelists.

Richard Rive, in *Emergency*, takes the South African struggle itself for his subject matter, and adopts a straightforward news report-type narrative framework for his presentation of the events of 1960 in Langa and Cape Town during the campaign against the pass laws (the

'Sharpeville' of the south). Though Rive avoids the romanticising myth-making pitfalls of Abrahams' fictional subject matter, nevertheless he carries over his predecessor's concentration on the psychological development of the individual hero. The historical and social context of the novel; the march on Cape Town on 28 March, the strike on the 29th, the protest march against the arrests on 30 March, the declaration of the State of Emergency and the resumé of the history of the liberation struggle, all function as a backcloth against which Andrew Dreyer can work back over his childhood and youth, search out his political orientation and identify his priorities.

Consequently there is no conflict between the traditional novel framework Rive adopts and the work's thematic significance. Where the problem (that is the *literary* problem) does arise is in the long didactic passages where Abe, Braam and Andrew hold long discussions on the issues at stake. Not only does Rive fail to evolve a sufficiently realistic dialogue – his characters speaking like university essays rather than heated human beings – but the discussions are intrusive and insufficiently related to the action of the novel to be accepted naturally by the reader. Hence they impede rather than push forward the functioning of the text as an instrument of the struggle, focusing the reader's attention on one character and his ethical dilemma rather than on the progress of the struggle. The literary conventions he adopts, though they may inhibit the novel's contribution to the struggle, nevertheless nicely convey the liberal education of the writer and his own hesitations concerning total commitment.

Alex La Guma, writing as a committed, active (rather than former) communist, out of the experience of a political activist inside his own country and outside it in exile, goes some way to detach himself from these ideological conventions. In his novel *In the Fog of the Season's End* there is a genuine attempt to eradicate the personality cult and the notion of the heroic leader figure. The revolution he depicts is not a heroic epic of platforms and seething masses, romantic imprisonments and popular deliriums, but a silent back-street affair of secret assignments, dreary trudging about with leaflets, and a constant haunting fear of detection, betrayal, and the repulsive and shameful realism of the torture cells. His main characters, Beukes, Tekwane and Isaac, are drained of much of their individuality in the interests of their functions as revolutionary units. La Guma is much too skilful a writer to present them as cardboard stereotypes, mouthpieces for didacticism and propaganda. The reader is always in full possession of their humanity, of their placement in a network of relationships – Beukes with his wife and child, Tekwane with his widowed mother, Isaac, more superficially, with his workmates – but this is all background detail in a way in which Udomo's relationship with Lois never is. Background in terms of the subject matter, in that these networks are only mentioned fairly briefly, but background also in terms of characterisation, for all these men have deliberately cut themselves off from connections in order to dedicate themselves entirely to their political activities, free from the distraction of domestic demands. (The impossibility of reconciling the two is emphasised in the presentation of Bennett, distracted from the simplest obligations by a demanding wife and his own fears for the safety of his family.)

Yet for all their single-minded dedication, none of these figures emerges as the romantic hero of the revolution: theirs is a drab and unexciting struggle, with little prospect of early success and no possibility of individual glory or power. La Guma underlines this subordination of the individual to a cause most emphatically in his account of the day of the strike, where he picks out various symbolic figures and charts their normal daily activity: the Washerwoman, the Bicycle Messenger, the Outlaw, the Child, to emphasise the outrageous cruelty of their deaths at the hands of the police, among the crowd gathered outside the Police Station. La Guma not merely makes no effort to conceal the artificiality of his literary device here, but actually stresses it typographically by his use of capital letters. For these four are more significant as representatives of their people, oppressed to the point of senseless obliteration, than they could ever be as individuals.

This combination of diverse stylistic devices reveals the extent of La Guma's literary skills enabling him to present the social and objective historical significance of events without divorcing his main characters from everyday reality or humanity. If he had attempted to individualise the victims of police brutality on the day of the strike it would have confused the reader and blurred the dialectical message: but if he had attempted to subordinate the characterisation of his main figures to his dialectics it would have emptied his message of all power to evoke a response from the reader. Beukes, Tekwane and Isaac are cogs in the machine of the movement, but they are sentient cogs, feeling not only in their capacities as functionaries, but also in their individual conscious-ness, the bruises suffered by the movement as a result of organised repression. And their attempts to try to heal the breaches, to put things together again so that the party can function, are attempts to heal their own psyches and find mechanisms to deal with their own hurts and fears. They work like moles in the dark, groping blindly, but testing each move, each contact first.

Yet despite La Guma's conscious efforts to introduce new literary devices tailored to his revolutionary theme, the novel's essential structure, its formal embodiment of the content, remains firmly situated in the mainstream of western literary tradition. The revolution in values has not yet transformed the genre. Western readers may perhaps be made uneasy by certain aspects of the novel – the absence of a search for identity on the part of the nominal hero, Beukes, or of any significant relationships between individuals which develop in the course of the story – but they are reassured by the conventional literary style (skilfully adapted though it may be, by its sparseness, to the impersonal nature of the message) and by the observance of such formal conventions as unity of plot, time and place (stressed by the recurrent newspaper headlines about the murder) and narrative devices.

But perhaps the novel's principal connection with the literary traditions of the West lies in its perspective rather than in any specific conventions employed by the author: in its presentation of its characters as isolated individuals. This perspective is so endemic to the bourgeois novel tradition as to undermine the foundations of La Guma's effort to devise a new literary form for his revolutionary content. For in spite of the socialist principles which inform his content, his message and his theme, there is no integration of social groups. Though all the characters we meet are in fact involved in cells and all their action in the novel is a result of the interaction of the members of the cells, we are never presented with these underlying relationships. Instead we see Beukes, Tekwane and Isaac functioning against a background of other people – Tommy, the men in the hostel, the office servants – but never interacting with them in significant action (i.e. action contributing to the development of the plot). The revolutionaries act alone, obeying instructions, and all contacts with outsiders are consequently drained of any vitality and reduced to casual encounters. This is taking things one stage further than the traditional bourgeois novelists, for they at least showed their individuals inter-relating with other individuals, and indeed much of the interest of these novels depends on the development of such inter-relationships and their significance as contributions to the character development of the principal figures.

There are several reasons for the isolation of La Guma's characters, both in terms of the literary work and in terms of the social context of the writer himself. La Guma is deliberately trying to convey the operations of a movement condemned to operate in secret, conditions which inevitably import isolation into procedures. But a liberation movement need not necessarily function in this way: Tlali, Mzamane,

Sepamla and Serote have a very different perspective and present closely related groups of individuals interacting and giving mutual support and indeed carrying out most operations in small groups most of the time. This may well have something to do with the condition of the liberation movement itself after the repressive blows it suffered in the early sixties (whereas in the eighties it had slowly built up strength and confidence, established its networks and perhaps changed its procedures). But it also has to do with the backgrounds of the writers.

La Guma, as a coloured, was subjected to a much more severely alienating upbringing than was usual for the African population. He was much more severely pressurised by western values within his own racial group, a great many of whom were more concerned with upward mobility than with community solidarity. Though Africans are also subjected to western education, an alien language and all the cultural and ethical values involved here, they gain some strength from very close-knit communities which not only have a long tradition of social co-operation but none of their members have anything to gain individually from attempts to identify with white behaviour patterns or white culture. Hence socially conscious coloured writers, who reject white-identification, tend to lack the community support available to their fellow black African writers. This is very obvious not only from the *content* of their writing, which tends to be more individualistic, but also from the styles and forms they adopt, which are much more closely based on the cultural traditions in which they have been so much more saturated than purely African writers. This is a pattern which crosses genre boundaries: Brutus and Nortje, as well as writers like Bessie Head, Richard Rive, and La Guma are equally isolationist and individualistic in approach. Thus a conflict is set up within their literary works: their absorption into a culture with which they are ideologically out of sympathy has insidious control over their artistic functioning.

FROM LIBERALISM TO LIBERATION

The novel in the eighties

The novelists of the eighties who undertook the literary documentation of the Soweto uprising escape from this ideological trap, not only through the strong support of their community but also as a consequence of the Black Consciousness Movement, an advantage they have, by virtue of their age and their geographical location in the black townships, over the three older novelists. (The way the coloured person is cut off from the black townships and the political ferment within them is well illustrated by the movements of the coloured hero of *Emergency*, Andrew Dreyer, between his respectable coloured suburb and Langa, which he enters illegally, through the fence. He is alienated from those to whom he is handing out leaflets. When the police arrive, he and his friend escape back to their own sections of the town, and although they face life on the run, they are not confined to the dual imprisonment of the black: imprisonment within the fenced-in location where he is permanently exposed to the risk of a further stage of detention in the prison cell.)

For the writers of the late seventies and eighties, the movement raised consciousness not only of identity, in its psychological operations, but also of cultural imperatives, among which was the need for new literary forms to carry the burden of literature's specific function within the movement, and finally, consciousness of a new audience for whose sake these forms were to operate.

Even before the introduction of Bantu Education black African writers had, as a rule, been much less drawn into involvement in western culture than other groups in the country, both because the education they had available to them was often inferior and because their own communities provided social, cultural and ethical values of their own. (There were exceptions like Ezekiel Mphahlele who became deeply soaked in English and American literature, but his opportunities were rare among the black community.) Coloured communities on the other hand provided no indigenous culture and all upwardly mobile individuals modelled themselves on white society. Thus even those Africans such as Sepamla who, by virtue of their age, were exposed to more of a western education, had sufficient community support to remain essentially African in outlook. They lacked the aesthetic convictions of established western traditions that inhibited approaches to the creation of a new form in the earlier novelists mentioned.

This is not to say that the creation of a new form was easy or that their efforts were instantly successful. There was, before 1976, a general feeling of the need for some socio-historical literary genre to document the stages in the struggle against apartheid: indeed Rive's and La Guma's works were efforts to fill this gap. But both these writers were in effect documenting from the outside, from a community on the fringes of the action (at that stage of the liberation struggle) and, in La Guma's case, ultimately from exile. It was only after the Soweto uprising that members of the African community began to speak out, and there are interesting formal similarities between the works they produce.

All of them focus on a group of people and abandon the western commitment to a single hero or heroine within the group of characters whose search for identity constitutes the theme of the novel. Even Sepamla's novel, which perhaps takes Mzi as its central character in western fashion, does not resolve itself around the young guerrilla's development but around the action in which he is involved. There are two main reasons for this shift. One is that the movement has, over the years, eliminated the concept of the individualistic leader and the impression given in all the books is one of a non-hierarchical organisational structure where individuals have the power of their function rather than operating by personal charisma and unilateral manipulations. Another is that the concern of all these novels is to show the development of political action rather than the development of character, and the action they are concerned with is essentially corporate and communal, unlike the isolated operations of Beukes and his peers in *In the Fog of the Season's End*. That is to say that whereas a western novel investigates social inter-relationship for its own sake, as an end in itself, the liberation novels of the eighties, though they pay as much attention, if not more, to this aspect of life, being in any case products of a much more community-oriented society, look for something beyond relationships – that is for the corporate functioning of families and friends within the liberation struggle. The struggle itself takes over, as it were, the role of the hero, and it is *its* development, rather than that of any particular person, with which we are concerned. This is perhaps the most radical structural change that has been effected in the recent black novels of liberation.

It is perhaps significant that it is a change which has not reached out to white novels, even though the novels of such writers as Gordimer and Brink have accepted the need for Africanisation, the need to set their novels in terms of the same struggle. For in their novels it is still the experiences of the individual within the struggle with which we are concerned – Maureen's difficulties in adapting to the tribal village, tribal values and tribal culture of her servant July in Nadine Gordimer's *July's People* (an interesting reversal of the Jim-comes-to-Joburg novels) and Ben's lonely pitching of himself against the forces of oppression in an effort to uphold the liberal ideology and faith in good intentions in André Brink's *A Dry White Season*.

This community focus in the black novels of the eighties is essential to set forth the guerrilla strategy of moving among the people like a fish in water. Indeed it is something closer than the relationship between fish and water, in the South African situation, for there is an elemental identity between the guerrillas and the society they move in – for the liberation fighters live with and are sheltered by their own families and friends, not merely by sympathetic township folk. The bonds between them are actual bonds of kinship or friendship, not merely bonds of identity of cause. Thus that support so essential for the survival of a revolutionary movement is provided by the very people most committed, by nature, to giving it.

This prominence of the community in turn makes another formal demand upon the novels: for so much of the burden of these novels has to be carried in the dialogue, since what is communicated between people provides the essence of the novel. In the conventional western novel, it is possible for straightforward narrative to carry much of the load if the writer happens to lack a talent for dialogue. But in the liberation novels the subject matter demands dramatic presentation of social interaction – a demand easily met by those writers who have a talent for capturing in English the speech rhythms of the mixed vernaculars of the townships, but one which can destroy the impact of a work if the writer has not such talent. For stiff and formal conversations can negate the force of any other literary device employed to convey the qualities of relationships.

Accepting the struggle as the determinant of literary method also brings the need for a different kind of unity within the novels. The original unities of time, place and action which have dominated western literature for so long (though admittedly each author has manufactured his or her own interpretation of the demands) have now become to some extent redundant in South Africa, for the dimensions of the struggle itself have taken over. Unity of time is imposed by the duration of the struggle itself, and those novels succeed best which manage to integrate the historical dimensions of the struggle (that is, back through time and also forward into the future) with the risings that form their particular subject matter. Unity of space is achieved by confining the places to the theatres of operation – but these can cover a great many places in South Africa itself, and extend to surrounding countries. Unity of action is imposed by the subordination of all activities to a central end. In a very real way here, life has taken over from literature and begun to dictate literary conventions and questions of style and form.

Plot construction has also been subordinated to the dynamics of political action. Hence the failure of Sepamla's attempt to impose a unified plot in *A Ride on the Whirlwind* in the classic novel tradition. It makes the action seem artificial and as a consequence hinders the functional impact of the work upon the reader. Other novelists such as Tlali succeed in avoiding this pitfall but then run into difficulties over cohesion of action as a consequence.

These new literary dynamics also obliterate the writer's freedom to impose a conventional ending on the novel: for the struggle, so far, has no end, and this fact turns each novel into an episode in a serial. Yet writers are left with the need to find some sort of artistic solution that will enable them to avoid leaving their readers frustrated and irritated at the end of the novel, while conveying to them the reality of the situation about which they have been reading.

Indeed the whole relationship of writer to reader, and literary work to reader has changed for South African liberation writers. While the bourgeois novel strove to educate the sensibilities, to make the reader more aware of the sensibilities of others, and to give more understanding about relationships, the liberation novel assumes this awareness as pre-existent and goes on to educate the political awareness of the readers, help them to understand the mechanisms of community action, and to deepen their commitment to a common cause. This is yet another modifier of literary methods, for the writer's aim is a very precise and specific one: it is easy enough, using the conventional methods of the West, to produce a work that so manipulates the readers as to fire up their enthusiasm to the point where, as soon as they have put the book aside, they rush out to join the struggle. But this is hardly the kind of recruit the movement would welcome, or who would prove useful. What the writers must rather do is to find literary techniques that will enable them to take the readers through a slow process of consciousness-raising, and leave the momentum of the struggle itself to complete the task for them. They are attempting to bring about the readers' inner growth so that they are able to re-identify themselves in positive, optimistic and active terms, rather than in the old negative, pessimistic and passive ones.

Obviously these new critical perceptions did not all come at once: there was no definite turning point; no theoretical deliberation concerning the direction of the new novel, with instructions from the party (as there was, for example, at times in revolutions under the direction of a very homogeneous political party such as, for example, in pre-liberation China). They emerged fitfully and hesitantly, out of practical discourse between writers who for personal and social, as well as ideological reasons, work together more closely than is usual for writers in less pressing circumstances. (Though political and geographical conditions have put severe restraints on the meetings of some of the four novelists involved in this study.) Nevertheless, it is possible to trace a general literary development in the course of the four novels, as they each grope towards a more appropriate form for their new content.

Miriam Tlali: *Amandla*

All four novels, Miriam Tlali's *Amandla*, Sipho Sepamla's *A Ride on the Whirlwind*, Mbulelo Mzamane's *Children of Soweto* and Mongane Serote's *To Every Birth Its Blood*, take the Soweto uprising as their core material. The novelists are responding to the need experienced by the whole writing community and voiced by Nadine Gordimer[1] to set down the history which they and their community are involved in making.

Setting down a liberation struggle in the making presents writers immediately with problems of perspective. The struggle, clandestine perforce and inevitably confused, not a phenomenon easily analysed and ordered, yields up a mine of bewildering material for writers who, themselves immersed in the centre of the whirlwind, are unable to make the neat artistic detachment of plot or theme and objective viewpoint customarily demanded by the western bourgeois novel form, even if they were to consider such a form suitable to their purpose.

One possible consequence of all this, and certainly a consequence evident in Miriam Tlali's novel, is a very confused literary product. *Amandla* certainly captures the immediacy of events and draws the reader into the confused apprehensions which must be the lot of many of the participants in such a period of social turmoil. She allows the reader to stumble on events, on connections between characters and on sequences of cause and effect in much the same state of bewildered ignorance as must have been the lot of many of the citizens of Soweto. This could have welded itself into a brilliant artistic play to draw the reader into significant experience of the action of the novel. But somehow it never does: it remains accident rather than design. The writer's rejection of western structural devices may have been as deliberate as it was necessary, nevertheless the confusion of the action merely seems to reflect a confusion in the mind of the writer which is never resolved. It may be that the black South African reader, familiar with township relationships and interconnections, is less at a disadvantage here than the western reader. And, after all, the novel is aimed at the black South African reader. However, there seems a low level of organisational awareness even on the part of the central characters, though their prototypes in the real event obviously constructed some loose organisational framework to control their activities and their destiny as much as they could in the teeth of accelerating events. Thus even for the black South African reader there is a failure to transmit an important element of revolutionary consciousness.

The novel opens with Sipho bringing news of the arrival of 'the terrorists' (a term which is not allowed to pass without discussion) to his friends Pholoso and Felleng (Pholoso's girlfriend). The 'terrorist's' confrontation with the army and the police took place on 29 April 1975. The friends' initial jubilation swiftly gives way to a grim realisation of the reality of the situation as Pholoso staggers back wounded and grieving over the death of their comrade Dumisani. He takes refuge at the house of 'T' Moremi. This quickened pace is maintained by an account of the simultaneous burning of municipality offices throughout Soweto, while the chorus of 'Power! Amandla!' chanted by the youths closes each narrative.

Time passes imperceptibly till by the tenth chapter (one third of the way through) the novel is looking back from the perspective of 16 June 1976, and the young students are living as fugitives secretly shifting from place to place in disguise to escape the police.

The action in which they are engaged is presented in a very fractured and disjointed fashion. The funeral, which in Mzamane focuses an entire book, though it gives the students a platform, is the last integrative piece of action. The following underground meeting puts forward no campaign plan but degenerates into a naïve discussion of codes, invisible inks and utopian vagaries about education. There are interludes of discussion between the elders which provide an opportunity to put forward a mass of background details and to sketch the general political scene: the grievances of Bantu Education, the Unity Movement, the Ten Point Programme, the Liberal Party, the Committee of Ten. Yet Tlali provides no peg to hang these on – as Mzamane and Serote do when they use a particular character to evoke certain stories or sketches of certain institutions.

Tlali uses the relationships of certain characters to introduce various themes – such as the triangular affair between Sergeant Mamabola's young wife Teresa and the young policeman Nicodemus who is in turn involved with Seipei, which brings in the questions of collaboration and betrayal and the measures taken by the young revolutionaries to deal with such problems.

The detention of Pholoso and his friends gives her the chance to describe the brutal ill-treatment of the prisoners and the methods of torture, and she combines Pholoso's escape with a description of the Zulu riots.

Tlali's problem arises from this attempt to incorporate, erratically, too much historical and political material in her framework. Instead of selecting a small number of events and limiting her historical and political explanation of these to what the situations themselves make necessary, she allows herself to be seduced into making comprehensive surveys and using situations as an excuse for serving them up to the reader. Thus Agnes and Joe's broken marriage or Gramsy's unveiling ceremony and illness are not the genuine focus of the women's gossip, but merely pretexts to introduce information about the students' campaign against alcohol, the arrests of the children or the enforcement of the 'Black Christmas' period of mourning and austerity. And the feast after the unveiling is merely a vehicle for a general discussion that ranges at length and at random from the problem of strategy and the Unity Movement to the white creation of a black middle class, from missionaries and capitalism to the notion that 'we are all guilty of collaborating with the system',[2] from an exposition of the revolutionary theory of non-collaboration based on the Ten Point Programme to the roles of multinationals, western countries, women and the food-growing programme.

The plot is belatedly resuscitated with the killing of the two policemen, Mamabolo and Nicodemus, before action is once again subordinated to hearsay in the account of Seipei's betrayal of Sipho and his and 'T' Moremi's imprisonment. The novel concludes with the death of Gramsy and the escape of Pholoso over the border – both of which events could have effected a successful resolution for the reader had either character had a more significant role, rather than appearing as one of many passive leaves blown hither and thither by the wind of events.

The work's ultimate flimsiness rests on this tendency to clothe ideas and information in situations, instead of the other way around, and in the absolute absence of any sense that the characters are a people in charge of their own destiny.

Sipho Sepamla: *A Ride on the Whirlwind*

Sipho Sepamla would appear to avoid all the pitfalls of over-diffusion by selecting a single hero and a single chain of events, though as we shall see, this in turn creates other problems. By focusing on the hero's mission – the elimination of the traitor policeman Batata – he achieves a very western unity of plot and a very tight control of his material. The other actors are all subordinated to Mzi's central action: although the schoolchildren have their own involvement and commitments, and indeed only Mandla and later, to a certain extent, Roy, have anything to do with Mzi and his mission, their doings are only recorded in so far as they relate to this central action.

Mzi's mission is introduced in the first pages, as he returns from guerrilla training abroad with very precise instructions about his task. His return is timed to coincide with what is disparagingly referred to as 'the children's revolution', so that advantage could be taken of the disorganisation incurred by it. Mzi's Soweto contact is an old revolutionary, Uncle Ribs, who is also connected with the group of young people at the centre of the uprising, and he introduces Mzi to Mandla, their leader. When Mandla begins to collaborate with Mzi it is the first time he has acted independently of the group, and this has its repercussion on the group's democratic system of organisation by discussion. They are immediately suspicious of such unilateral involvement, feel that they have no credentials for Mzi and therefore no way of telling whether or not he is working for the system, and resent Mandla's unilateral involvement which threatens their pattern of collective leadership.

With Mzi and Mandla's bombing of the police station, the pace quickens and simultaneously the police net begins to close in: with a permanent police watch on Mandla's home, a price on his head and the ever-closer attentions of informers like Noah Witjie, Mzi, Mandla and the student group are increasingly at risk. Mandla's injury after he and Mzi are stopped by the police and escape is only a mild foretaste. Keke's indisciplined accidental explosion at Sis Ida's house, where all the students are living, leads to the arrest of Sis Ida and the entire group except for Sello and Don Montsho who escape.

A pattern of interrogation, torture and attempted bribery and trickery develops as the police attempt to get closer on the trail of Mandla. (They do not know about Mzi, who is in none of their records.) Yet the student group are not without their sympathisers, even among the police ranks, and Sergeant Ndlovu gives forewarning of Uncle Ribs's impending arrest, enabling him to escape to Botswana. The bombing of Batata's house and Mandla's killing of Sergeant Rampa in mistake for Batata increase the police pressure even further. Gradually all that remain of the group are dispersed: Don Montsho and Sello follow Uncle Ribs to Botswana, and are followed in turn by Ribs's wife, Sis Joyce, and finally by Mandla; and after accomplishing his mission by killing Batata, Mzi himself makes for Swaziland.

This tight plot and tempered form enables us to 'read' the situation in Soweto in a way that Tlali's more confused account does not. But once again one has to pause and ask *whose* reading is facilitated? The international white readers' or the South African blacks'? It may well be that for the product of Bantu Education, untrained in western literary conventions, the convolutions of *Amandla* are as accessible as the elegant simplicity of *A Ride on the Whirlwind*. Moreover the price of

Sepamla's elegance is reductionism: his novel gives a simple, almost naïve account of an incredibly complex situation, and in doing so falsifies reality by turning the material of history and indeed tragedy into a sophisticated form of light entertainment – a 'good read', an action-packed novel of adventure and suspense.

Moreover the formal restrictions intervene in the actual content of the novel. The emasculation of the student group (they carry out no operations in the novel, and their only significant action is Keke's accident which leads to their discovery by the police) is not merely a matter of the author wishing to concentrate attention upon Mzi the guerrilla, but is also a function of the form. Were they to be active in the novel, the formal pattern would be broken and the uncompromising drive of the plot towards the elimination of Batata would be blurred. As if to emphasise this single fixed purpose, the students are not merely deprived of significant action within the plot, but actually literally *put out of action* as one of the inevitable results of Mzi's and Mandla's attempts upon the policeman. For suspicion falls upon them and they are hauled in to be interrogated and tortured concerning acts in which they played no part. Roy's death in the torture cell is the ultimate stage of this metaphorical obliteration.

This brings us to the fundamental weakness of Sepamla's novel as a record of the struggle. For it is not a record of the people's struggle – the communal contribution by the great majority of the populace to the overthrow of a system which oppresses them. In *A Ride on the Whirlwind* it is the rider and not the whirlwind of which we are conscious: we see, not the people making their own revolution, as they do in Mzamane's or Serote's novels, or even, confusedly, in Tlali's, but the people having it made for them by an outside agent, trained and instructed by outsiders to carry out an assignment among people who know him as little as he knows them. It might be argued that this is merely a question of perspective: that in fact Sepamla merely happens to be focusing on a single facet of the struggle that happens to be in the hands of a stranger. Yet Sepamla was under no compulsion to make this choice, and therefore must be held responsible for its implications. Moreover the reactions of the characters do not permit of this interpretation. From the outset there is unease and distrust among the Sowetans: Uncle Ribs is irritated by the brash insensitivity and the arrogant recklessness of the freedom fighter; the student group never wholly accept him, suspecting him as an imposter, or resenting his usurpation of their initiative. All the characters indeed except Mandla are reduced from participants to spectators upon Mzi's arrival. They are acted upon by their saviour as much as by their oppressors, and reduced to passivity instead of reifying themselves by their actions as black consciousness required.

I would suggest that this malaise is a consequence of an attempt to conform to western plot structure. And indeed Sepamla shows his consciousness of the displacement effect in the group's discussions of Mzi and his part in the struggle. But it all remains at the level of discussion, there is never any resolution in action. Sepamla is evidently uneasy with the formal resolution he has chosen, but nevertheless he carries it through to the end and so commits himself to the western tradition with all that it implies.

Another aspect of the novel which contributes towards its failure to establish African revolutionary form is the weakness of the dialogue which might otherwise have served to establish group dynamics. Occasionally, as in the shopkeeper Tandabantu's recital to Sis Ida of the police search for his missing son, with its repetitive narrative and vigorous idioms, Sepamla strikes an authentic note:

> ' . . . They wanted to know the whereabouts of Fanyana. They said I should know, I am his father. They said I've hidden him. Tell me, where can I hide a child as big as Fanyana, a whole eighteen-year-old? They poured salt into my body wound, that's what they did, accusing me of lies. They have no shame, humiliating me and threatening me as they did in full view of my customers. Thixo uyazi, if I had a gun I would have died with one of them today. Never in my whole life have I been called a liar. By amakhwenkwe – boys! Raa!'
> 'Shame on them, tata!'
> 'What should I have said? I know where he's gone to when I didn't? Did they expect me to shit him out? Raa! These dogs!'[3]

Yet when it comes to the language of the struggle itself, Sepamla's dialogue is curiously flat and deadening. There is an awkwardness, a lack of power and a dinginess of metaphor in, for example, Uncle Ribs's pronouncements, as though he is reciting a speech written by someone else and imperfectly committed to memory:

> This moment gives birth this minute to a marriage of convenience, a marriage destined to change the course of history in the country. God knows brothers we shall take the fight into the enemy's camp. An eye for an eye; a tooth for a tooth. I shudder to think of the outcome of this marriage.[4]

It is difficult to account for the contrast between the dynamism of the first speech and the vapidity of the second, but the failure to verbalise the revolutionary zeal of the main characters is a major obstacle to the book's successful reification of the struggle.

It is thus not only Sepamla's weaknesses that militate against his success, but also his strengths: had his dialogue been truer to life within the revolutionary exchanges, it might have offset the alienation effect of his skilled manipulation of the traditional western literary plot structure. As things stand, both the inappropriateness of the perfectly handled form and the lifelessness of the dialogue undermine the novel's impact.

Mbulelo Mzamane: *The Children of Soweto*

It would perhaps be possible to argue that the novel's inertness is a result of Sepamla's position as an outsider, a sympathetic observer rather than a mainstream participant in the liberation politics and struggle of 1976. And indeed at this point he was less wholeheartedly committed to the liberation movement than many of his younger colleagues. He did not know the schoolchildren and was not privy to their daily involvement, nor was he likely to be *au fait* with the liberation organisations in exile.

However the two other novels still to be considered do not suffer from this fault, although their writers were both outsiders during 1976. Mzamane was in exile throughout the period, though able to pay occasional visits to his family; Serote was in America, unable to return even for visits. Their alienation, however, was geographical rather than intellectual or emotional, so perhaps, in the end, it may in fact be a question of identification determining the potency of the literary document. Sepamla's fullest commitment resulted from the experience of the uprising (see *The Soweto I Love*) rather than predated it.

Mzamane's book brings to the fore the role of the students in the events in 1976 in an organised way which Tlali fails to do and which Sepamla does not attempt. The entire perspective, apart from a brief, self-contained interlude concerned with the white man Johannes Ventner, is that of the student group; and we meet them first in their academic setting, for Mzamane records the very beginnings of the troubles within the schools – something which none of the other writers has attempted.

The style he adopts is something of an innovation as regards contemporary novels, though it has its precedents both in the articles of some of the *Drum* writers in the fifties in South Africa and in the first person narratives of the eighteenth century, such as Robinson Crusoe or Tristram Shandy. (Nor can Mzamane plead African innocence of English forebears; he is after all a lecturer in English Literature). His use of the first person is very different from that typical of the late nineteenth and twentieth-century autobiographical novelists. Sabela the narrator is just that – a voice that records events, a provider of information; he is no introspective, searching for identity, he does not develop through experience, we never see into his soul; even his opinions are never individualised but are representative of the whole group of students. The tone is partly narrative and partly documentary: Mzamane seeks, perhaps even more than to tell the story of the activities of the students, to set those activities firmly in their sociological and historical context. Hence the narrative is frequently broken off in order to provide information on the background and activities of recently introduced characters: the history of Ma Vy and her gangster-girlfriend daughter, and her part in the struggle as the founder of the Shebeen Owners' Association; the background of Chabeli and Rathebe and the saga of their interventions in black affairs in Soweto and the homelands; a character assessment of Bra P which attempts to explain his social and political influence, his great wealth and generosity and the power he derives from his charisma; the political involvement of all of Bella's family and their history of banning and imprisonment as the penalty for their activities. It is an irritating technique for a novelist to employ (at least for the western reader – an African reader, used to different story-telling techniques, may respond quite differently), for the narrative is perpetually frustrated by long interruptions, but it does enable Mzamane to convey large quantities of information in a fairly easily digestible form, the reader's interest being maintained by curiosity about the character.

Woven among the passages of narrative and documentary is a thread of comic escapades, picaresque in character, centring on the two rogue school teachers Pakoe and Pakade whose principal devotion is to drink and whose major interaction with their students consists of the extortion of renewable loans to fund their religious observances in the shebeens. The firebrand Mick is another of the comic figures. True to the picaresque tradition, their less admirable characteristics are satirised: the schoolteachers' cowardice and prevarication, Mick's indiscipline and his wildness, together with his comic malapropisms. Yet Mzamane also touches upon their very real contributions to the struggle – the teachers in the way they have alerted their pupils to the real history and culture of their people, in spite of a school syllabus deliberately devised to evade such issues, and Mick's incisive grasp of the revolutionary situation, of the directions the group ought to be taking and his ability to organise fast and efficient action, all of which constitute his genuine leadership potential, maverick though he may be.

The novel is divided into three books, each dealing with the 1976 Soweto uprising from a different angle. The first book, 'My Schooldays in Soweto', gives an evaluation of the entire Bantu Education issue, recording the history of student response in one particular school both to that and to the decision to use Afrikaans as a major medium of instruction. The second book, 'The Day of the Riots', is a brief reaction to events from the perspective of a white man accidentally trapped in Soweto during the uprising, and of his unwilling black protectors. The third and much the most substantial book, 'The Children of Soweto', covers the period after 16 June, from the perspective of the student leaders within the framework of Munthu's murder, the nights of mourning and his funeral. This book takes in the much wider community issues that lay behind the uprising and the community action which grew out of the children's rebellion.

From the first few pages it is evident there is to be no attempt at sophisticated plot structure of the kind that introduces us to the guerrilla Mzi and his mission that forms the basis of the plot in *A Ride on the Whirlwind*. Instead there is a garrulous introduction, not to the main characters but to the clowns, Pakoe and Pakade. Though the style is formal and literary, the tone is township gossip – a blend of personal reminiscence, anecdote, comment and narrative. The narrator makes himself and his friends Khulu and Monty known to the reader in passing, but they are not distinguished in any way – they merely provide a more chatty and personal channel for the narrative than the objective third person would do.

In the course of the first pages we pick up details of the school background – the headmaster, his assistant head, and his rival in love, Dladla, the unpopular carpentry teacher. We find out the school-children's attitudes towards Bantu Education with its focus on carpentry and home economics in place of the academic subjects such as science that would enable them to enter the professions and the useful technical subjects such as motor mechanics or electronics that would prepare the non-academic children for the requirements of daily life in the townships. Pakoe and Pakade's shebeen life and full-time commitment to drinking convey the despair experienced by teachers bound by such restrictions, even of those teachers who have found ways of subverting the syllabus and teaching real history and culture as well as dispensing the adulterated material necessary for passing examinations.

The first book also charts the beginnings of the Students' Representative Council in this particular school, from the early debates concerning the introduction of Afrikaans to the negotiations with the police for the release of their teachers and fellow students, using the school's senior staff as their representatives. Once the SRC has come out into the open, police harassment leads to a demonstration which in turn is met with tear gas, bullets and tanks. Refusing to be intimidated the students return violence for violence and all buildings connected with the authorities – municipal offices, post offices, government beer halls, schools – are razed by fire. Positions harden as the Department of Bantu Education requires all students to sign an undertaking to desist from damaging the school or risk expulsion, and the students react with a mass boycott forcing the authorities to withdraw the letter and extend registration deadlines for examinations in an attempt to entice the children back to school. Tricked by this apparent softening, and needing to avoid individual victimisation, the students return only to find their leaders are rounded up. It is at this point that the students call an emergency meeting and elect the head, the deputy head and Dladla as their delegates to negotiate with the police for the release of their history teacher Nkululeko and the student leaders. The success of the delegation does not, however, resolve the situation, and leaves the SRC organising layers of back-up leadership while deciding not to register for examinations until the remaining students are released.

The second book, 'The Day of the Riots', gives an indirect perspective on 16 June through the predicament of a black family having to work out what to do with a trapped white colleague while the children rampage in the streets. When there is a knock at the door they hide him in the coal hole in the yard, and there is a narrative flashback to the demonstration that day which the police had initially attempted to disperse by referring to the Riotous Assemblies Act – a law the children had never heard about – then by firing tear gas canisters which the children inactivated by covering them with wet cloths, and finally with bullets, which killed some students but incited the rest to riot. Buildings and vehicles associated with whites were burned, and stray whites killed.

A later flashback describes their journey to Sipho's house, when they were stopped by a mob of very small children and only negotiated to safety by Sipho's diplomacy and the bribe of a ride in the car.

Meanwhile Sipho, his wife and their friends agonise over the conflict between their innate humanitarian impulse to keep Venter safe and the danger this protection might bring upon their children. Their solution is to shelter him till the small hours then drive him home to white Johannesburg hidden in the boot of the car.

The first book covers the events and feelings leading up to 16 June. The second book captures some of the atmosphere of that day. The third book, 'The Children of Soweto', the most intensely realised of them all, covers the community action and conscientisation born out of the deaths of that day.

It opens, poignantly and dramatically, with a simple statement of fact – 'We buried him on Sunday' – which carries the full weight of all the grief of that day of deaths, those years of slaughter, those centuries of oppression, and together with the following sentence:

> There were several other funerals being held all over the township that Sunday, funerals of others who had died in the shootings earlier that week[5]

epitomises all the material of this climactic book. Muntu, the dead friend, is an obvious symbol for Hector Petersen and Mzamane uses his death, the nights of the wake and the funeral as the framework for all his content.

After this initial reference to the funeral and brief reminiscences of Muntu's childhood, Mzamane takes his reader back into a vivid narrative account of the day itself – the assembly of the children from all the schools, the confrontation with the police and the savage onslaught that caused Muntu's slow bleeding death. Brought to the scene, Muntu's elder sister takes the body in her arms and braves the police in the street once again as she searches for a way to get her brother to the hospital. In her grief and wrath she turns on the questioning police: 'First you kill my brother, then you ask what's the matter with him'[6] and drives home the enormity of the black police's betrayal:

> You would shoot your own children for a miserly thirty pieces of silver. I could peel you like peaches and God himself would call it justice. You are incomplete; the human parts of you are missing. Sies![7]

Bra P, the influential father figure of Soweto, pacifies the police and rescues Sindi and her dying brother from this confrontation, though Muntu dies in the car before they can reach hospital.

The student group meets to take stock of all that has happened in the house of Bella, one of their number whose family has a long history of involvement in the black struggle, and whose father is currently paying the price of his commitment on Robben Island. The meeting gives Mzamane the opportunity to survey the press reports of the day, and to show the impact of these fictions upon the students who are fired to further action by their disgust with white editorial control even over black newspapers and the writings of black journalists.

As they recognise that the battle with the system is likely to prove a long one, they begin to discuss means of building up community support and solidarity. They combine compassion with political acumen in their decision to organise a mass collection for the bereaved families, to institute a national week of mourning calling for abstention from work, school, celebrations, outings, drinking and sports events.

The reports of the arrests, including those in hospital wards, sharpen their awareness of the danger of their position as the police begin to gather information. They go underground, shifting meeting and sleeping places, Muntu's house is their only regular calling point.

After the meeting Micky begins his organisation of the simultaneous burning of all government buildings throughout Soweto and the rest of the students gather at Bra P's place to draft their leaflet calling on Soweto to observe the week of mourning. Bra P provides them with typing and duplicating facilities, and agrees, albeit reluctantly, to try to persuade his colleagues to call off the football fixtures for the mourning period. He returns the next day with the duplicated leaflets, agreement from the sports associations to cancel the fixtures, the ominous news of Bella's arrest and a list of wanted ringleaders whose names (including all the student leaders) the police had extorted from prisoners in custody.

Mzamane moves from the secret group enclosed in Bra P's house to an account of what was happening out in the township. With his customary comic touches he relates the progress of the fund-raising campaign which captures its donations by a mixture of wit, bravado and organisation – catching all the workers as they rush for buses and trains on their way to work, so that they give to avoid being detained, 'persuading' taxi drivers to add a compulsory levy to all fares, and bus drivers to subscribe fares by reselling old bus tickets collected by organised groups of children, drawing in the support of the gangs and the tsotsis, in their battle against the police, of the shebeen keepers in their collections in the shebeens and of the businessmen and traders who become generous in their gifts to the bereaved out of a mixture of solidarity and good business sense. Even shoplifters and pick-pockets turn Robin Hoods on the occasion and give their pickings to the needy:

A truly altruistic spirit gripped the people's minds and their hearts and a compassionate feeling pervaded all our relationships. It was the perfect example of the collective goodness and generosity of a deeply troubled community.[8]

The fund-raising brings the students into closer relationships with various community groups and leads to gradual co-operation between them. The founding of the Shebeen Owners' Association is a case in point, which began to negotiate with the students for closure of the shebeens at certain periods. Organisation defused the tensions and resolved the conflicting demands of students, customers and owners.

In their meeting with Rathebe and Chabeli they try to extend their influence to township government affairs. Rathebe's and Chabeli's activities on the School Board and on the Urban Bantu Council, their collaboration with the system, enabling them to maintain a pretence of dialogue and a reality of increasingly ruthless control, had long disgusted the community. Urged to resign by the Students' Representative Council they give apparent consent. Although they later renege on this, the connection has been made between the student protest and the wider arena of black and white politics – an important preliminary to the election of the Committee of Ten. In other areas, too, the student example lights a torch – their school principal resigns and five hundred teachers follow his example, clarifying the extent of black refusal of Bantu Education.

The nights of mourning that had provided the cover for the group's meetings climax in a funeral whose political message is borne in its outward form – the horse-drawn cart, the procession – as much as in its explicit verbal tributes. The tributes themselves show the breaking down of formal boundaries in life as much as in art: the address given by the Anglican Dean of Johannesburg, Father Mpilo Tutu, the traditional ceremonial of the funeral service, is followed by a brief speech by the headmaster focusing on Bantu Education and by poems written by the student revolutionaries. The police contribution to the breaking down of formal boundaries consists of gunning down the mourners while they bury those they had gunned down in the streets.

The funeral is such a powerfully depicted climax that the novel loses something of its impetus as it goes on to record the march of the schoolchildren on John Vorster Square, the killing of the policeman, Hlubi, the spread of unrest through the country and the dispersal of the students:

We were the children of the new diaspora, we, the children of

Soweto, germinating everywhere we went little new seeds of vengeance, hatred, bitterness, wrath, on the fertile soil of our hearts . . . [9]

However, Mzamane's principal interest, from the beginning, has been documentary authenticity rather than perfection of artistic form, so this hasty summary of events and attempt at assessment and self-criticism with which the novel closes, narrated from exile in Botswana, is consistent with his aims. Moreover the refusal to fabricate a neat fictional ending prevents the artistic form from perverting the reader's interpretation.

One might ask why Mzamane does not, in that case, choose to write straightforward documentary instead of a novel, if the needs of reportage are to supersede the demands of literary form. While I have no special insight into the author's motives, there are various criteria which suggest themselves as possible reasons. The novel form allows him to condense and focus the conglomeration of incidents that took place in Soweto between the early months of 1976 and the middle of 1977. An attempt to present the period with absolute accuracy would inevitably result in a fairly shapeless and confusing narrative. Such an account might be of inestimable value to the historian or the political analyst, but it would have little impact on the general reader and would contribute little to the conscientisation of the masses in South Africa. And one can be sure that one of Mzamane's principal aims in writing the book was to contribute to this very explicit programme mounted by black writers of the seventies and eighties. (Of course, the masses are not going to read such novels, but so close is the integration of intellectuals and ordinary people in the current situation that material filters down to them automatically through the ideas, conversation and attitudes of those who do read.)

The fictional form gives him a licence to condense, sharpen the focus and slightly rearrange the sequence of events to achieve maximum emotional stimulus. The events in the third book of the novel, for example, which are compressed into the space between the death and the funeral, actually took place at intervals throughout the year following the momentous day of 16 June. Nor was the leadership of the Soweto Students' Representative Council as apparent to the majority of Sowetans as it appears to be in this narrative; yet to present their role with niggling accuracy would undermine the effect of the work.

Yet Mzamane has struck a happy balance: he has not simplified issues, events or details to the extent that Sepamla has. Sepamla, by allowing literary considerations to be his ruling force, has drained his rendering of the Soweto uprising of its life-blood. Mzamane has succeeded in maintaining the complexity of the period while clearing a path for the reader to follow so that he can grasp the essentials without being ensnared by the confused tangles of the undergrowth. By approaching 16 June first through the build-up of feeling in the schools, second through the predicament of the trapped white man, and finally retrospectively through the grief and activism of the student leaders, Mzamane is able to reach out and incorporate a great many of the most important issues of the period. In this way the reader begins to perceive the ramifications in a way in which the reader of *Amandla* or *A Ride on the Whirlwind* never does.

He has escaped, too, from the trap of the individual hero, and the detrimental effect of this on the function of the literary form. Rive's focus on the individual anguish of Andrew Dreyer in *Emergency* negates the popular uprising and reduces it to the level of back-cloth to a hero's search for self-realisation. Mzamane's 'I' is not this individual-ised, self-engrossed 'I', but the almost anonymous 'I' or 'eye' of the reporter who exists to transmit information, not to intrude his personality on the reader. Sabelo is amalgamated first with the small group of students within the school and later with the larger group of the SRC leadership. This yields very different results from the spot-lighting of the single guerrilla fighter in *A Ride on the Whirlwind*. For though Mzi is not the conventional western literary hero in search of an identity, it is nevertheless around his actions that the entire plot revolves, and his status not only undermines the importance of the student group, but also paralyses their function. In *The Children of Soweto* it is the group that acts, that holds the initiative, and their planning and organisation is responsible not only for their own activities but also for much that occurs in the community at large.

Thus Mzamane has succeeded in incorporating this shift in values within the literary form itself. Yet he has achieved this at some cost. For the group of characters, like the narrator himself, have some of the anonymity of figures in a newspaper report. Mzamane's focus is upon the broad canvas of historical events and social movements, rather than on the relationships of a group of individuals:

> The book has been written to preserve the memory of these events, as in the 'tales' of my people I was told as a child. In this 'tale' I see little need to delineate individual character sharply because the community as a whole is the hero. My book is a record of the attempt to create a new collective consciousness, for which Black Consciousness in South Africa stands.[10]

Bella, Micky, Nina and the others are seen in terms of their activities rather than in terms of their relationships.

This does not prevent Mzamane from revealing his mastery of idiomatic exchanges, especially in the banter between the two rogue teachers and the students, where the mixture of English, Afrikaans and the vernacular languages conveys the vigour and humour of the streets. Yet where the reader is most moved by speech it is at times of rhetorical intensity when a simple character speaks out – the graveside speeches and poems, Sindi's berating of the police at the death of her brother – rather than during exchanges.

Yet the suppression of individuality and of relationships is only one way to the goal of converting individual to community-consciousness. Indeed it is by the intensity of his realisation of people and their interaction that Mongane Serote makes his most significant contribution to the literature of combat.

Mongane Serote: *To Every Birth Its Blood*

Serote's conception of literary function in this his first novel, as it had been in his later poetry, is very close to that of Mzamane and other contemporary black writers: he, too, is seeking a form that will 'articulate the people's problems and complaints and . . . project their collective aspirations'.[11] He, too, would subscribe to the refusal to separate out '"documentary" literary genres and "imaginative" genres',[12] and he, too, firmly rejects the individualist orientation of liberal humanist literary values. Yet he reaches his goal by a very different path from that of the three other writers considered, a path which raises many questions as we attempt to trace it out – questions about form, about presentation of character and about the handling of relationships.

For the aesthetics to which Serote and the more politicised of the black consciousness writers have subscribed, an aesthetics which Michael Vaughan dubs 'black populism',[13] radically rejects the centralisation of the individual and the mediation of literary themes through 'sensitively *individualized* experiences and interactions'.[14] And yet the most powerful aspects of Serote's novel are the sensitively individualised experiences and interactions of its characters, especially of Tsi and John.

Moreover the novel apparently focuses in the first part on the individual figure, whether he be hero or anti-hero, of Tsi, and in the second part on John, in authentic liberal-humanist tradition. A traditional western critic would, however, take issue with this apparent switch of central figure on formal grounds: the novel is apparently broken in two by its shift from Tsi and his family to John and the wider group of friends peopling the second part: the first part telling the tale of an individual, the second that of a group.

Yet it has to be asked where this apparent focus on individuals leads: certainly not to Tsi's or John's discovery of their identity, as is usually the case in the standard liberal-humanist novel. Rather, Tsi and John lend themselves to the exploration of changes in the consciousness of an entire population, and are individualised the better to realise the process at work. And this break in the form serves the same end: in the two parts of the novel Serote is exploring two levels of change: conscientisation and politicisation. The use of two separate characters enables him to achieve this on a much broader canvas than a single character would, for he is able to follow through the changes in different personality types with different motivations and different qualities of experience.

Though Serote's novel covers the same historical period as Tlali's, Sepamla's and Mzamane's, it is less concerned than the other three with the documentation of events than with the chronicling of transformations of consciousness during the momentous years that led up to the 1976 uprising, and that were activated as a consequence of the political activity that grew out of it. The transformations are worked out in the political development first of Tsi, then of John.

Each character begins with non-involvement – indeed with a deliberate rejection of knowledge, so strong is the instinct to avoid those responsibilities that come with acknowledgement. In this sense the process of consciousness is parallel for Tsi and John. Yet although this might seem to give the novel a two-part parallel structure, there are significant differences in the starting point, the pace and the finishing point of the two sections. The structure indeed seems to recall the repetition effects of traditional oral poetry, though here the repetition is rarely exact but at each instance introduces some subtle element of change that gives the literary work its progressive impetus.

Tsi's development starts from the base line. He is a drunken escapist whose entire consciousness is confined to the negative impulses of revolt, rejection, hopeless bitterness. Even Tsi's most intimate relationships, with his wife, his parents, his siblings are contaminated by his condition of despair. And yet the opening of the novel is not as nihilistic as this assessment may seem to indicate. The affection of Lily and Tsi's homecoming in the opening chapter is powerfully evoked, despite Tsi's evocation of his (that is, his people's) state of endemic homelessness: 'I knew that another time was coming when we would have to be in the street again.'[15] Yet, driven by his chronic restlessness, Tsi wanders out of the refuge of home to the murdering streets and the wilderness of the shebeens. The incident of the murdered man brings into focus Tsi's inability to fuse feeling and action in any way at this stage of his existence: he does not, out of fear, go to the man's assistance, and he rejects very violently Moipone's curiosity after the event:

> 'They killed him,' Moipone said at last. 'Let's go see.'
> 'You want to eat him?' I said, becoming angry.
> 'No, but maybe we know him.'
> 'Fuck it, if we knew him, we should have gone to him before they killed him.'[16]

The incident epitomises the helplessness of a people who have been victimised to such an extent that they turn on each other in inverted aggression, and who are too manipulated by fear to go to each other's assistance.

The visit to his grandfather's grave marks the first step in his progress towards awakened consciousness. There is of course the symbolism of communing with the ancestors, not only for reassurance, for authority, but also in search of roots, of identity, but there is also the conversation with Old Man Zola that catches onto this symbolism and draws it into the realm of real life. The old man's rambling greetings, inquiries and information about their respective families serve to reinstate Tsi within the security of the community in the way every such meeting and greeting does in a traditional society. And his own history of his political involvement, evoked by the references to Tsi's imprisoned brother Fix, recently arrested for his political activities, forces Tsi to register (even if at this stage he does not necessarily take cognisance of) the historical dimensions of the struggle – dimensions emphasised by their symbolic climb up the hill away from the cemetery:

> When I looked back, I saw the steep hill which he had climbed at that slow pace, stopping to ponder, at times almost beginning to cry, laughing, walking on, thinking about the past, the future[17]

and by the symbolism of the fresh vegetables and fruit – growth and fruition in the midst of all the destruction and death – which the old man buys and shares before they part.

The first step, however, is a step in a journey whose direction is by no means always forward. Tsi is still hampered by his inability to communicate, his refusal to face up to situations, and this aspect of his character is reflected as in a mirror by his brother Ndo, who comes from the shebeen bringing news of the police visit to their parents to ask about their brother Fix. The brothers skirmish with words, evasions, accusations, the truth momentarily acknowledged in rare and brief outbursts: 'Ja, all this means that I am a coward.'[18] But Ndo then immediately takes refuge in dwelling on Fix's stupidity in getting himself into the trap. Although Tsi is not as politically naïve as his brother Ndo, and tries to put an end to such pointless accusations, he is only a little less articulate than Ndo with his repeated 'shut up!' and his smashing of the coffee cup to prevent dialogue.

Nevertheless the confrontation serves to help focus Tsi's feelings about Fix, as had the meeting with Old Man Zola, so that when Anka urges him to visit Nomsisi, his brother's wife, astonished that he had not already seen her, he finally complies despite his initial refusal springing from an automatic reluctance to place himself in a situation where he can't communicate: 'Look, I can't talk to Nomsisi. That is all.'[19] Once again, it is knowledge that Tsi is fighting by his apparent inability to communicate, for once he does begin to talk to Nomsisi and listen, he has to face the realisation that she, as well as his brother Fix, is in the Movement, and to carry the fear for her which that realisation brings. Disorientated by this moment of consciousness –

> I fear this feeling. It knocks me down . . . Suddenly, not knowing where to go . . . Lost. Big man I am. Lost . . . [20]

– Tsi escapes into drunkenness, unconsciousness, only to be shown that there is no such escape for the likes of him, by the rude knocking of the police in the night.

Faced, at last, with Lily's anger and the necessity of acknowledging the consequences of his actions, his childish evasion of responsibility (he had squandered the pass money Lily had given him on beer) he takes another positive step and borrows the money to pay his pass dues.

Serote emphasises the subservience of action to consciousness by alternating episodes of narrative with episodes of reflection. After the police raid and the visit to the pass office, Tsi falls into a long reverie on his father and mother in which he tries to come to terms with the past and the future of the black man, the black family in South Africa. As he reaches into his own past he recognises the impossibility of putting his finger on the truth about it – everything is so fragmented that any attempt to 'bring it out' would involve a great deal of fiction:

> Yet somehow it seems important to know where you come from,
> what happened; it seems important to link you to the present, so you
> can order the future, which is supposedly built for you.[21]

Yet the mere mention of the future seems a bitter mockery. He remembers his mother's assertion that their father had fought for their future: 'Which future?'[22] and experiences violently conflicting feelings of sympathy for and anger towards the father whose face is filled with a defeat he refuses to accept, and who asks if he will have grandchildren:

> What for? Where is the future they will take in their hands? . . .
> What will I tell your grandchildren? That you cried when you were
> dying? . . . That when Fix was gone we waited, we waited for him to
> come back? That you waited. That I waited.[23]

(Tsi's growing impatience with black passivity is evident, even though as yet he sees no channel for action.)

The contrapuntal musings are set against a piece of Coltrane's music – a common stylistic device of Serote's – and both lyric and reflections ultimately converge on the idea of home, bringing Tsi to the realisation that, for his people, home was a place of defeat, that the old people had worn out all their strength and all their lives in a fruitless attempt to build a home and a future. Yet the conclusion is not a moment of despair, but of seminal tension: 'There was silence in the house now, as if something was going to snap.'[24] Not an ending, but a beginning, and the lines of poetry which open the following chapter (the only chapter, in fact, so introduced) underline the moment's thematic implications:

> Where, where does a river begin
> to make, to take its journey
> where does a river begin
> to take its journey to the sea?[25]

It is, indeed, a turning point for Tsi, a point, if not of active commitment, at least of involvement, of acceptance of knowledge. And the price of that involvement is demanded immediately in the form of a week in prison.

Tsi's first actual moment of knowledge comes as he gives his wife Nomsisi's message and recognises that Lily as well as Nomsisi is involved in the Movement:

It was as I said that, that I realised, I knew, I feared. Where, where
does a river begin?[26]

And the dawn of knowledge is indeed the loss of innocence:

> We were born, and we had come to be witnesses of life, distorted by
> time and by place. Everything that we could claim immediately left
> bloodstains on our fingers. Here we go again . . . Fix. Pule.
> Moipone. Old Man Zola. Where does the river begin, on its journey
> to the sea?[27]

The narrative passes (again in its ceaseless backwards and forwards
flow) via memories of boyhood in Lesotho and the streets of Alexandra
with his friend Boykie to the car journey the two of them take on behalf
of their newspaper, reporter and photographer together. Thus the
passage seems direct from boyhood to the prison cell, from companionship in childish play to companionship in torture. In the course of the
first part of their journey, Boykie spells out the political consequences
of that knowledge Tsi has arrived at in his reflections on his people's
history:

> You know that it is only in our memory that this is our land. We
> imagine that we have a home, we know that in reality, if there was a
> quick way that these settlers could wipe us out, they would, and if
> they did not need our labour they would.[28]

He emphasises the fact that it is not just a question of morality, but
more importantly, of power. In order to convince the mass of the
people to lead the revolution, a few well-organised people have to
demonstrate that power is a possibility, and that it is the function of the
Black Students' Organisation to mount this demonstration, yet

> that is only a stage, just a stage in our battle to reclaim a home for
> ourselves.[29]

On the heels of Boykie's pronouncements about power comes the
physical confrontation with it as the police stop their car, beat them
both up and take them to a police station before, eventually, setting
them free, presumably because of Boykie's attempt to photograph a
previous victim of their abuse, beaten to death by the roadside. As they
attempt to absorb the full horror of this experience – 'we are a defeated
people'[30] – they are stopped again, taken to the police station and

assaulted a second time, apparently because their faces, distorted out of recognition by the first police beating, do not match the photographs in their passes. In the full horror of the beating, the humiliation, the squalor, Tsi calls on his grandmother and recalls her words:

> Child you must know, in the darkness of your past, where you came from, and in the faint future where you are going . . . We tried to show you everything, we loved you, took your hand and walked with you. One day you will have to remember that you are alone, among other people, and that you have a journey to make.[31]

By the end of his week in prison Tsi, alone in his cell, had learned his grandmother's lesson, and his journey had begun: 'I realised where I was and knew that the only thing I had was my journey.'[32]

Though, typically, despite resolutions to the contrary, he is unable to communicate his experience to his family and his secretiveness generates a temporary alienation similar to earlier ones mentioned, Serote had in fact begun to comprehend more about family relationships and their place in the schema of the struggle. And the remaining section of Part I does in fact shift to the conscientisation of the family: his father and mother, brought by the experience of Fix's imprisonment to a new perception of the situation, begin to attend freedom funerals. Mary, who had been turned out of the house after giving birth to Oupa (a central figure in Part II) is found by Tsi and gradually eased back into the family circle. Tsi's job as an extension worker brings him not only a measure of prosperity, but also confrontation with the police. The section ends, significantly, with a family gathering in which the manifestation of the unity of the family, the overcoming of former breaches, the harmony of feeling between the generations, symbolises the growth of solidarity among the community. The tone is set for Part II by the discussion between Tsi's parents of their visit to Fix, and their recognition of the high spirits and confidence of Fix and his fellow prisoners: the struggle is moving forward despite all the previous setbacks and disharmonies, and the mood is one of determined and calm optimism. Tsi's father, who has hitherto figured only as an embodiment of silent confusion and defeat is the one who pronounces the new creed:

> Now I know what it means . . . When people's minds are made up, nothing can stop them. I never used to know that the way I know it now. It is as if you are reliving your life . . .[33]

The first part of the novel covers the period before the 1976 uprising, in a general, non-specific way. It has no close historical detail in the way that Mzamane's novel has. The second part begins with the aftermath of that uprising and records the kind of organisation it gave rise to. Of the many possible reasons for the omission of the uprising itself from the novel, two suggest themselves as possibly important. One is that Serote himself was not in South Africa at that time, but, like his character Yaonne, was studying in America and dependent for his news on the self-censored letters of his wife, family and friends and on the newspaper and television reports. (The full horror of his predicament is brought out by Yaonne.) The second is that the book is concerned not with events, but with consciousness. Even if Serote had been present, it might well have been that he would still have chosen to emphasise the effects of the uprising on people's minds in terms of moving forward their commitment to the struggle.

Whatever the reason, the coverage of the uprising is confined to John's memory of the killing of his fiancée Nolizwe as she ran towards her dead brother, shouting abuse at his murderers, the police. And it is typical of Serote's intensely poetic style that the most powerful evocation of those days is through dramatic monologue – John's recollection of Onalenna's rendering of the poem 'My people the streets are clean now' which commemorated the horror of the experience within the framework of the next step forward:

> We remove the blood, its not nice to walk on
> We remove the bodies
> It would be terrible to see the dogs eat them
> And then we hope
> Hope for what?
> That they won't come again
> That they know we don't like what they are doing?
> No
> I know we know much more than that
> We are people
> Who have struggled a long long time
> Now we have to use the lessons of our struggle![34]

There is a direct thematic link here, despite the division of the book into two parts and the change of narrative perspective from Tsi to John, with Tsi's acknowledgement that the journey had begun in chapter 4 – a link underlined by the poetic form. Onalenna's poem neatly sets in its context the incessant repetition of black history, conveying the terror of all the bloodshed and destruction they have to deal with much more tellingly by its savagely ironic understatement, and contemptuously dismissing the futile liberal hopes of reform. The lesson does not need to be spelled out – the logic of history itself sets down the necessity for active resistance.

The structure of this part of the book parallels the structure of the first part to some extent, delving into the consciousness of an individual as part of the analysis of changing patterns of consciousness among the population at large, and then spreading out to take in how it affects a wider group. The difference is that the concentration on an individual is for a much shorter period (acquaintance with Tsi helps the reader to 'read' John without so much background detail); the individual's consciousness is very early meshed with the consciousness of a group in the second part, and the group is much wider and less homogeneous. It is as though Serote had conceived his form as two waves of consciousness – one which swells and disperses and apparently reaches no goal, but which in fact is swept back into and increases the force of the second wave – a wave which swells to a torrent as the movement gathers momentum and engulfs numberless people and places in its forward impulse.

Yet the starting point for John has some similarities with the starting point for Tsi. Although John, unlike Tsi, has had a history of political involvement to the point of imprisonment, after Nolizwe's death he manifests the same refusal to know, to get involved, to discuss matters, that had characterised Tsi. He spends time with friends who are actively involved and yet refuses to recognise their involvement, deliberately excluding himself not only from their activities, but even from any response to what they do:

> In time, all these silences created more complex silences. One day they would have to talk about Nolizwe; now they never did. One day they would have to talk about Yao; now they never did. One day they would have to talk about the days of Power and the schoolchildren. Now they never did. If anyone dared to talk John made it clear that that had nothing to do with him. Pushed, he either exclaimed or shrugged, that was all.[35]

As John's commitment is gradually educed and nourished in his talks with Dikeledi and Onalenna, through the reading of letters from Yaonne, Onalenna's husband, and ultimately in talks with the young Oupa, Tsi's nephew, whose responsibility it eventually becomes to lead John through the final stages of recruitment, so the complex web of interconnections makes clear the corporate nature of the process. This is not the journey of an individual, examining his soul and working through a philosophical justification of the need for commitment to a movement that will, in the last resort, turn to violence to achieve its objectives. It is the socialisation of one who has allowed introspection and private grief to deflect him from the needs of his community – a community which is not a philosophic abstraction, but is composed of his closest friends and relatives and their connections, spreading outward in an ever-increasing circle. So when John is finally recruited, he is not recruited alone, but with Dikeledi, whose family has a long history of involvement, and whose father has just been imprisoned for his leadership in the struggle. Thus the long flashback giving the history of Mr Ramono's family life and involvement in the movement is no digression but a deliberate focus on the historical dimensions of the struggle.

There are specific narrative events in this section of the book: the policeman Mpando is killed; a bomb is planted in central Johannesburg; the four police chiefs responsible for identifying ringleaders are eliminated; farmers throughout the country witness their ranches fired and their prison workers and cattle set free. However, unlike Sepamla and Mzamane, who use events as the main focus of their novels, Serote merely uses them as milestones in the chronicle of the movement in time, in space and in people's lives and relationships: for he seeks the whole ethos and quintessence of the struggle. He takes the reader back to the earlier days of the struggle with Michael Ramono, Mmaphefo and Hlase – a leader in the earlier struggle in Sekhukhuniland – and forward to the day (now alas arrived) when the bombs would fall in Botswana and Mozambique.

Botswana and Mozambique are also the final points (in the novel) of the chronicle of the movement in space. The early part of the book locates the action very firmly within the streets of Alexandra, the township Serote regards as home, but gradually the circle is widened and extended to include white Johannesburg, the townships of Soweto, Walmanstadt, the village outside Pretoria, Sekhukhuniland, Umlazi, and then finally the scene shifts with many of the characters into exile in Botswana: 'The land is up on its legs, it knows no rest'[36] as Mmaphefo says towards the end. And it is by tracing his characters in brief cameos as they disperse through the country and neighbouring countries that Serote manages to sketch in the geographical dimensions of the struggle and its wildfire spread through the land.

But it is the chronicle of the movement in the people who compose it, in their relationships, their shifting consciousness, their bonds of affection, the mutual support they give each other and even their tensions and conflicts that forms the core of Serote's novel and gives it all its intensity and depth. The tenderness between Onalenna and Dikeledi and John in his grief, between Onalenna and Yaonne in their separation, between Dikeledi and her mother and sister in their family tragedy, between John and Oupa and Dikeledi in their visit of consolation – a tenderness that, like the struggle, spreads outwards to Mmaphefo, Russia, Hlase, Tuki, Thembo – these safety nets of affection provide the foundation of the profound humanism that underlies the violence of the struggle. Yet Serote is careful also to measure the cost of commitment in terms of relationships, in the separation of Themba and Granny and the special care needed for their child Fidel as a consequence of the split. Granny had been unable to absorb the silences and uncertainties forced upon Themba by his involvement, and yet the man she retreats to for security also becomes a casualty of the struggle. By his speedy, indeed almost frenetic (yet it is not frenetic because the reader has gradually grown accustomed to the involvement of all the characters earlier in the novel) switches from group to group and place to place at the end of the novel, Serote manages to convey the density of relationships supporting the military effort in a way that, so far, in the novels of combat is unique. He provides for his reader a map of the psychogenesis of the struggle, charting its growth and development from the first seeds in the stubborn stony soil of Tsi's mind to the point where it incorporates the consciousness of all the characters in the novel.

CONCLUSION

The appearance, this decade, of these four novels, whatever the critical response may be to their individual achievements, adds another dimension to the development of South African literature. The advancement of the long prose narrative form not only solidifies its claim to critical attention by establishing it as more than the passing phenomenon of a few collections of short stories and poems, but also takes the literature into the domain of the dominant literary form on its own terms. It substantiates its claim by its formal innovations as much as by its social content. Just as the social forces in South Africa present a marked contrast to those in the West over the last few decades, where, as Lucien Goldmann argues, 'forces of contestation . . . no longer exist or are disappearing', so a literature in that country has evolved which is totally different from Europe's, where 'the literature of revolt has gained only a relatively secondary place in the recent development of contemporary literature.'[37]

These novels, together with previous black South African writing, belong to a new category of literature. They have a more direct, less mediated relationship with the forces of history and politics than western novels, seeking, indeed, a much more interventionist role than their counterparts in the West would dare to lay claim to, and seeking also access (through indirect transmission via the whole consciousness and world view of readers who in South Africa are integrated in daily life with the illiterate mass) to a mass audience – a mass audience already receptive to literature through its exposure to street and community theatre and oral poetry. There have been revolutionary literatures before, but this is the first revolutionary literature in English that has taken over the entire literary production of a country, and integrated professional writers and spare time writers from all social classes in a common cause. There may be writers still producing material in English that has nothing to do with the revolutionary situation, but it is not getting distributed or finding a market. White writers who, some years ago, *were* writing on other topics have either fallen silent or been drawn into the cataclysmic force of the struggle, whatever their standpoint.

This is why the experiments with form of these four novelists are so crucial. Not because these authors can be designated South Africa's leading writers; not because their novels are outstanding literary creations – I have pointed out earlier the irrelevance of such criteria – but because they are attempting to mark out a new path and, at this point in history, it seems to be the only possible path for South African literature to take.

Whereas the western novel has developed from tracing the individual's search for identity and values to the point where the individual has disappeared into the mists of existentialism or modernism, with only sporadic attempts to produce a novel with a collective subject (one thinks of the revolutionary community of Malraux's *La Condition Humaine*), as abortive as parallel political developments, in South Africa the concatenation of a long-term revolutionary struggle and a heroic essay at constructing an appropriate literary tradition is resulting in the development not of a new novel form, but of a new range of novel forms which have certain elements in common while allowing for differences of approach.

The South African writers have not only had the political context in which to take the development of the novel of the collective subject to a point which European writers were never able to reach; they also have a social environment much more conducive to its evolution. For individualism has never really established itself in African society in South Africa, despite the fact that capitalism is more firmly entrenched there than in any other African country, and consequently it has never nourished the body of its literature, notwithstanding the novels of Abrahams and Rive. The African tradition itself, with its communal principles and (in Southern Africa) its democratic values, has blended with the socialist ideology accepted by the majority of its writers. All four novels bear traces of this African tradition; some bear more than a trace. Mzamane consciously sets out to continue the traditional role as tale-teller; Serote employs many of the stylistic devices of the praise poets; all four would endorse the theory to which Mzamane subscribes of the public role of the African artist and audience – accountability.[38]

This is a point at which the emergent South African novel tradition diverges most sharply from the western tradition. For in the West the novel's role has, from the first, been critical and oppositional (we can see this transferred also to the West African novel), whereas in South Africa, emerging as it has done as a cultural weapon, a force in the liberation struggle, it has taken over the affirmative role of the praise poem within the community, reinforcing and promoting the community values, taking up the community action and rendering it back to them celebrated and perpetuated.

It is in this sense that the novels are truly autobiographies of the group, records not only of their deeds and of the advancement of the movement in which both novels and writers participate, but also of the evolution of their consciousness. They are accounts of how a people learned to know themselves by their experience of living in the time and the circumstances to which they were bound; of how involvement, at first accidental, something external in which they were passive and acted upon, eventually becomes deliberate, something they have internalised, a process in which they are the collective agent.

It is a curious kind of autobiography for, as well as being the record of a collective rather than an individual, it introduces an entirely new relationship between text and readership. There is now no question of writers, as manipulators, attempting to work upon and influence the attitudes of their readers, for in the South African novels their readers are in effect the subject of the book, their actions are the book's content, and the writers are themselves a part of the readership, the subject, and the content. For they too are only individuals in the great collective of the struggle, participators rather than instigators, and it is their self-identification with the people, the processes, the development of consciousness they write about that gives them their authority.

All four writers are recording this collective consciousness, and their success has to be measured by their impact on their readership, by the extent to which they make an understanding of this collective consciousness accessible to the average reader. Thus Miriam Tlali, in confining herself to a simple reflection of the events and discussions in the townships during the mid-seventies, is holding back from major organisational interference, though she may have succeeded in avoiding the false consciousness effected by western literary form (which by imposing an organised structure and effecting a resolution would falsify the material's complexity and its unresolved state) in recording only the real consciousness of the community, not their potential consciousness. Her readers gain from her novel a simple reflection of events a little less vivid and immediate than that to be gained by actual experience. She does nothing to transform the reader's consciousness. Sepamla, aware of the need for structure, but unable to produce an innovative form, falls back on a western structural pattern which perverts the real consciousness into false consciousness, leaving the reader with a spectator's rather than a participator's grasp of events. Mzamane breaks away from conventional form, and however disjunct his three books with their multiplicity of styles may seem, does succeed in giving the reader some kind of ordered hold both on the events of the mid-seventies and on some strands of the history of the struggle leading up to that climactic year of 1976. To a certain extent, then, at the level of information and, in the third book, occasionally, at the level of the emotions, he is intervening in the consciousness of his readers in order to transform it into potential consciousness. The reader is left with a strong impression of a continuum, a historical process.

Perhaps the most intense intervention in consciousness, however, is Serote's. For by his subtle use of characterisation, by subjecting history, will, human fallibility and the strengths of human relationships to the consciousness of individuals, he is able to give to his chosen reader – the black South Africans engaged in the liberation movement, and any outsiders, of any colour, who desire to submit themselves to the black South African world view – a literary experience by which they become aware of their own conscientisation, and the moral imperatives to which they have to respond.

All of these writers, however, are engaged in a common effort to enable their readers to reappropriate their culture, and to contribute to that cultural base which the liberation movement has recognised as a fundamental necessity for the movement of a nation towards its liberation.

6 Conclusion

The novelists of the eighties represent the latest stage in an on-going journey of self-discovery that has been taking place as long as black South African poets, novelists, writers and actors, have been creating cultural works.

The journey of black South African writers who write in English has taken them from a departure point of willing acceptance of the English cultural values of their education to arrival at their literary destination: the conscious construction of an organic African literature for South Africa. That journey has taken them through many stages: through a state of negation in which they were tortured by self-disgust and horror at their own and their people's defeated apathy – 'the pulling out of the innards'[1] as Mafika Gwala calls it – on to a stage of emergent consciousness, and finally to the proud confidence of a people actively in control of their own historical destiny.

The literature itself has made a contemporaneous journey, for all that its presence has been fractured and fragmented by government obstruction. It has travelled from the earliest historically-oriented output of the missionary presses, through white-oriented protest literature to the less individualistic community-oriented conscientisation literature of the Black Consciousness Movement and has arrived finally at the generative documentation of the liberation struggle as mass movement. Literature has undergone a metamorphosis from a vehicle of expression to a vehicle of propagable function. It is a literature which writers have laboured to construct by sifting all the African and European languages, all cultures ancient, rural, urban and modern, and the economics, history, and politics of their country for elements that can serve their purpose. They have fashioned a culture in which people are able to confront their government with all the questions that are most meaningful and most critical for the mass of their people; a culture which undermines by its dialectic all the anodyne

251

values that have been foisted on them by alien cultural assumptions. What is this talk of artistic freedom, Mongane Serote has asked of a society that has neglected to provide food, space to live and work in, and light in the evening? What does it mean to a woman who works eight hours in a factory, commutes for two hours, and then returns to an evening of child-care and cooking?

> The 'artistic freedom' the oppressor culture so often admires is a worthless irrelevance to that woman: 'art for art's sake' would only take her even further away from challenging the miseries of her life. The oppressor's very concept of culture, rather than leading people to deal with their own realities, serves to confuse and distract . . . It is not sufficient for culture to reflect an awareness of oppression and exploitation; such awareness only becomes meaningful when it leads to action to end that oppression. Culture is not only awareness, but the expression of that awareness.[2]

And what of the critics? What role do they play in the scheme of things? Lewis Nkosi's definition of the writer has peculiar aptness for the critic of contemporary black South African literature: 'The (critic) is like someone with a telescopic lens trained on a target which is constantly moving on.'[3] They cannot fall into the stable role that has traditionally been theirs in the West, nor rest on the associated critical assumptions. Yet the rejection evinced by black writers in many of their statements is a rejection of that traditional role and the value judgements inherent in it, not a rejection of the function of criticism itself. For if a black South African aesthetic is to be firmly established and developed, it is necessary that a black-oriented critical theory takes account of the social, political and economic context in which the works are produced, describes the formal and linguistic innovations as they appear, and wrests the critical criteria to be applied to the writing away from obsession with literary value (a criticism which today in South Africa is even being used as a tool of censorship) and towards assessments of cultural function. In the course of this the critic has to be able to distinguish real function from intended function, and so demystify the arena of literature as to enable both readers and writers to become aware of the underlying implications both of the individual works and of the processes by which they are reproduced, distributed, read and evaluated. It is only by laying bare the socio–political operations of literature that writers are empowered to unite intent and effect, and take control of their own literary production in the interests of the ideology to which they subscribe. In this process the critical contribution can be immensely valuable.

For black South African writers are doing more than creating a language, a style, new forms, substituting collectivism for individualism both intrinsically in the work and in the very act of composition. They are building up a discourse within which it is possible for ordinary people to discuss and understand their history, to recognise the mechanical structures of their oppression, to discover and take charge of their own identities in the face of all the forces working towards their alienation or even erasure, and, finally, to work out a strategy for momentum. This is the point at which discourse becomes material power, and at which writers provide the cultural context, the language, the self-confidence, the condition of readiness for action in which the liberation struggle can take place. (The freedom funerals are a perfect example of the functioning of this discourse, by which an occasion for mourning has been turned into an occasion for affirmation and celebration, death transformed into an assertion of the will to survive.)

This is not to suggest that all the problems have been solved, that an immaculate conception has been brought to fruition in the realm of black South African literature. The achievements of many writers often fall short of their aims and intentions. Sound aesthetic theory does not necessarily result in flawless literary practice. A great many of the writers, hampered by youth or inexperience or lack of skill, produce material as untainted by functional power as it is by scornfully-dismissed literary value. Language is also still a major problem: writers are making heroic efforts to solve it and are in the process of creating a very vital, flexible and expressive organic literary language that assimilates very closely to the natural speech of the people. But it is not yet identical with the speech of the people in the published writings – though in plays such as *Woza Albert* and *Asinamali* it *is* and the English speaker requires a great deal of translation. And there will remain for many years yet the problem both of illiteracy, complete or functional, and of the many for whom reading will never be the source of pleasure or entertainment. The oral performances of poetry and the township plays go some way towards filling this gap between the literary artefact and the people, but this is no solution for the novel or the short story.

Nevertheless, such difficulties do not invalidate the literature's claim to speak for the great mass of the people. For their dialectics are not a purely literary preserve. The autobiographical mode in which the writer speaks as representative of the people has been transferred to the way people live their lives in today's South Africa. World-famous leaders and the humblest political prisoners claim to suffer, not as individuals, but as embodiments of an entire nation's struggle for freedom:

> I am in prison as the representative of the people and of your organization, the African National Congress, which was banned. What freedom am I being offered while the organization of the people remains banned? . . . I cannot and will not give any undertaking at a time when I and you the people are not free.[4]

Winnie Mandela writes her story, not as an individual, but as the story of every ordinary African woman subjected to the life-long harassment by the state which they all have to endure. Young aspirant writers now publish their eyewitness accounts of township disturbances in short book-form because in critical times such as these, the humblest individual's experience assumes universality, the 'we' has become 'the most of us' in very truth.

The transference of this discourse from the realms of literature to the realms of everyday life, the metastasis of culture into power will, I think, come to be seen in hindsight as one of the most interesting cultural developments of the twentieth century. The black literature of South Africa (and indeed black music and black art) has reached a point of total identity with the liberation movement: as Mongane Serote explained:

> What direction the liberation struggle takes in the 1980's . . . that is the direction of the black South African poet.[5]

Signs seem to indicate as I write, in August 1986, that the escalation of the struggle will involve yet another disjunction, another disruption of literary production. But it will not now be the kind of literary sterility of the 1960s, while the liberation movement licked its wounds, picked up the fragments and attempted to patch together the fabric of their tradition. Culture itself is now in an immeasurably stronger position; even if individual literary works cease, for a time, to be produced, the discourse has been established, the cultural context created, and whatever temporary disruptions may occur, they are occurring as part of a programme of resistance rather than as part of a programme of repression.

> we have become silent
> listen
> only if you listen can you hear footsteps
> rolling quietly like the clouds

one day
when the day comes
and the night moonless and starless
is dragged and is gone
we shall sing a song
a song
which transforms
the misery of the millions
the millions who starved . . .
a song
in life and action
breaking the night and building a day
when we will live free
to work and build our land.[6]

Notes

INTRODUCTION

1. Though the policies of apartheid and separate development sought to preserve African languages and traditions, this was part of a wider programme to confine the 'Bantu' to their tribal cultures; it took no account of the degree of tribal integration that had taken place, and very little account of the natural linguistic developments within the black communities – developments which were never towards greater purity. The major liberation movements therefore view this official tampering with African cultures as part of the machinery of repression.
2. Recent work by Couzens and others demonstrates much more fully than has hitherto been shown, the operations of African tradition within the work of those early writers. See Daniel Kunene's new translation of Mofolo's *Chaka* and Tim Couzens' editions of Dhlomo.
3. A shebeen is a drinking place run, illegally, by African women, usually in their own homes. Thus while it serves the function of a bar, and is often the scene of wild drinking bouts, it has the character of a family living room.
4. See R. Kavanagh, *Theatre and Cultural Struggle in South Africa* (London: Zed Books, 1985) p. 33.

CHAPTER 1

1. Mafika Gwala, *No More Lullabies* (Johannesburg: Ravan Press, 1982) p. 10.
2. Terry Eagleton, *Literary Theory: An Introduction* (Oxford: Basil Blackwell, 1983) p. 21.
3. Athol Fugard, John Kani & Winston Ntshona, 'The Island', *Statements* (London & Capetown: Oxford U.P., 1974) p. 62.
4. Eagleton, *Criticism and Ideology: A Study in Marxist Literary Theory* (London: Verso, 1978) p. 49.
5. Donald Woods, *Biko* (New York & London: Paddington Press, 1978) p. 130.
6. See Denis Duerden & Cosmo Pieterse (eds), *African Writers Talking* (London: Heinemann, 1972) p. 158.
7. Nadine Gordimer, 'English-Language Literature and Politics in South

Africa' in Christopher Heywood (ed.), *Aspects of South African Literature* (London: Heinemann, 1976) p. 118.

8. Nadine Gordimer, 'The Novel and the Nation in South Africa', in G. D. Killam (ed.), *African Writers on African Writing* (London: Heinemann, 1973) p. 52.

9. Lewis Nkosi, 'Fiction by Black South Africans', *Home and Exile and Other Selections*, 2nd edition (London & New York: Longman, 1983) p. 137.

10. Ibid., p. 5.

11. Essop Patel (ed.), *The World of Nat Nakasa: Selected Writings of the Late Nat Nakasa* (Johannesburg: Ravan Press, 1975) p. 82.

12. Nkosi, *Home and Exile* II, p. 25.

13. Aelred Stubbs (ed.), *Steve Biko: I Write What I Like* (The Bowerdean Press, 1978) p. 164.

14. Gordimer in Christopher Heywood (ed.), *Aspects of South African Literature*, p. 118.

15. Alex La Guma in Duerden and Pieterse (eds), *African Writers Talking*, p. 93.

16. Gordimer in Christopher Heywood (ed.), *Aspects of South African Literature*, p. 119.

17. Ezekiel Mphahlele, *The African Image*, 1st edition (London: Faber & Faber, 1962) p. 108.

18. Ibid., p. 38.

19. Olive Schreiner, *Story of an African Farm* (London: T. Fisher Unwin Ltd, 1924) p. 106.

20. Nadine Gordimer and Lionel Abrahams (eds), *South African Writing Today* (Harmondsworth: Penguin, 1967).

21. Dennis Brutus, 'Protest Against Apartheid', in C. Pieterse & D. Munro (eds), *Protest and Conflict in African Literature* (London: Heinemann, 1974) pp. 93–4.

22. See *Publications and Entertainment Act 1963* Section 6, *Statutes of the Republic of South Africa, Classified & Annotated from 1910*.

23. *House of Assembly Debates, Republic of South Africa, 18 Jan.–15 March, 1963*, vol. 5, columns 532–3.

24. *Publications Act No. 42 of 1974, Statutes R.S.A.*

25. *Publications Act No. 42 of 1974, Statutes of R.S.A.*, Section 52.

26. Ibid., Section 8.

27. Alfred Hutchinson, *Road to Ghana* (London: Gollancz, 1960) p. 15.

28. Jonathon Paton, 'Censorship & the University', in J. S. Paton (ed.), *The Grey Ones: Essays on Censorship* (Johannesburg: Ravan Press, 1974) p. 8. Quoted from a memorandum on banned books of literary merit by Professor Colin Gardner, no reference given.

29. Nadine Gordimer, 'Apartheid and Censorship', in J. S. Paton (ed.), *The Grey Ones*, p. 5.

30. Lewis Nkosi, *Home and Exile*, 1st edition (London: Longmans, 1965) p. 119.

31. Ibid., p. 121.

32. Nadine Gordimer, *The Black Interpreters* (Johannesburg: Spro-Cas/Ravan, 1973) p. 51.

33. Nkosi, *Home and Exile* I, p. 121.

34. Ibid., p. 46.
35. G. D. Killam (ed.), *African Writers on African Writing*, p. 10.
36. Nkosi, *Home and Exile* I, p. 50.
37. G. D. Killam (ed.), *African Writers on African Writing*, p. 33.
38. See Nkosi, *Home and Exile* I, p. 17.
39. Marx & Engels, *The German Ideology*, 1865–6, quoted in Terry Eagleton, *Marxism and Literary Criticism* (London: Methuen, 1976, reprinted 1983) p. 4.
40. From *A Contribution to the Critique of Political Economy* (1859), quoted ibid., p. 4.
41. 'Notebook' December 1968, quoted in Christopher Heywood (ed.), *Aspects of South African Literature*, p. 169.
42. Woods, *Biko*, p. 124.
43. Hazel Barnes, *Sartre* (London: Quartet Books, 1974) p. 120.
44. Ibid.
45. Ezekiel Mphahlele, 'Renewal Time', preface to *The Unbroken Song* (Johannesburg: Ravan, 1981) p. x.
46. Barnes, *Sartre*, p. 111.
47. Iris Murdoch, *Sartre* (London: Fontana, Collins, 1967) p. 71.
48. David Lodge (ed.), *Twentieth Century Literary Criticism* (London: Longmans, 1972) pp. 276–90.
49. Ibid., p. 289.
50. Robert Kavanagh, *South African People's Plays* (London: Heinemann, 1981) pp. xxiii–xxiv.
51. Eagleton, *Marxism and Literary Criticism*, p. 22.
52. Ibid., p. 24.
53. Ibid., p. 26.
54. Jacques Alvarez Peryre, *The Poetry of Commitment in South Africa* (London: Heinemann, 1984) p. 215.
55. Mothabi Mutloatse, *Forced Landing Africa South, Contemporary Writings* (Johannesburg: Ravan Press, 1980) p. 5.
56. Eagleton, *Marxism and Literary Criticism*, p. 62.
57. Mutloatse, *Forced Landing*, p. 5.
58. Quoted in Eagleton, *Marxism and Literary Criticism*, p. 24.
59. Ibid., pp. 24–5.
60. Allistair Sparks, 'A poet's anger revives ideals of Steve Biko', *Observer*, 18 September 1983, p. 13.
61. Eagleton, *Literary Theory*, p. 90.
62. Eagleton, *Criticism and Ideology: A Study in Marxist Literary Theory* (London: Verso Editions, 1978) p. 56.
63. Eagleton, *Literary Theory*, pp. 208–9.
64. Ibid., p. 209.
65. Ibid., p. 196.
66. Ibid., p. 141.
67. Ibid., pp. 108–9.
68. Ibid., p. 109.
69. Ibid., p. 112.
70. David Lodge (ed.), *Twentieth Century Criticism*, p. 371.
71. Ibid., p. 376.
72. Ibid., p. 377.

73. Ibid.
74. Ibid.
75. Ibid., p. 379.
76. Ibid., p. 380.
77. Ibid., p. 383.
78. Ibid.
79. Ibid.
80. Ibid., p. 384.
81. Ibid., p. 338.
82. Northrop Frye, *Fables of Identity: Studies in Poetic Mythology* (New York: Harcourt Brace & World, 1963) pp. 12–13.
83. Lodge (ed.), *Twentieth Century Criticism*, p. 187.
84. Ibid.
85. See Barnes, *Sartre*, p. 71.
86. N. Chabani Manganyi, *Mashangu's Reverie and other essays* (Johannesburg: Ravan Press, 1977) pp. 55–6.
87. Ibid., p. 60.
88. Ibid., p. 66.
89. Ibid., p. 67.
90. Eagleton, *Literary Theory*, p. 214.
91. Cliff Slaughter, *Marxism, Ideology and Literature* (London: Macmillan, 1980) p. 179.
92. Ibid., p. 182.
93. See ibid., pp. 90–100.
94. Eagleton, *Literary Theory*, p. 215.
95. Eagleton, *Criticism and Ideology*, p. 55.
96. Slaughter, *Marxism, Ideology and Literature*, p. 57.
97. Ibid.
98. Eagleton, *Literary Theory*, p. 203.
99. Ibid.
100. Slaughter, *Marxism, Ideology and Literature*, p. 145.
101. Ibid., p. 174.
102. See summary of Benjamin's 'The Author as Producer', ibid., p. 181.
103. Eagleton, *Criticism and Ideology*, p. 84.
104. Eagleton, *Literary Theory*, p. 74.
105. Ibid., p. 89.
106. Ibid., p. 125.
107. See ibid., p. 191.
108. Slaughter, *Marxism, Ideology and Literature*, p. 47.
109. Eagleton, *Criticism and Ideology*, p. 135.

CHAPTER TWO

1. Ezekiel Mphahlele, preface to *The African Image*, 1st edition (London: Faber & Faber, 1962) p. 16.
2. Ezekiel Mphahlele, preface to *The African Image*, 2nd edition (London: Faber & Faber, 1974) p. 10.
3. N. Chabani Manganyi, *Exiles and Homecomings: A Biography of Es'kia Mphahlele* (Johannesburg: Ravan Press, 1983) p. 2.

4. Ezekiel Mphahlele, *Voices in the Whirlwind and Other Essays* (London: Macmillan, 1972) p. 160.
5. *Voices in the Whirlwind*, p. 127.
6. Ibid., p. 157.
7. Ibid., p. 127.
8. Ibid., p. 128.
9. *The African Image* II, p. 21.
10. *Voices in the Whirlwind*, p. 198. He goes on to argue that with development and the inequalities that follow in its train, culture now requires an economic base. This is one of the points at which his train of thought is not immediately apparent – an idea in germination rather than fruition, perhaps.
11. Ibid., p. 121.
12. Ibid.
13. Ibid., p. 127.
14. Ibid., p. 198.
15. Mphahlele, *The African Image* II, p. 15.
16. Ibid., p. 29.
17. Ibid.
18. Ibid., pp. 48–9.
19. Ibid., p. 30.
20. Mphahlele, *Voices in the Whirlwind*, p. 169.
21. *The African Image* I, p. 93.
22. *The African Image* II, p. 41.
23. *Voices in the Whirlwind*, p. 15.
24. Ibid., p. 198.
25. Ibid., pp. 76–7.
26. *The African Image* II, p. 27.
27. Ibid., p. 28.
28. Ibid.
29. Ibid., p. 30.
30. Ibid., p. 248.
31. Ibid., pp. 247–8.
32. *The African Image* I, p. 93.
33. *The African Image* II, p. 35.
34. Ibid., pp. 246–7.
35. André Brink, *A Dry White Season* (London: W. H. Allen, 1979).
36. Nadine Gordimer, *July's People* (London: Jonathan Cape, 1981) p. 8.
37. Ibid., p. 152.
38. Mphahlele, preface to *The African Image* II, p. 9.
39. *The African Image* I, p. 19.
40. Ibid.
41. Ibid., p. 20.
42. *Voices in the Whirlwind*, pp. 15–16.
43. Ibid., p. 16.
44. Ibid., p. 196.
45. *The African Image* II, p. 89.
46. Ibid.
47. Ibid., p. 93.
48. Ibid.

49. Ibid.
50. Ibid.
51. Ibid., p. 84.
52. Ibid., p. 88.
53. Ibid.
54. Ibid., p. 92.
55. *Voices in the Whirlwind*, p. 3.
56. Ibid., p. 66.
57. Ibid.
58. Ibid., p. 116.
59. Larry Need, 'The Black Arts' Movement', *The Drama Review*, vol. 12, no. 4 (T40) Summer 1968, p. 29, quoted in *Whirlwind*, p. 65.
60. Ibid.
61. *Voices in the Whirlwind*, p. 98.
62. *The African Image* II, p. 244.
63. *Voices in the Whirlwind*, p. 144.
64. Ibid., p. 128.
65. Ibid., p. 127.
66. Ibid., p. 131.
67. *The African Image* II, p. 70.
68. *The African Image* I, p. 193.
69. *Voices in the Whirlwind*, p. 150.
70. *The African Image* II, p. 247.
71. Ibid., p. 36.
72. *The African Image* I, pp. 91–2.
73. Ibid., p. 27.
74. *Voices in the Whirlwind*, p. 46.
75. Ibid., p. 120.
76. *The African Image* II, p. 82.
77. Ibid., p. 30.
78. Mafika Gwala, 'Writing as a Cultural Weapon' in M.J. Daymond, J. Jacobs, Margaret Lenta (eds), *Momentum: On Recent South African Writing* (Pietermaritzburg: University of Natal Press, 1984) p. 50.
79. Ibid.
80. Mphahlele, *Voices in the Whirlwind*, p. 4.
81. Ibid., p. 54.
82. Ibid., p. 16.
83. Ibid., p. 17.
84. Ibid., p. 100.
85. Ibid., p. 111.
86. Ibid., p. 113.
87. Mphahlele, *The African Image* II, p. 23.
88. N. Chabani Manganyi, *Exiles and Homecomings*, p. 120.
89. *Voices in the Whirlwind*, p. 74.
90. Ibid.
91. *The African Image* II, p. 269.
92. Ibid., p. 244.
93. *Voices in the Whirlwind*, p. 70.
94. *The African Image* I, pp. 28–9.
95. Ibid., p. 121.

96. *Voices in the Whirlwind*, p. 76.
97. Ibid.
98. Ibid., p. 24.
99. *The African Image* II, p. 11.
100. Ibid., p. 13.
101. *Voices in the Whirlwind*, p. 54.
102. Ibid., p. 7.
103. Ibid., p. 120.
104. *The African Image* II, p. 245.
105. *The African Image* I, p. 94.
106. *Voices in the Whirlwind*, pp. 3–4.
107. Ibid., p. 12.
108. *The African Image* II, p. 239.
109. *Voices in the Whirlwind*, p. 99.
110. Ibid.
111. Ibid., p. 65.
112. *The African Image* II, p. 249.
113. Ibid., p. 70.
114. Ibid., p. 85.
115. Ibid., p. 71.
116. Ibid., pp. 91–2. Quoted from Fanon, *The Wretched of the Earth* (New York: Grove Press, 1968) p. 233.
117. Ibid., p. 248.
118. *The African Image* II, p. 194.
119. Ibid., p. 194.
120. Ibid., pp. 269–70.
121. 'The Tyranny of Place', *New Letters*, ed. David Ray, vol. 40, no. 1, University of Missouri, Kansas City, p. 83.
122. Ibid.
123. *The African Image* II, p. 28.
124. Ibid., pp. 200–201.
125. *Voices in the Whirlwind*, p. 151.
126. 'Looking In: In Search of Ezekiel Mphahlele', interview with N. C. Manganyi, *Looking Through the Keyhole* (Johannesburg: Ravan Press, 1981) p. 44.

CHAPTER 3

1. Mongane Serote, *No Baby Must Weep* (Johannesburg: Ad Donker, 1975) p. 29.
2. Northrop Frye, 'Specific Continuous Forms: The Novel', in Robert Murray Davies (ed.), *Modern Essays in Criticism* (New Jersey: Prentice Hall Inc., 1961) p. 34.
3. Damian Grant, *Realism* (London: Methuen, 1970) p. 52.
4. Eagleton, *Marxism and Literary Criticism*, p. 31.
5. Iris Murdoch, *Sartre*, p. 37.
6. Nadine Gordimer, 'The Novel and the Nation in South Africa', in G. D. Killam (ed.), *African Writers on African Writing*, p. 37.
7. Manganyi, *Mashangu's Reverie*, p. 63.

8. The association of black skin with an inbred tendency to steal is astonishingly bedrocked in the minds of many white South Africans – see Sipho Sepamla's 'The Bookshop', *Hurry Up To It* (Johannesburg: Ad Donker, 1975), pp. 13–14 and Oswald Mtshali's 'Always a Suspect', *Sounds of a Cowhide Drum* (London: Oxford U.P., 1971) p. 28.
9. Frantz Fanon, *Black Skin White Masks* (London: MacGibbon & Kee, 1968) p. 118.
10. See Eagleton's summary of Lukács' attitude to realism and the writer in *Marxism and Literary Criticism*, p. 50.
11. N. Chabani Manganyi, *Looking Through the Keyhole* (Johannesburg: Ravan, 1981) pp. 59 & 61.
12. Manganyi, *Exiles and Homecomings*, pp. 54–5.
13. Manganyi's comment on a statement by Becker in *The Denial of Death*, *Looking Through the Keyhole*, p. 55.
14. Roy Pascal, *Design and Truth in Autobiography* (London: Routledge & Kegan Paul, 1960) p. 177.
15. Ian Watt, *The Rise of the Novel* (Harmondsworth: Penguin, 1963) p. 78.
16. Pascal, *Design and Truth in Autobiography*, p. 182.
17. Ibid., p. 193.
18. Ibid., p. 194.
19. Athol Fugard, *Statements*, p. 38.
20. See Dugmore Boetie, *Familiarity is the Kingdom of the Lost* (London: Barrie & Rockcliff, The Cresset Press, 1969).
21. See Todd Matshikiza, *Chocolates For My Wife* (Cape Town, Johannesburg: David Phillip, 1982).
22. Quoted in the Foreword by A. J. Polley to Peter Wilhelm and James Polley (eds), *Poetry in South Africa, Selected Papers from Poetry 74* (Johannesburg: Ad Donker, 1976) p. 8.
23. Quoted by Pascal in *Design and Truth in Autobiography*, p. 58.
24. See ibid., p. 51.
25. Bloke Modisane, *Blame Me On History* (London: Thames & Hudson, 1963) p. 73.
26. See Manganyi's preface to *Mashangu's Reverie*.
27. Ibid., p. 20.
28. Modisane, *Blame Me On History*, p. 73.
29. Ibid., p. 55.
30. Ibid., p. 67.
31. Ibid., p. 70.
32. Ezekiel Mphahlele, *The Wanderers* (London: Macmillan, 1971) p. 279.
33. Alfred Hutchinson, *The Road To Ghana* (London: Gollancz, 1960) p. 131.
34. Ibid.
35. Nkosi, *Home and Exile* I, pp. 109–10.
36. Manganyi, *Mashangu's Reverie*, p. 12.
37. Mphahlele, *The Wanderers*, p. 121.
38. Nkosi, *Home and Exile* I, p. 32.
39. Ibid., p. 33.
40. Manganyi, *Mashangu's Reverie*, p. 24.
41. Nkosi, *Home and Exile* I, p. 91.
42. Ibid., p. 92.

43. Ibid., p. 123.
44. See ibid., p. 47.
45. Ibid., p. 46.
46. *Staffrider Magazine* (Johannesburg: Ravan Press, vol. 2, no. 4, Nov./Dec. 1979) p. 48.
47. Nkosi, *Home and Exile* I, p. 35.
48. Ibid., p. 11.
49. Ibid., pp. 12 and 10.
50. Ibid., p. 12.
51. Noni Jabavu, *Drawn in Colour: African Contrasts* (London: John Murray, 1960) p. 3.
52. Ibid., p. 188.
53. Modisane, *Blame Me On History*, p. 5.
54. Ibid., p. 10.
55. Donald Woods, *Biko*, p. 130.
56. D. J. Enright, *Memoirs of a Mendicant Professor* (London: Chatto & Windus, 1969) p. 11.
57. Hazel Barnes, *Sartre*, p. 71.
58. Matshikiza, *Chocolates For My Wife*, p. 126.
59. Manganyi, *Looking Through the Keyhole*, p. 30.
60. Manganyi, *Mashangu's Reverie*, Preface.
61. *Looking Through the Keyhole*, p. 59.
62. Nkosi, *Home and Exile*, Preface to first edition, 1965.
63. *Home and Exile* II, p. 31.
64. Ibid., p. 95.
65. Jabavu, *Drawn in Colour*, p. 189.
66. Ibid., p. 50.
67. Ibid., p. 49.
68. Another work which conveys the shortcomings of South African legal trials without didactic comment, by allowing the police and prosecution witnesses to convict themselves, is the play *The Biko Inquest* by J. Blair and N. Fenton (London: Rex Collings, 1978).
69. Interview with the author, July 1978.
70. Explained in the course of a general discussion covering many of the events and characters, in an interview with the author, July 1978.
71. N. Chabani Manganyi, *Exiles and Homecomings: A Biography of Es'kia Mphahlele* (Johannesburg: Ravan, 1983) p. 7.
72. Ibid., p. 6.
73. Ezekiel Mphahlele, *Down Second Avenue* (London: Faber & Faber, 1971) pp. 158–9.

CHAPTER 4

1. Mongane Serote, *Selected Poems*, M. Mzamane (ed.), (Johannesburg: Ad Donker, 1982) p. 142.
2. *Pelculeff Newsletter* (Gaborone, Botswana, I, no. 1, Oct. 1977) p. 32.
3. See M. Mzamane 'Black Consciousness Poets in South Africa 1967–1980', D. Phil. thesis prsented to Sheffield University 1983, pp. 64–75.
4. See ibid, p. 83.

5. Mongane Wally Serote, *Yakhal'inkomo* (Johannesburg: Renoster Books, 1972) p. 47.
6. Serote, 'Lost and Found World', *Yakhal'inkomo*, p. 21.
7. *Yak.*, p. 4.
8. Mongane Serote, *No Baby Must Weep* (Johannesburg: Ad Donker, 1975) p. 45.
9. Ibid., p. 46.
10. Mzamane, 'Black Consciousness Poets', p. 83.
11. *Yak.*, p. 48.
12. Ibid., p. 28.
13. Ibid., p. 22.
14. Mongane Serote, *Tsetlo* (Johannesburg: Ad Donker, 1974) p. 59.
15. Ibid., p. 60.
16. Ibid.
17. Ibid., p. 13.
18. *Yak.*, p. 29.
19. Ibid.
20. Ibid.
21. Ibid.
22. Ibid.
23. *Tsetlo*, p. 47.
24. Ibid., pp. 47–8.
25. *Yak.*, p. 38.
26. *Tsetlo*, p. 20.
27. *No Baby Must Weep*, p. 56.
28. *Tsetlo*, pp. 22–4.
29. *No Baby Must Weep*, p. 33.
30. Ibid., pp. 33–4.
31. *Yak.*, p. 20.
32. Ibid., p. 47.
33. *Tsetlo*, p. 56.
34. *No Baby Must Weep*, pp. 52–3.
35. Ibid., p. 53.
36. Serote, *Behold Mama, Flowers* (Johannesburg: Ad Donker, 1978) pp. 71–2.
37. Ibid., p. 20.
38. Ibid., p. 75.
39. *Yak.*, p. 10.
40. *Behold Mama, Flowers*, p. 36.
41. Ibid., p. 19.
42. Ibid.
43. Ibid., p. 49.
44. Ibid., p. 68.
45. Ibid., p. 29.
46. Ibid., p. 13.
47. *Yak.*, p. 19.
48. Ibid., p. 40.
49. Ibid., p. 41.
50. Ibid., p. 12.
51. Ibid., p. 9.

52. Ibid., p. 43.
53. *Tsetlo*, p. 53.
54. Ibid.
55. Ibid.
56. Ibid., p. 54.
57. Ibid.
58. Ibid.
59. *Yak.*, p. 21.
60. Ibid., p. 27.
61. Ibid.
62. Ibid., p. 37.
63. Ibid.
64. Ibid., p. 38.
65. Ibid., p. 8.
66. 'I Will Wait', ibid., p. 36.
67. Ibid., p. 13.
68. Ibid., p. 16.
69. Ibid.
70. *Tsetlo*, p. 41.
71. Ibid., p. 42.
72. *Yak.*, p. 26.
73. Ibid.
74. Ibid., p. 44.
75. Ibid.
76. *Tsetlo*, p. 34.
77. Ibid.
78. Ibid., p. 58.
79. Ibid., p. 61.
80. Ibid., p. 62.
81. Interview with M. Mzamane. See 'Appendix', 'Black Consciousness Poets in South Africa', p. 349.
82. Ibid., p. 351.
83. Ibid., p. 352.
84. *Behold Mama, Flowers*, p. 49.
85. *No Baby Must Weep*, p. 20.
86. T. S. Eliot, *Collected Poems* (London: Faber, 1963) p. 203.
87. *Yak.*, p. 52.
88. *Behold Mama, Flowers*, p. 26.
89. Ibid., p. 47.
90. See ibid., p. 49.
91. See *Yak.*, p. 52.
92. *No Baby Must Weep*, pp. 28–9.
93. *Tsetlo*, pp. 27–31.
94. Ibid., p. 30.
95. Ibid., p. 31.
96. See James A. Snead, 'The Black Trope of Repetition'; in Henry Louis Gates Jr. (ed.), *Black Literature and Literary Theory* (London & New York: Methuen, 1984).
97. *Yak.*, p. 16.
98. *No Baby Must Weep*, p. 7.

99. Ibid., p. 61.
100. Ibid., p. 25.
101. Ibid.
102. See ibid., pp. 28–9.
103. Ibid., p. 32.
104. Ibid., p. 36.
105. Ibid., p. 37.
106. Ibid., p. 46.
107. Ibid., p. 48.
108. Ibid., p. 49.
109. Ibid., p. 61.
110. Mzamane, 'Black Consciousness Poets in South Africa', p. 137.
111. *Behold Mama, Flowers*, p. 14.
112. Ibid., p. 16.
113. Ibid., pp. 15–17.
114. Ibid., p. 15.
115. Ibid., p. 18.
116. Ibid., p. 19.
117. Ibid., pp. 19–20.
118. Ibid., p. 21.
119. Ibid., p. 25.
120. Ibid., p. 26.
121. Ibid., p. 34.
122. Ibid., p. 49.
123. Ibid., p. 57.
124. Ibid., p. 59.
125. Ibid.
126. Ibid., p. 60.
127. Ibid., p. 61.
128. The difficulty a white readership has in grasping this role, in comprehending the different psychological processes at work in the coming to consciousness of an African growing up in a community is evidenced by the utterly unconvincing portrait of Max Solo, an African would-be revolutionary, in Jack Cope's *My Son Max* (London: Heinemann, 1977).
129. *No Baby Must Weep*, p. 21.
130. Ibid.
131. Ibid., pp. 47–8.
132. Ibid., p. 52.
133. Ibid., pp. 60–61.
134. *Behold Mama, Flowers*, p. 14.
135. Ibid.
136. Ibid., p. 16.
137. See ibid., pp. 19–20.
138. See ibid., p. 23.
139. Ibid., p. 22.
140. Ibid.
141. Ibid., p. 24.
142. Ibid., p. 26.
143. Ibid., pp. 28–9.
144. Ibid., p. 35.

145. Ibid., p. 42.
146. Ibid., p. 45.
147. Ibid., p. 56.
148. Serote, *Selected Poems*, p. 142.
149. *Behold Mama, Flowers*, p. 67.
150. Serote, *The Night Keeps Winking* (Gaborone, Medu Arts Ensemble, 1982) p. 17.
151. *Behold Mama, Flowers*, p. 82.
152. Ibid., p. 68.
153. Ibid.
154. Ibid., p. 70.
155. Ibid.
156. Ibid.
157. Ibid., p. 71.
158. Ibid.
159. Ibid., pp. 71–2.
160. Serote, *Selected Poems*, p. 142. Various specious reasons were given by the publisher for cutting this and other poems before publication – another example of the unofficial censorship devices to which South African writers are subject.
161. Ibid.
162. Ibid.
163. Ibid., p. 139.
164. *Behold Mama, Flowers*, p. 86.
165. Ibid., p. 78.
166. 'No More Strangers', *Selected Poems*, p. 135.
167. Ibid.
168. Ibid., pp. 142–4.
169. Ibid., p. 135.
170. *No Baby Must Weep*, p. 32.
171. *Behold Mama, Flowers*, p. 75.
172. Ibid., p. 45.
173. *No Baby Must Weep*, pp. 60–61.
174. *The Night Keeps Winking*, p. 13.
175. *Selected Poems*, p. 142.
176. *The Night Keeps Winking*, p. 6.

CHAPTER FIVE

1. See Nadine Gordimer, *The Black Interpreters*, p. 14.
2. Miriam Tlali, *Amandla* (Johannesburg: Ravan Press, 1980) p. 230.
3. Sipho Sepamla, *A Ride on the Whirlwind* (Johannesburg: Ad Donker, 1981) p. 32.
4. Ibid., p. 34.
5. Mbulelo Mzamane, *The Children of Soweto: a Trilogy* (Harlow: Longman, 1982) p. 77.
6. Ibid., p. 86.
7. Ibid.
8. Ibid., p. 151.

9. Ibid., p. 244.
10. Mbulelo Mzamane, 'The Uses of Traditional Oral Forms in Black South African Literature' in Landeg White and Tim Couzens (eds), *Literature and Society in South Africa* (Harlow: Longmans, 1984) pp. 147–8.
11. Ibid.
12. Vaughan in *Literature and Society in South Africa*, p. 200.
13. See ibid., p. 209.
14. Ibid., p. 197.
15. Mongane Serote, *To Every Birth Its Blood* (Johannesburg, Ravan Press, 1981) p. 1.
16. Ibid., p. 7.
17. Ibid., p. 15.
18. Ibid., p. 19.
19. Ibid., p. 33.
20. Ibid., p. 45.
21. Ibid., p. 59.
22. Ibid., p. 58.
23. Ibid., p. 60.
24. Ibid.
25. Ibid., p. 65.
26. Ibid., p. 69.
27. Ibid., p. 70.
28. Ibid., p. 78.
29. Ibid., p. 79.
30. Ibid., p. 88.
31. Ibid., p. 89.
32. Ibid.
33. Ibid., p. 162.
34. Ibid., p. 173.
35. Ibid., p. 176.
36. Ibid., p. 322.
37. Lucien Goldmann, *Cultural Creation in Modern Society* (Oxford: Blackwell, 1977) p. 63.
38. See Landeg White and Tim Couzens (eds), *Literature and Society*, p. 148.

CONCLUSION

1. Mafika Gwala, 'Writing as a Cultural Weapon' in M. J. Daymond, J. U. Jacobs and M. Lenta (eds), *Momentum on Recent South African Writing* (University of Natal Press, 1984) p. 39.
2. Wally Serote, 'The Politics of Culture', *Sechaba*, March 1984, p. 28.
3. Lewis Nkosi, *Tasks and Masks: Themes and Styles of African Literature* (Harlow: Longman, 1981) p. 80.
4. Mandela's reply to Botha read in Jubulani Stadium in Soweto on 10 February 1985, quoted in Winnie Mandela, *Part of My Soul* (Harmondsworth: Penguin, 1985) p. 146.
5. Quoted by Mafika Gwala in *Momentum on Recent South African Writing*, p. 53.
6. Mongane Serote, *The Night Keeps Winking*, p. 22.

Bibliography

As this book attempts to construct a critical approach from the comments and discussions of the writers themselves, in addition to examining literary works, the division of the bibliography into primary and secondary sources is a somewhat equivocal process. Moreover the rejection of strict genre definitions by the writers themselves renders genre classification inappropriate. I have therefore adopted a very general categorisation in the hope that it would bring a little order to the bibliography without betraying the critical values of those black South African writers on whom this book is based.

PRIMARY SOURCES

I Fiction, Poetry, Drama, Biography, Autobiography and Prose Works

Abrahams, Peter *Return to Goli* (London: Faber, 1953).
—*Tell Freedom* (London: Allen & Unwin, 1954).
—*A Wreath for Udomo* (London: Faber, 1956).
Biko, Steve *I Write What I Like* (London: Heinemann, 1979).
Black Orphens, Beier, U. and Jahn, J. (eds), Ibadan, 1957–1968.
Blair, Jon and Fenton, Norman *The Biko Inquest* (London: Rex Collings, 1978).
Boetie, Dugmore *Familiarity is the Kingdom of the Lost*, Simon, B. (ed.), (London: Cresset, 1969).
Brink, André *A Dry White Season* (London: W. H. Allen, 1979).
Brutus, Dennis *A Simple Lust* (London: Heinemann, 1973).
—*Stubborn Hope* (London: Heinemann, 1978).
Classic, Nakasa, Nat (ed.), Johannesburg, 1963–1967.
Feinberg, Barry (ed.) *Poets to the People: South African Freedom Poems*, enlarged edition (London: Heinemann, 1980).

Fugard, Athol *Notebooks 1960–1977*, Benson, M. (ed.), (London: Faber, 1983).

'The Island', *Statements* (Oxford University Press, 1974).

Gordimer, N. and Abrahams, L. (eds) *South African Writing Today* (Harmondsworth: Penguin, 1967).

Gordimer, N. *July's People* (London: Jonathan Cape, 1981).

Gordimer, N. & Abrahams, L. (eds) *South African Writing Today* (Harmondsworth: Penguin, 1967).

Gwala, Mafika Pascal *Jol'inkomo* (Johannesburg: Ad Donker, 1977).

—*No More Lullabies* (Johannesburg: Ravan, 1982).

Head, Bessie *When Rainclouds Gather* (London: Heinemann, 1972).

—*Maru* (London: Heinemann, 1972).

—*A Question of Power* (London: Heinemann, 1974).

Hutchinson, Alfred *Road to Ghana* (London: Gollancz, 1960).

Jabavu, Nontando *Drawn in Colour* (London: John Murray, 1960).

—*The Ochre People: Scenes from South African Life* (London: John Murray, 1963).

Kgositsile, Keoropetse *The Word is Here: Poetry from Modern Africa* (New York: Doubleday, 1973).

La Guma, Alex *In the Fog of the Season's End* (London: Heinemann, 1972).

Lomak, A. and Abdul, R. (eds) *3,000 Years of Black Poetry* (New York: Dodd, Mead, 1970).

Manganyi, N. Chabani *Exiles and Homecomings: A Biography of Es'kia Mphahlele* (Johannesburg: Ravan, 1983).

Matshikiza, Todd *Chocolates For My Wife* (Cape Town, Johannesburg: David Phillip, 1982).

Matshaba, Mtutuzeli *Call Me Not a Man* (Johannesburg: Ravan, 1979).

Modisane, Bloke *Blame Me On History* (London: Thames & Hudson, 1963)..

Mokgatle, Naboth *The Autobiography of an Unknown South African* (London: Hurst, 1971).

Mphahlele, Ezekiel *Man Must Live and Other Stories* (Cape Town: African Bookman, 1947).

—*Down Second Avenue* (London: Faber, 1959).

—*In Corner B* (Nairobi: East African Publishing House, 1967).

—*The Wanderers* (London: Macmillan, 1972).

—*Chirundu* (Johannesburg: Ravan, 1979).

—*The Unbroken Song* (Johannesburg: Ravan, 1981).

Mutloatse, Mothabi *Forced Landing Africa South, Contemporary Writings* (Johannesburg: Ravan, 1980).

Mzamane, Mbulelo *The Children of Soweto: a Trilogy* (Harlow: Longman, 1982).

Nakasa, Nat *The World of Nat Nakasa*, Patel, Essop (ed.) (Johannesburg: Ravan, 1975).

New Classic, Sepamla, S. (ed.), Johannesburg, 1975– .

New Coin, Butler, G. (ed.), Grahamstown, 1965– .

Nkosi, Lewis *Home and Exile*, 1st edition, London: Longman, 1965; 2nd revised edition, Harlow: Longman, 1983.

Nortje, Arthur *Dead Roots* (London: Heinemann, 1973).

Rive, Richard *Emergency* (London: Faber, 1964).

Royston, Robert (ed.) *Black Poets in South Africa* (London: Heinemann, 1974).

Sepamla, Sipho *The Soweto I Love* (London: Rex Collings, 1977).

—*A Ride on the Whirlwind* (Johannesburg: Ad Donker, 1981).

Serote, Mongane *Yakhal'inkomo* (Johannesburg: Renoster Books, 1972).

—*Tsetlo* (Johannesburg: Ad Donker, 1974).

—*No Baby Must Weep* (Johannesburg: Ad Donker, 1975).

—*Behold Mama, Flowers* (Johannesburg: Ad Donker, 1978).

—*To Every Birth Its Blood* (Johannesburg: Ravan, 1981).

—*Selected Poems*, Mzamane, M. (ed.) (Johannesburg: Ad Donker, 1982).

—*The Night Keeps Winking* (Gaborone: Medu Arts Ensemble, 1982).

Staffrider Magazine, Johannesburg, 1978– .

Themba, Can *The Will to Die* (London: Heinemann, 1972).

Tlali, Miriam *Amandla* (Johannesburg: Ravan, 1980).

Woods, Donald *Biko* (New York: Paddington Press, 1978)

Zwelonke, D. M. *Robben Island* (London: Heinemann, 1973).

II Other Primary Sources

Including theoretical works of criticism, philosophy, culture and politics

'Against Apartheid Culture: Document Submitted by the A.N.C. of South Africa to the Lisbon Conference', *Sechaba*, London, vol. 11, 4th quarter, 1977.

Barnes, H. *Sartre* (London: Quartet Books, 1974).

Brink, André *A Chain of Voices* (London: Faber, 1982).

Camus, Albert *The Rebel* (Harmondsworth: Penguin, 1962).

Daymond, M. J., Jacobs, J. U. and Lenta, M. (eds) *Momentum on Recent South African Writing* (Pietermaritzburg: University of Natal Press, 1984).

Duerden, D. and Pieterse, C. (eds) *African Writers Talking* (London: Heinemann, 1972).

Fanon, Frantz *The Wretched of the Earth*, Preface by J. P. Sartre (London: MacGibbon & Kee, 1965).

—*Black Skin White Masks* (London: MacGibbon & Kee, 1968).

—*Towards the African Revolution* (Harmondsworth: Penguin, 1970).

Gordimer, N. *The Black Interpreters* (Johannesburg: Spro/Cas Ravan, 1973).

—'English-Language Literature and Politics in South Africa', *Journal of South African Studies*, Oxford, vol. 2, no.2, April 1976.

Heywood, Christopher (ed.) *Aspects of South African Literature* (London: Heinemann, 1976).

House of Assembly Debates, Republic of South Africa, vol. 5, 1963.

Index on Censorship (London: Writers & Scholars International, 1972–).

Killam, G. D. (ed.) *African Writers on African Writing* (London: Heinemann, 1973).

La Guma, Alex 'Culture and Liberation', *Sechaba*, London, vol. 10, 4th quarter, 1976.

—*Apartheid: A Collection of Writings on South African Racism by South Africans* (New York: International Publisher, 2nd printing, 1972).

Langa, Mandlankosi 'Review of No Baby Must Weep', *Pelculeff Newsletter*, Gaborone, vol. 1, no. 1, Oct. 1977.

Marx, K. and Engels, F. *On Literature and Art* (Moscow: Progress Publishers, 1976).

Manganyi, N. Chabani *Mashangu's Reverie and Other Essays* (Johannesburg: Ravan, 1977).

—*Looking Through the Keyhole* (Johannesburg: Ravan, 1981).

—(ed.) *Bury Me At the Marketplace. Selected Letters of Es'kia Mphahlele 1943–1980* (Johannesburg: Skotaville, 1984).

Mphahlele, Ezekiel 'The Non-European Character in South African English Fiction', M.A. Thesis submitted to University of South Africa, 1956.

—*The African Image*, 1st edition, London: Faber, 1962; 2nd revised edition, London: Faber, 1974.

—*Voices in the Whirlwind and Other Essays* (London: Macmillan, 1972).

—'The Tyranny of Place', *New Letters*, University of Missouri, vol. 40, no. 1, Oct. 1973.

—'Review of Southern African Literature: An Introduction by Stephen Grey', *African Studies*, Johannesburg, Witwatersrand University Press, vol. 41, no. 1, 1982.

Murdoch, Iris *Sartre* (Fontana: 1967).

Mzamane, Mbulelo 'Black Consciousness Poets in South Africa 1967–1980, with Special Reference to Mongane Serote and Sipho Sepamla,' Ph.D. thesis submitted to University of Sheffield, 1983.

Nkosi, Lewis 'South Africa: Literature of Protest', *A Handbook of African Affairs*, Helen Kitchen (ed.) (London: Pall Mall Press, 1964).

—*Tasks and Masks. Themes and Styles of African Literature* (Harlow: Longman, 1981).

Pieterse, C. and Munro, D. (eds) *Protest and Conflict in African Literature* (London: Heinemann, 1969).

Sartre, J. P. *What is Literature?* (New York: Philosophical Library, 1949).

Serote, Wally 'The Politics of Culture', *Sechaba*, March 1984.

Sparkes, Allister 'A Poet's Anger Revives Ideals of Steve Biko', *Observer*, 18 Sept. 1983, p. 13.

Trotsky, Leon *Literature and Revolution* (Chicago: University of Michigan Press, 1971).

Vaughan, Michael 'Literature and Politics: Currents in South African Writing in the Seventies', *Journal of South African Studies*, vol. 9, no. 1, Oct. 1982.

White, L. and Couzens, T. (eds) *Literature and Society in South Africa* (Harlow: Longman, 1984).

Wilhelm P. and Polley, J. (eds) *Poetry in South Africa: Selected Papers from Poetry '74* (Johannesburg: Ad Donker, 1976).

III Books and Articles on Censorship

Black, M. K. 'Publications Bill is a Grave Threat to Freedom', *Forum*, Johannesburg, vol. 9, no. 10, Jan. 1961.

'Books Banned in South Africa', *U.N. Notes and Documents*, March 1971.

'Censorship Law Explained. Is Possession of Banned Books Illegal?', *Cape Times*, Editorial, 21 Aug. 1964.

Fairburn, James 'New Legislation to Control "Undesirable Literature"', *Forum*, vol. 8, no. 10, Jan. 1960.

Gordon, L. 'South Africa's Press: the Press Code and Council', *Race Relations News*, Johannesburg, vol. 39, no. 7, July 1977.

Index on Censorship, London, 1972–1985.

Mzamane, M. 'The Fifties and Beyond', *New Classic*, 4, 1977.

Nkosi, Lewis: 'From Veld Lovers to Freedom Fighters', *T.L.S.*, 21

Nov. 1980, p. 1341.

Paton, J. S. (ed.), *The Grey Ones: Essays on Censorship* (Johannesburg: Ravan, 1974).

Plomer, William *Celebrations* (Cape Town: Cape Poetry Paperbacks, 1973).

'Publications and Entertainments Act 1963' and 'Publications Act No. 42 of 1974', *Statutes of the Republic of South Africa, classified and annotated from 1910.*

SECONDARY SOURCES

I Fiction, Poetry, Drama, Biography, Autobiography, Prose

Benson, Mary *At the Still Point* (London: Chatto & Windus, 1971).

—*Nelson Mandela* (Harmondsworth: Penguin, 1986).

Carim, Enver *A Dream Deferred* (London: Allen Lane, 1973).

—*Golden City* (Berlin: Seven Seas, 1973).

Cope, Jack *My Son Max* (London: Heinemann, 1977).

Couzens, Tim and Vasser, Nick (eds) *H. I. E. Dhlomo: Collected Works* (Johannesburg: Ravan, 1985).

Enright, D. J. *Memoirs of a Mendicant Professor* (London: Chatto & Windus, 1969).

Gordimer, N. *The Late Bourgeois World* (London: Jonathan Cape, 1966).

Kunene, Daniel *A Seed Must Seem to Die* (Johannesburg: Ravan, 1981).

Kunene, Mazisi *Zulu Poems* (London: André Deutsch, 1970).

Legun, C. and M. *Robert Sobukwe: The Bitter Choice* (New York: Excalibur Books, 1968).

Mandigoane, Ingoapele *Africa My Beginning* (Johannesburg: Ravan, 1979).

Mandela, Winnie *Part of My Soul*, Benjamin, A. (ed.) (Harmondsworth: Penguin, 1985).

Mattera, Don *Azanian Love Song* (Johannesburg: Skotaville, 1983).

Mofolo, Thomas *Chaka*, transl. Daniel Kunene (London: Heinemann, 1981).

Mtshali, Oswald *Sounds of a Cowhide Drum* (Oxford University Press, 1972).

Nkosi, Lewis *Mating Birds* (London: Constable, 1968).

Paton, Alan *Towards the Mountain* (Cape Town: David Philip, 1980).

Plomer, William *Turbott Wolfe* (London: Hogarth Press, 1925).

—*Double Lives* (London: Jonathan Cape, 1943).

—*At Home – Memoirs* (London: Jonathan Cape, 1958).

Rive, Richard *Writing Black* (Cape Town: David Philip, 1981).

Schapera, I. *Praise poems of Tswana Chiefs* (Oxford University Press, 1965).

Schreiner, Olive *The Story of an African Farm* (London: T. Fisher Unwin, 1924, and Greenwich: Conn. Fawcett, 1960).

South African People's Plays, selected and introduced by Kavanagh, R. M. (London: Heinemann, 1981).

Wells, H. G. *Experiment in Autobiography* (London: Gollancz, 1934).

Woods, Donald *Asking for Trouble* (London: Gollancz, 1980).

II Other Secondary Sources

Including theoretical works of criticism, culture, politics, philosophy and literary theory

Althusser, Louis *For Marx* (London: Allen Lane, 1969).

Anozie, Sunday, D. *Structural Models and African Poetics Towards a Pragmatic Theory of Literature* (London: Routledge & Kegan Paul, 1981).

Barthes, Roland *Writing Degree Zero* (London: Jonathan Cape, 1967).

Berger, John *Art and Revolution* (London: Writers & Readers Publishing Co-op, 1969).

Bernstein, Hilda *For Their Triumphs and Their Tears: Women in Apartheid* (London: I.D.A.F., 1978).

Bhabha, Homi 'Representation in the Colonial Text' in *The Theory of Reading*, Gloversmith, F. (ed.) (Sussex: Harvester Press, 1984).

Brink, André *Mapmakers: Writing in a State of Siege* (London: Faber, 1983).

Caudwell, Christopher *Illusion and Reality: A Study of the Sources of Poetry* (London: Lawrence & Wishart, 1946)..

Cohen, D. L. and Daniel, J. (eds) *Political Economy of Africa: Selected Readings* (Harlow: Longman, 1981).

Clingman, Stephen 'The Consciousness of History in the Novels of Nadine Gordimer', D.Phil. thesis submitted to the University of Oxford, 1983.

—'History from the Inside: the novels of Nadine Gordimer', *Journal of Southern African Studies*, vol. 7, no. 2, April 1981.

Cook, David *African Literature: A Critical View* (London: Longman, 1977).

Davies, Robert Murray *The Novel: Modern Essays in Criticism* (New

Jersey: Prentice Hall, 1969).

Eagleton, Terry *Exiles and Emigrés: Studies in Modern Literature* (London: Chatto & Windus, 1970).

—*Criticism and Ideology: A Study in Marxist Literary Theory* (London: Verso Editions, 1978).

—*Marxism and Literary Criticism* (London: Methuen, 1976).

—*Walter Benjamin or Towards a Revolutionary Criticism* (London: Verso & N.L.B., 1981).

—*Literary Theory: An Introduction* (Oxford: Blackwell, 1983).

Eagleton, T. and Fuller, P. 'The Question of Value: A Discussion', *New Left Review*, 142, Nov.–Dec. 1983.

February, Vernie 'Review: Sipho Sepamla – *The Soweto I Love*', *African Literature Today*, 10, 1979.

Fish, Stanley *Is There A Text in This Class? The Authority of Interpretative Communities* (Cambridge, Mass.: Harvard University Press, 1980).

Foucault, M. *Language, Counter-Memory, Practice, Selected Essays and Interviews* (Oxford: Blackwell, 1977).

Frye, Northrop *Fables of Identity: Studies in Poetic Mythology* (New York: Harcourt Brace & World, 1963).

Gates, H. L. Jr. 'The "Blackness of Blackness": A Critique of the Sign and the Signifying Monkey', *Critical Enquiry*, vol. 9, no. 4, June 1983.

—*Black Literature and Literary Theory* (London: Methuen, 1984).

Gerard, Albert, S. *Four African Literatures* (Berkeley: University of California Press, 1971).

Goldmann, Lucien *Towards a Sociology of the Novel* (London: Tavistock Publications, 1975).

—*Cultural Creation in Modern Society* (Oxford: Blackwell, 1977).

—*Method in the Sociology of Literature* (Oxford: Blackwell, 1981).

Gramsci, Antonio *Selections from the Prison Notebooks* (London: Lawrence & Wishart, 1971).

Grant, Damian *Realism* (London: Methuen, 1970).

Gray, Stephen *Southern African Literature* (London: Rex Collings, 1979).

Halperin, John (ed.) *The Theory of the Novel: New Essays* (Oxford University Press, 1974).

Herbstein, Denis *White Man, We Want to Talk to You* (Harmondsworth: Penguin, 1978).

Hewitt, Douglas *The Approach to Fiction: Good and Bad Readings of Novels* (London: Longman, 1972).

Hirson, Baruch *Year of Fire, Year of Ash. The Soweto Revolt: Roots of* a Revolution? (London: Zed Press, 1979).

Howells, Christina *Sartre's Theory of Literature* (London: Modern Humanities Research Assoc., 1979).

Iyasare, Solomon 'Modern African Literature: The Question of Ideological Commitment', *West African Journal of Modern Languages*, University of Ibadan, no. 2, Sept. 1976.

Jameson, Frederic *The Political Unconscious, Narrative as a Socially Symbolic Act* (London: Methuen, 1981).

Kavanagh, Robert *Theatre of Cultural Struggle in South Africa* (London: Zed, 1985).

Leitch, R. G. 'Nortje: Poet at Work', *African Literature Today*, 10, 1979.

Lindfors, Bernth 'Dennis Brutus and his Critics', *West African Journal of Modern Languages*, University of Ibadan, no. 2, Sept. 1976.

Lodge, David (ed.) *Twentieth Century Criticism* (London: Longman, 1972).

Lukács, Georg *The Meaning of Contemporary Realism* (London: Merlin Press, 1963).

—*The Theory of the Novel* (London: Merlin Press, 1978).

Marx, K. and Engels, F. *The German Ideology Part One*, Arthur, C. J. (ed.) (London: Lawrence & Wishart, 1970).

Moore, Gerald *The Chosen Tongue* (London: Longman, 1969).

Nojara, Emmanuel *Art and Ideology in the African Novel: A Study of the Influence of Marxism on African Writing* (London: Heinemann, 1985).

Obuke, Okpure 'South African History, Politics and Literature: Mphahlele's *Down Second Avenue* and Rive's *Emergency*', *African Literature Today*, 10, 1979.

Olney, James *Tell Me Africa. An Approach to African Literature* (New Jersey: Princeton University Press, 1973).

Pascal, Roy *Design and Truth in Autobiography* (London: Routledge & Kegan Paul, 1960).

Pereyre, Jacques Alvarez *The Poetry of Commitment in South Africa* (London: Heinemann, 1984).

The Politics of Interpretation, Critical Inquiry, vol. 9, no. 1, Sept. 1982.

Rich, Paul 'Tradition and Revolt in South African Fiction', *Journal of South African Studies*, vol. 9, no. 1, Oct. 1982.

Roscoe, Adrian *Uhuru's Fire: African Literature East to South* (Cambridge University Press, 1977).

Sachs, A. *The Sail Diary of Albie Sachs*, adapted by Edgar, D. (London: Rex Collings, 1978).

Sampson, Anthony *Drum: A Venture into New Africa* (London:

Collins, 1956.).

Sharrett, Bernard *Reading Relations: Structures of Literary Production* (Brighton: Harvester Press, 1982).

Slaughter, Cliff *Marxism, Ideology and Literature* (London: Macmillan, 1980).

Smith, Roland *Exile and Tradition: Studies in African and Caribbean Literature* (London: Longman, 1976).

Spearman, Diana *The Novel and Society* (London: Routledge & Kegan Paul, 1966).

Spender, Stephen *The Making of a Poem* (London: Hamish Hamilton, 1955).

Steiner, George *Language and Silence* (Harmondsworth: Penguin, 1969).

Visser, N. W. (ed.) 'Literary Theory and Criticism of H. I. E. Dhlomo', *English in Africa*, vol. 4, no. 2, 1977.

Wake, Clive 'Poetry of the Last Five Years', *African Literature Today*, 10, 1979.

Watt, Ian *The Rise of the Novel* (Harmondsworth: Penguin, 1963).

Wellek, René *A History of Modern Criticism 1750–1950* (London: Jonathan Cape, 1955).

Williams, Raymond *Problems in Materialism and Culture: Selected Essays* (London: Verso & N.L.B., 1980).

Index